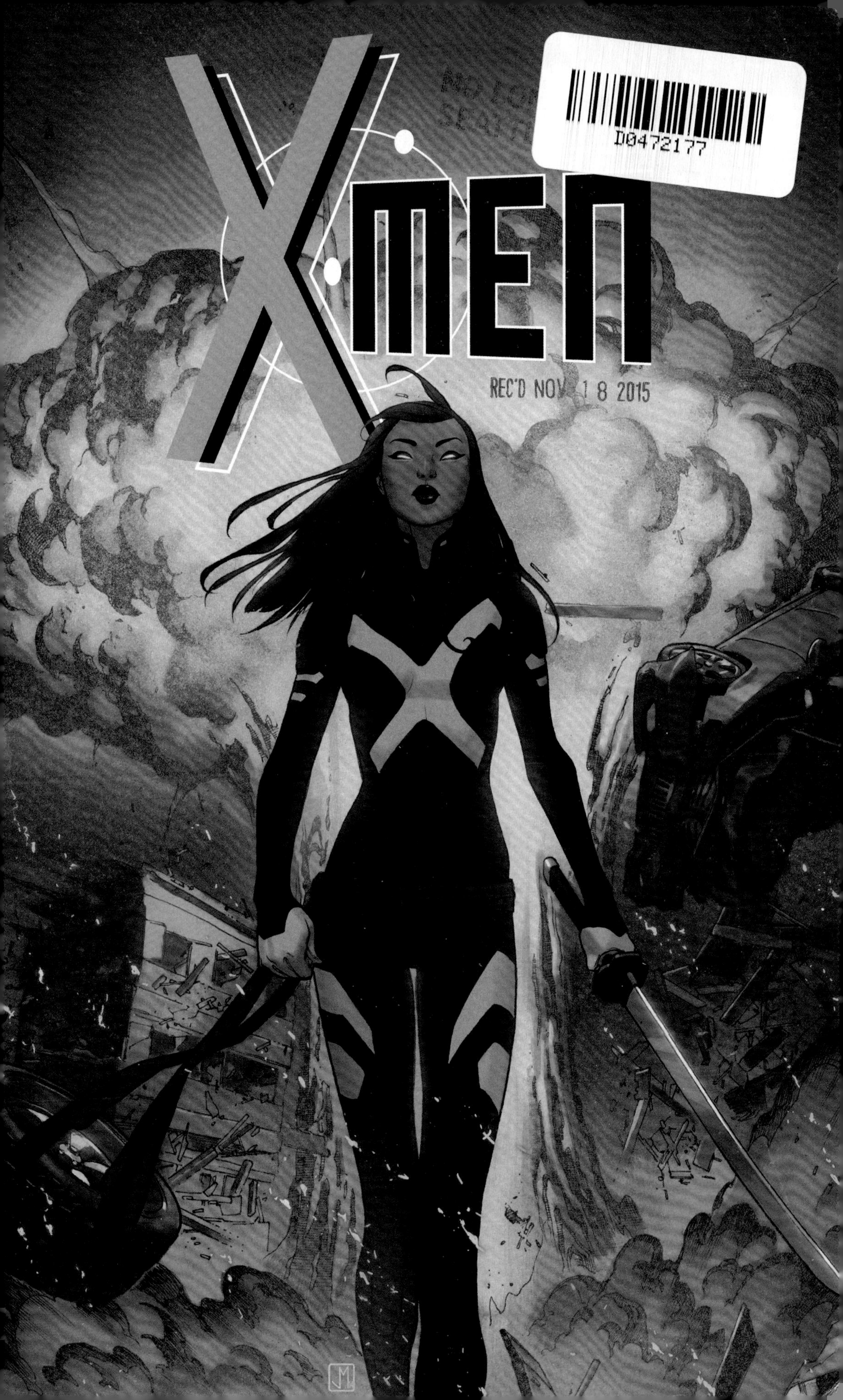
X MEN

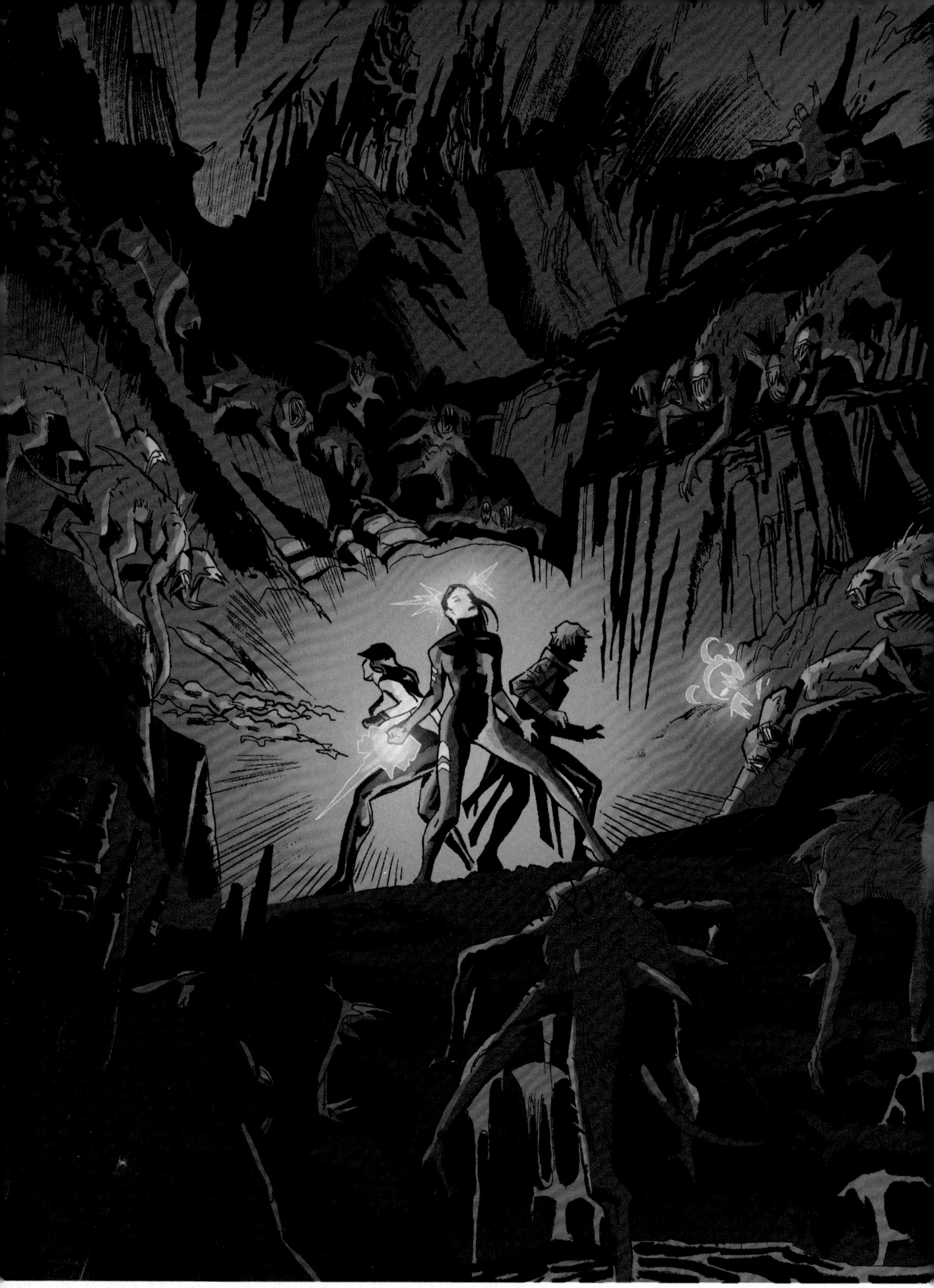

THE BURNING WORLD

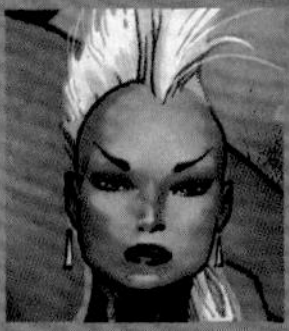

STORM

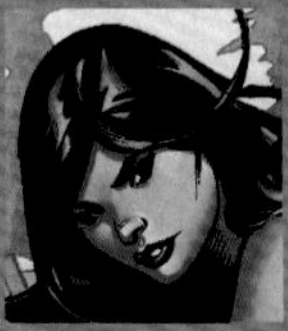

MONET

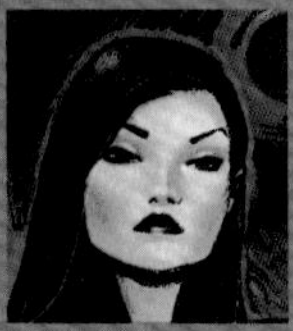

PSYLOCKE

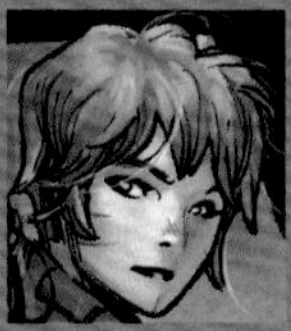

RACHEL GREY

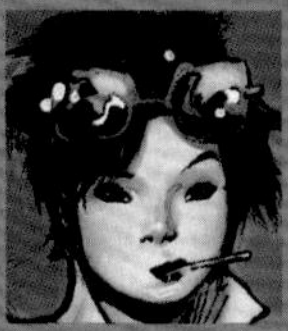

JUBILEE

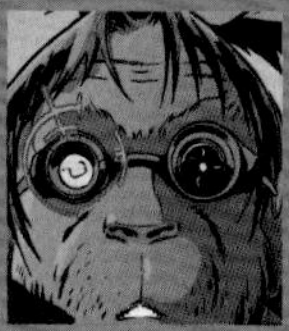

BEAST

G. WILLOW
WILSON
WRITER

ROLAND
BOSCHI
WITH JAVI FERNANDEZ (#24)
PENCILERS

JAY
LEISTEN
(#23-24)

ROLAND
BOSCHI
(#24-26)

MARK
PENNINGTON
(#24-25)

JAVI
FERNANDEZ
(#24)

HARVEY
HUGONNARD-BERT
(#25)

INKERS

LEE
LOUGHRIDGE
COLORIST

TRAVIS
LANHAM
LETTERER

COVER ART: **TERRY DODSON & RACHEL DODSON** (#23-24 & #26)
AND **JORGE MOLINA** (#25)
ASSISTANT EDITOR: **ALANNA SMITH**
EDITOR: **DANIEL KETCHUM**
X-MEN GROUP EDITOR: **MIKE MARTS**

X-MEN CREATED BY STAN LEE & JACK KIRBY

COLLECTION EDITOR: **JENNIFER GRÜNWALD** ASSISTANT EDITOR: **SARAH BRUNSTAD**
ASSOCIATE MANAGING EDITOR: **ALEX STARBUCK** EDITOR, SPECIAL PROJECTS: **MARK D. BEAZLEY**
SENIOR EDITOR, SPECIAL PROJECTS: **JEFF YOUNGQUIST** SVP PRINT, SALES & MARKETING: **DAVID GABRIEL**

EDITOR IN CHIEF: **AXEL ALONSO** CHIEF CREATIVE OFFICER: **JOE QUESADA**
PUBLISHER: **DAN BUCKLEY** EXECUTIVE PRODUCER: **ALAN FINE**

X-MEN VOL. 5: THE BURNING WORLD. Contains material originally published in magazine form as X-MEN #23-26. First printing 2015. ISBN# 978-0-7851-9726-3. Published by MARVEL WORLDWIDE, INC., a subsidiary of MARVEL ENTERTAINMENT, LLC. OFFICE OF PUBLICATION: 135 West 50th Street, New York, NY 10020. Copyright © 2015 MARVEL No similarity between any of the names, characters, persons, and/or institutions in this magazine with those of any living or dead person or institution is intended, and any such similarity which may exist is purely coincidental. **Printed in Canada.** ALAN FINE, President, Marvel Entertainment; DAN BUCKLEY, President, TV, Publishing and Brand Management; JOE QUESADA, Chief Creative Officer; TOM BREVOORT, SVP of Publishing; DAVID BOGART, SVP of Operations & Procurement, Publishing; C.B. CEBULSKI, VP of International Development & Brand Management; DAVID GABRIEL, SVP Print, Sales & Marketing; JIM O'KEEFE, VP of Operations & Logistics; DAN CARR, Executive Director of Publishing Technology; SUSAN CRESPI, Editorial Operations Manager; ALEX MORALES, Publishing Operations Manager; STAN LEE, Chairman Emeritus. For information regarding advertising in Marvel Comics or on Marvel.com, please contact Jonathan Rheingold, VP of Custom Solutions & Ad Sales, at jrheingold@marvel.com. For Marvel subscription inquiries, please call 800-217-9158. **Manufactured between 5/22/2015 and 6/29/2015 by SOLISCO PRINTERS, SCOTT, QC, CANADA.**
10 9 8 7 6 5 4 3 2 1

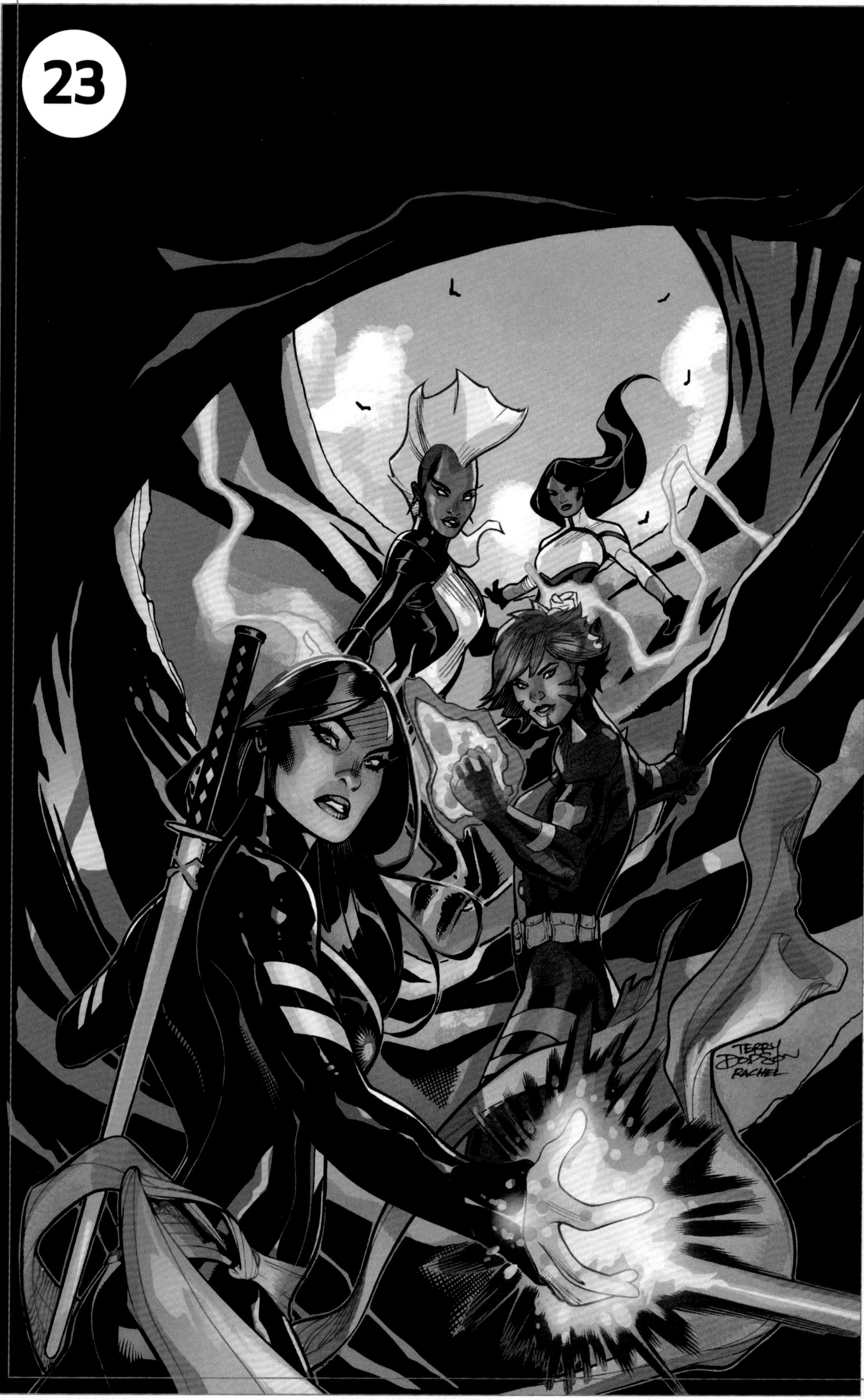
23
TERRY DODSON RACHEL

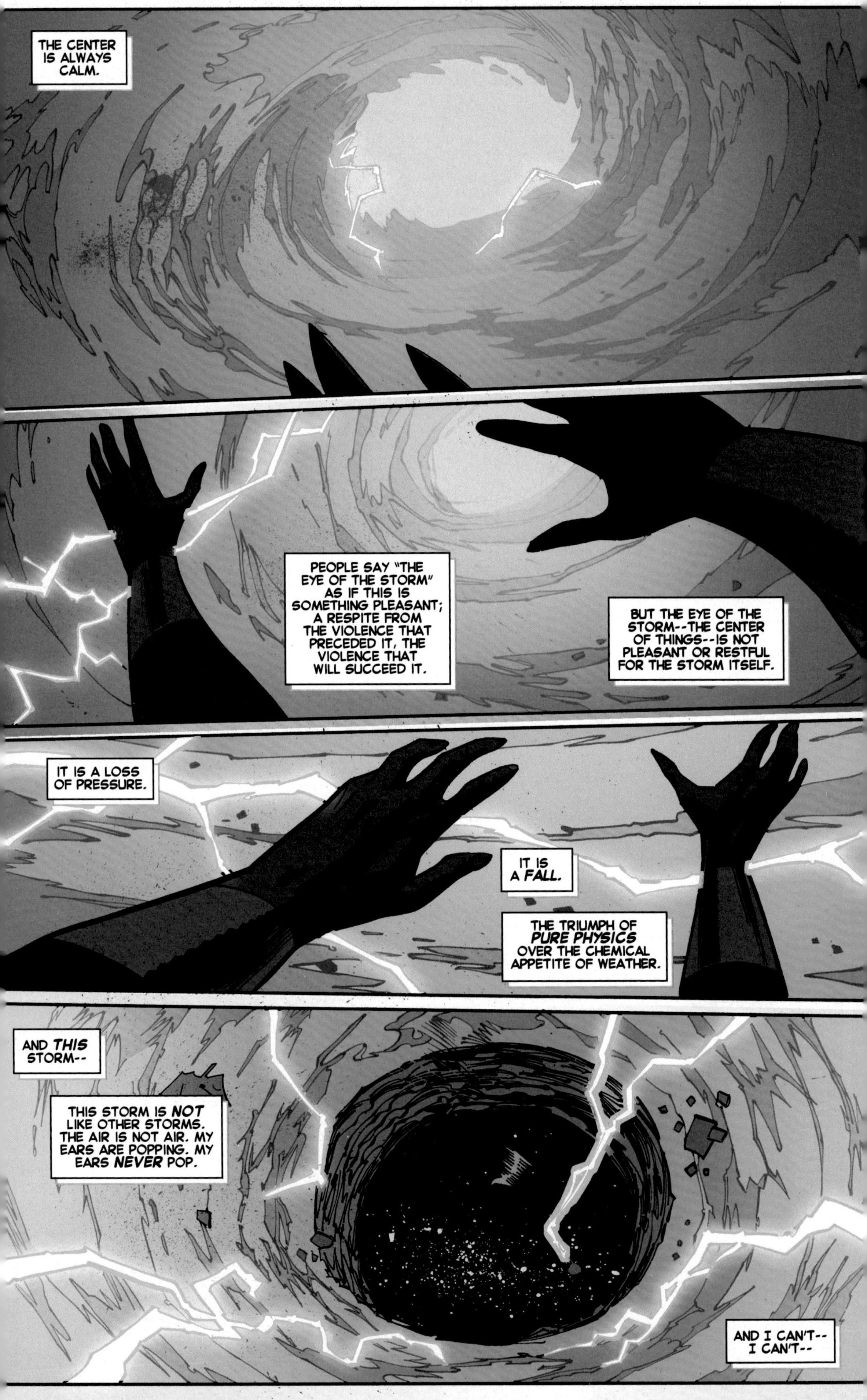
THE CENTER IS ALWAYS CALM.
PEOPLE SAY "THE EYE OF THE STORM" AS IF THIS IS SOMETHING PLEASANT; A RESPITE FROM THE VIOLENCE THAT PRECEDED IT, THE VIOLENCE THAT WILL SUCCEED IT.
BUT THE EYE OF THE STORM--THE CENTER OF THINGS--IS NOT PLEASANT OR RESTFUL FOR THE STORM ITSELF.
IT IS A LOSS OF PRESSURE.
IT IS A *FALL.*
THE TRIUMPH OF *PURE PHYSICS* OVER THE CHEMICAL APPETITE OF WEATHER.
AND *THIS* STORM--
THIS STORM IS *NOT* LIKE OTHER STORMS. THE AIR IS NOT AIR. MY EARS ARE POPPING. MY EARS *NEVER* POP.
AND I CAN'T-- I CAN'T--

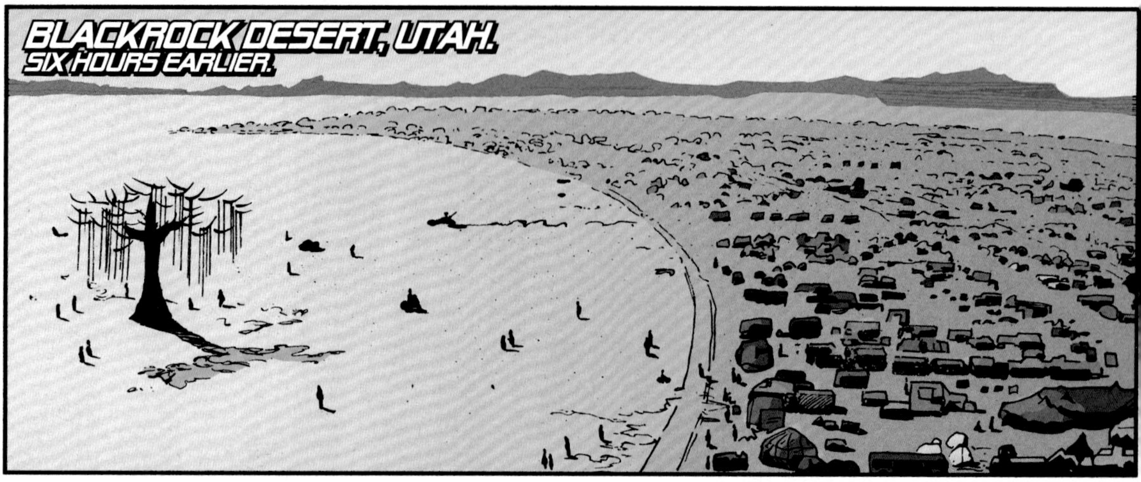

BLACKROCK DESERT, UTAH.
SIX HOURS EARLIER.

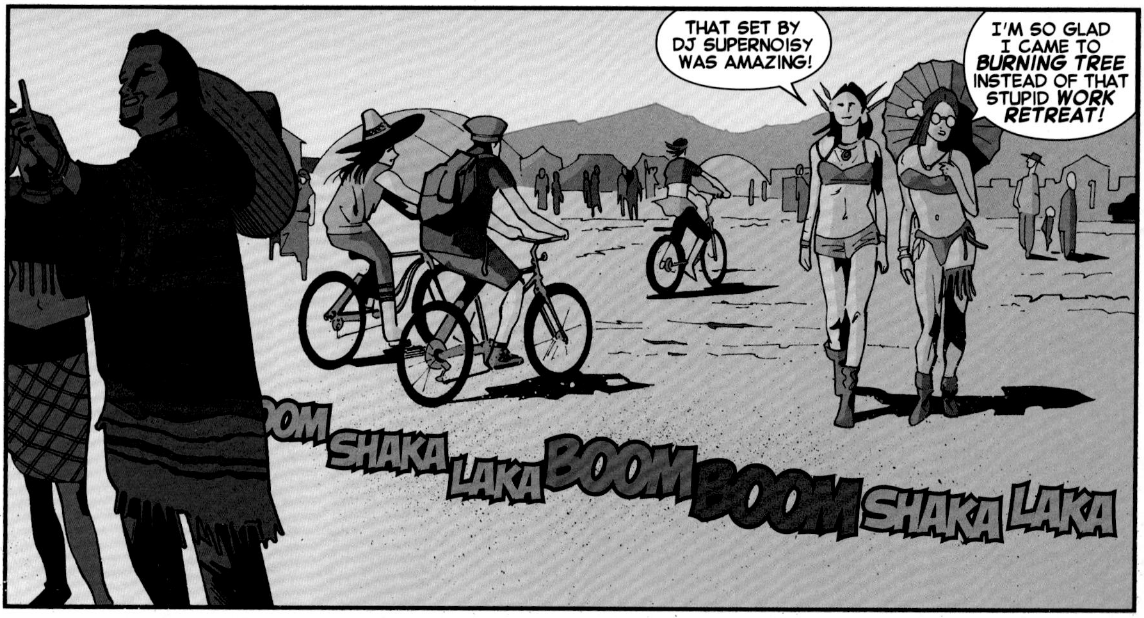

THAT SET BY DJ SUPERNOISY WAS AMAZING!
I'M SO GLAD I CAME TO BURNING TREE INSTEAD OF THAT STUPID WORK RETREAT!
OOM SHAKA LAKA BOOM BOOM SHAKA LAKA

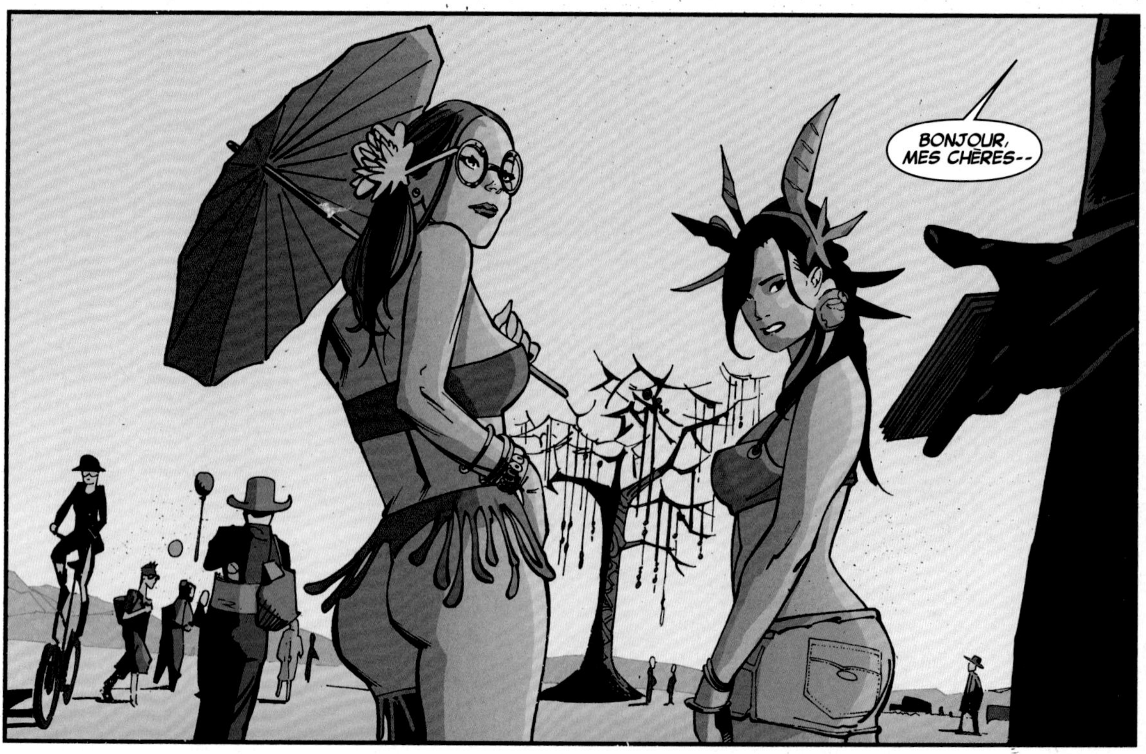

BONJOUR, MES CHÈRES--

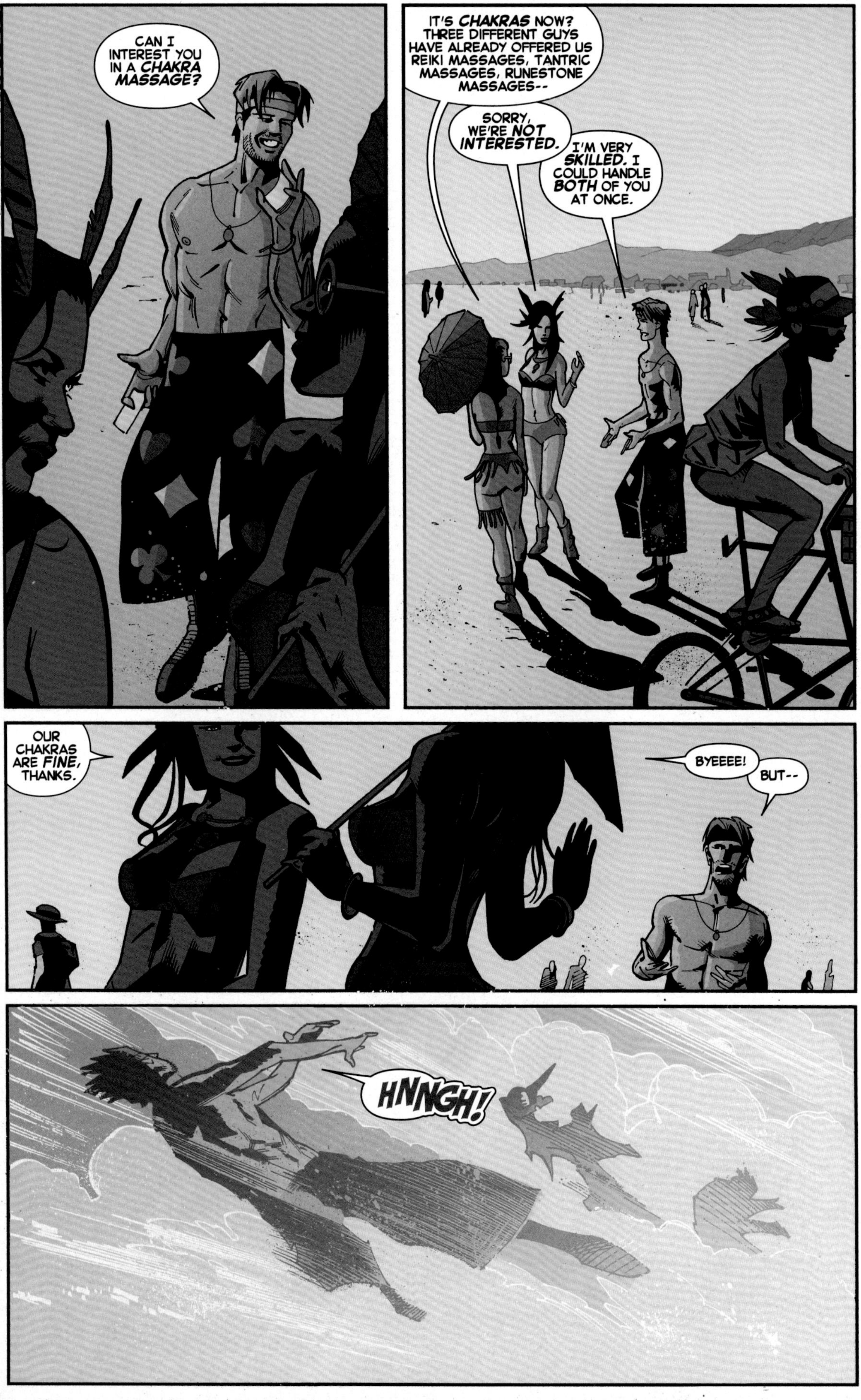
CAN I INTEREST YOU IN A CHAKRA MASSAGE?
IT'S CHAKRAS NOW? THREE DIFFERENT GUYS HAVE ALREADY OFFERED US REIKI MASSAGES, TANTRIC MASSAGES, RUNESTONE MASSAGES--
SORRY, WE'RE NOT INTERESTED.
I'M VERY SKILLED. I COULD HANDLE BOTH OF YOU AT ONCE.
OUR CHAKRAS ARE FINE, THANKS.
BYEEEE!
BUT--
HNNGH!

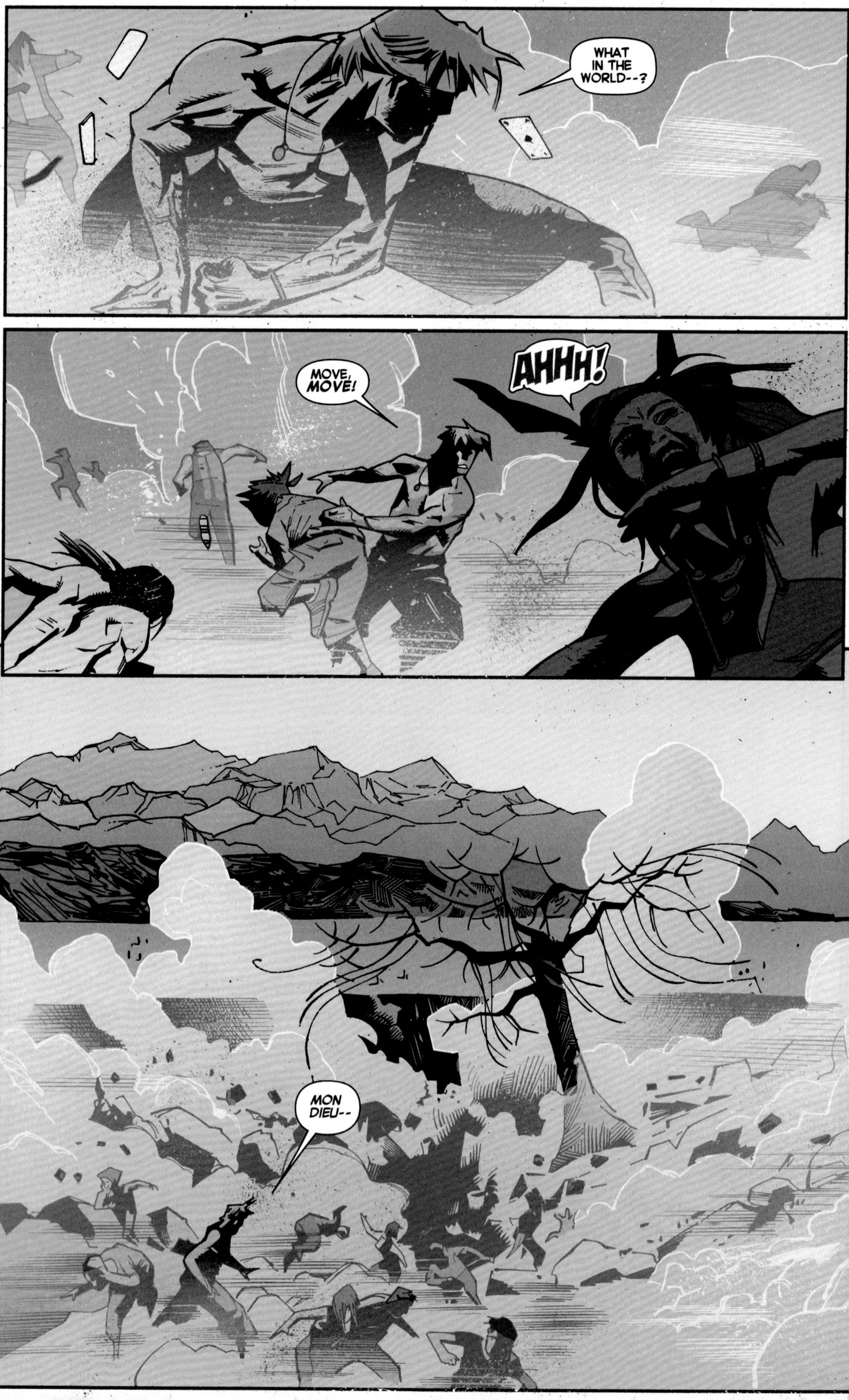
WHAT IN THE WORLD--?
MOVE, MOVE!
AHHH!
MON DIEU--

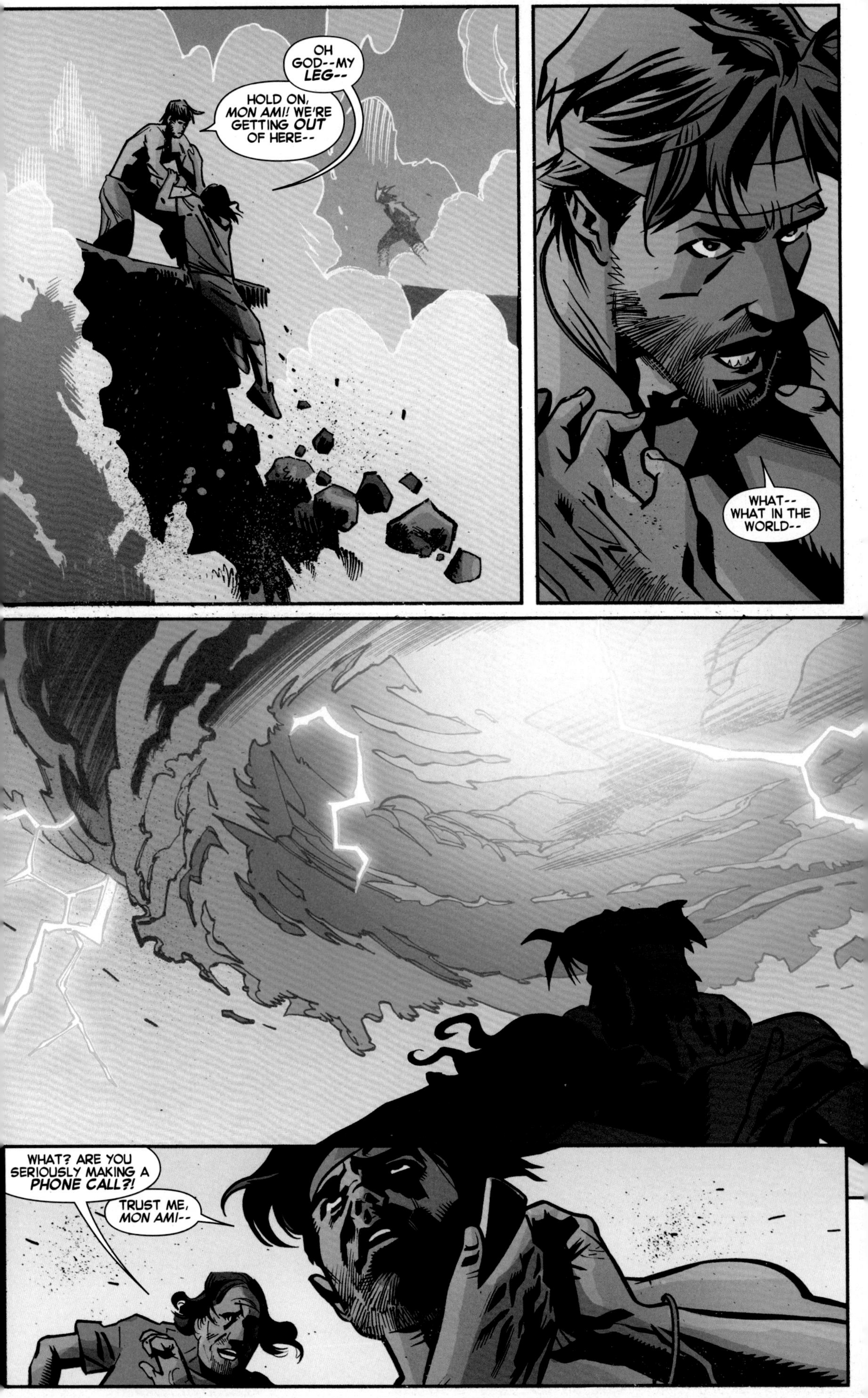
OH GOD--MY LEG--
HOLD ON, MON AMI! WE'RE GETTING OUT OF HERE--
WHAT-- WHAT IN THE WORLD--
WHAT? ARE YOU SERIOUSLY MAKING A PHONE CALL?!
TRUST ME, MON AMI--

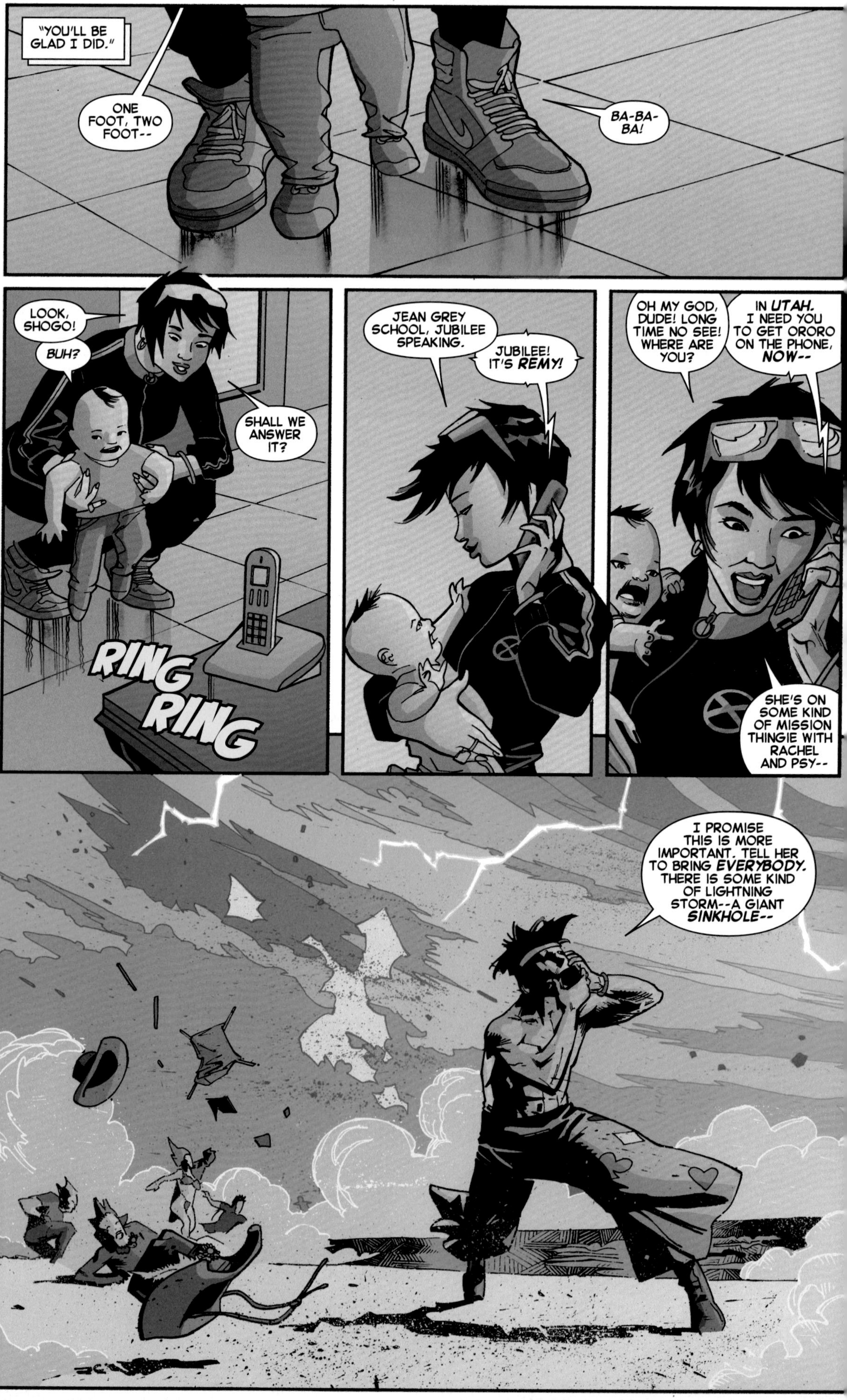
"YOU'LL BE GLAD I DID."
ONE FOOT, TWO FOOT--
BA-BA-BA!
LOOK, SHOGO!
BUH?
SHALL WE ANSWER IT?
RING RING
JEAN GREY SCHOOL, JUBILEE SPEAKING.
JUBILEE! IT'S REMY!
OH MY GOD, DUDE! LONG TIME NO SEE! WHERE ARE YOU?
IN UTAH. I NEED YOU TO GET ORORO ON THE PHONE, NOW--
SHE'S ON SOME KIND OF MISSION THINGIE WITH RACHEL AND PSY--
I PROMISE THIS IS MORE IMPORTANT. TELL HER TO BRING EVERYBODY. THERE IS SOME KIND OF LIGHTNING STORM--A GIANT SINKHOLE--

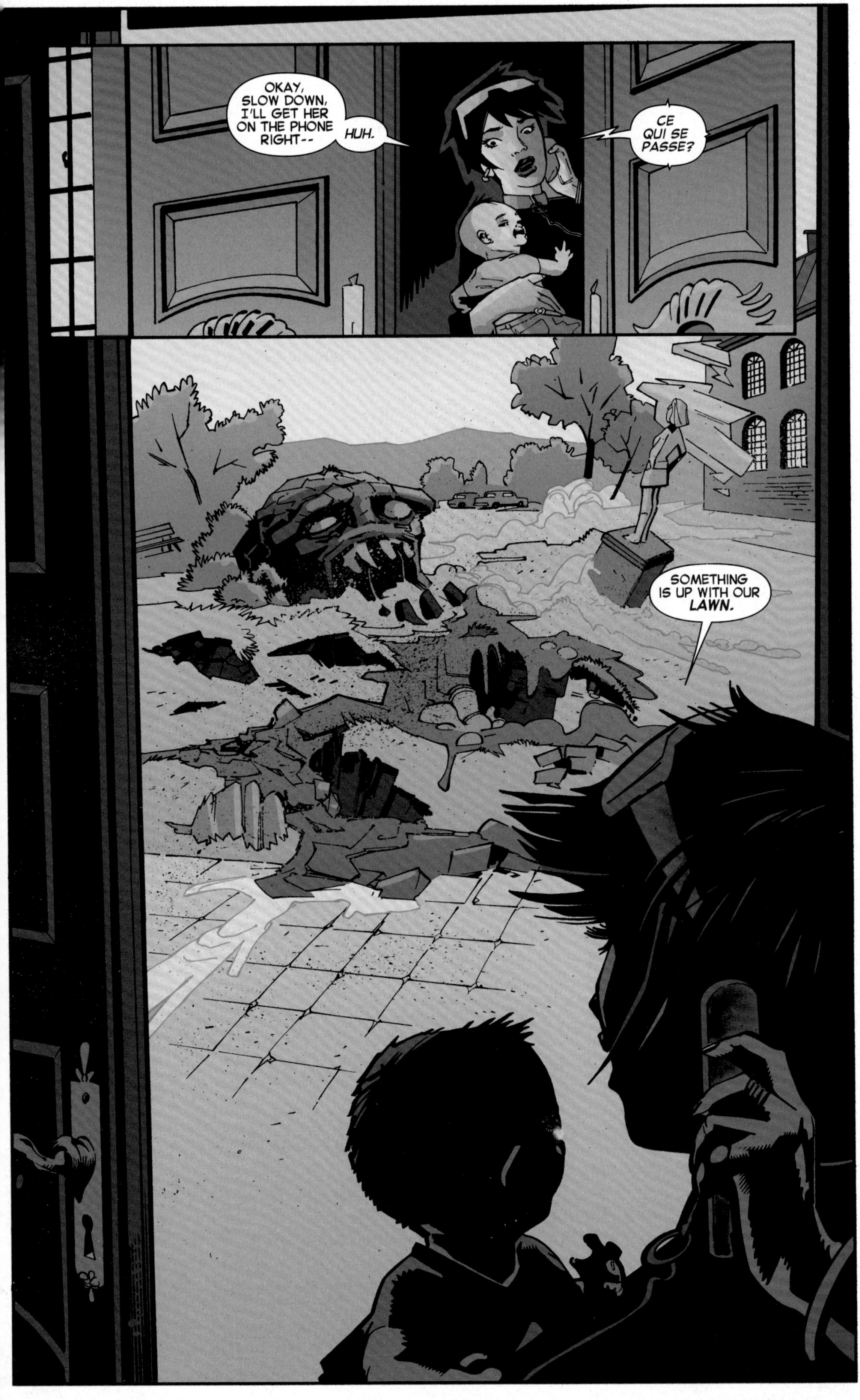

OKAY, SLOW DOWN, I'LL GET HER ON THE PHONE RIGHT--
HUH.
CE QUI SE PASSE?
SOMETHING IS UP WITH OUR LAWN.

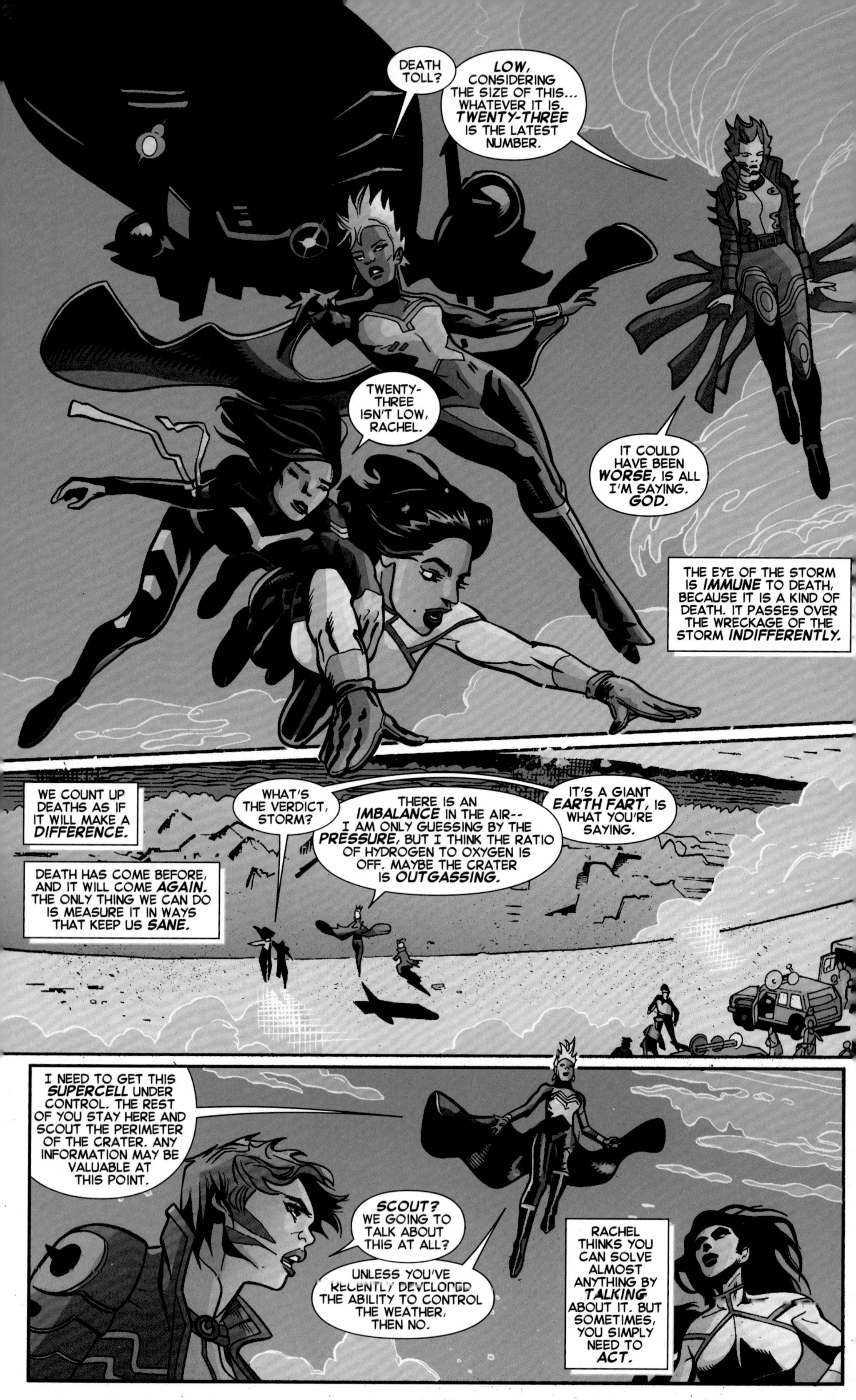
DEATH TOLL?
LOW, CONSIDERING THE SIZE OF THIS... WHATEVER IT IS. TWENTY-THREE IS THE LATEST NUMBER.
TWENTY-THREE ISN'T LOW, RACHEL.
IT COULD HAVE BEEN WORSE, IS ALL I'M SAYING. GOD.
THE EYE OF THE STORM IS IMMUNE TO DEATH, BECAUSE IT IS A KIND OF DEATH. IT PASSES OVER THE WRECKAGE OF THE STORM INDIFFERENTLY.
WE COUNT UP DEATHS AS IF IT WILL MAKE A DIFFERENCE.
DEATH HAS COME BEFORE, AND IT WILL COME AGAIN. THE ONLY THING WE CAN DO IS MEASURE IT IN WAYS THAT KEEP US SANE.
WHAT'S THE VERDICT, STORM?
THERE IS AN IMBALANCE IN THE AIR-- I AM ONLY GUESSING BY THE PRESSURE, BUT I THINK THE RATIO OF HYDROGEN TO OXYGEN IS OFF. MAYBE THE CRATER IS OUTGASSING.
IT'S A GIANT EARTH FART, IS WHAT YOU'RE SAYING.
I NEED TO GET THIS SUPERCELL UNDER CONTROL. THE REST OF YOU STAY HERE AND SCOUT THE PERIMETER OF THE CRATER. ANY INFORMATION MAY BE VALUABLE AT THIS POINT.
SCOUT? WE GOING TO TALK ABOUT THIS AT ALL?
UNLESS YOU'VE RECENTLY DEVELOPED THE ABILITY TO CONTROL THE WEATHER, THEN NO.
RACHEL THINKS YOU CAN SOLVE ALMOST ANYTHING BY TALKING ABOUT IT. BUT SOMETIMES, YOU SIMPLY NEED TO ACT.

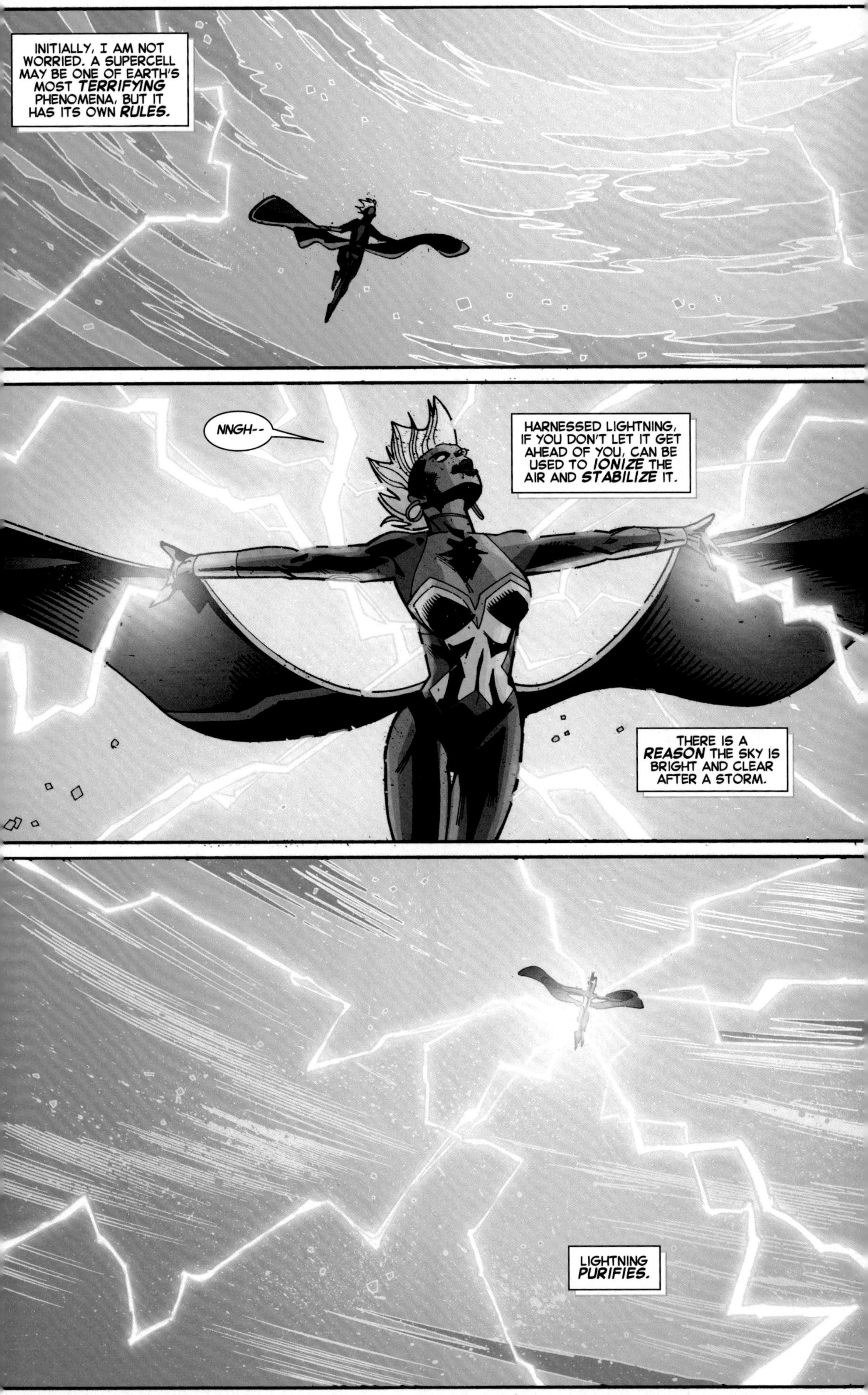
INITIALLY, I AM NOT WORRIED. A SUPERCELL MAY BE ONE OF EARTH'S MOST TERRIFYING PHENOMENA, BUT IT HAS ITS OWN RULES.
NNGH--
HARNESSED LIGHTNING, IF YOU DON'T LET IT GET AHEAD OF YOU, CAN BE USED TO IONIZE THE AIR AND STABILIZE IT.
THERE IS A REASON THE SKY IS BRIGHT AND CLEAR AFTER A STORM.
LIGHTNING PURIFIES.

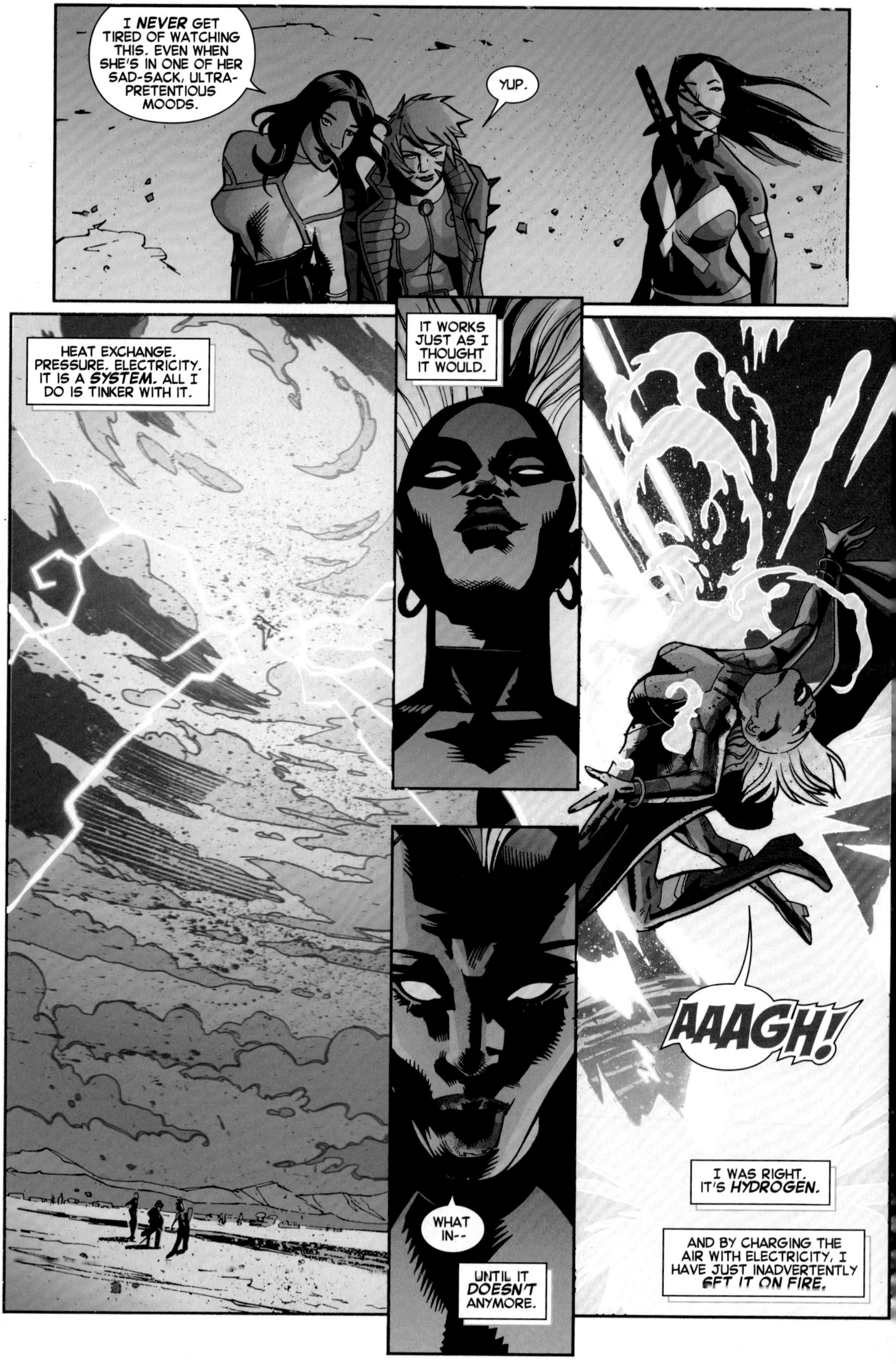

I NEVER GET TIRED OF WATCHING THIS. EVEN WHEN SHE'S IN ONE OF HER SAD-SACK, ULTRA-PRETENTIOUS MOODS.
YUP.
HEAT EXCHANGE. PRESSURE. ELECTRICITY. IT IS A SYSTEM. ALL I DO IS TINKER WITH IT.
IT WORKS JUST AS I THOUGHT IT WOULD.
UNTIL IT DOESN'T ANYMORE.
WHAT IN--
AAAGH!
I WAS RIGHT. IT'S HYDROGEN.
AND BY CHARGING THE AIR WITH ELECTRICITY, I HAVE JUST INADVERTENTLY SET IT ON FIRE.

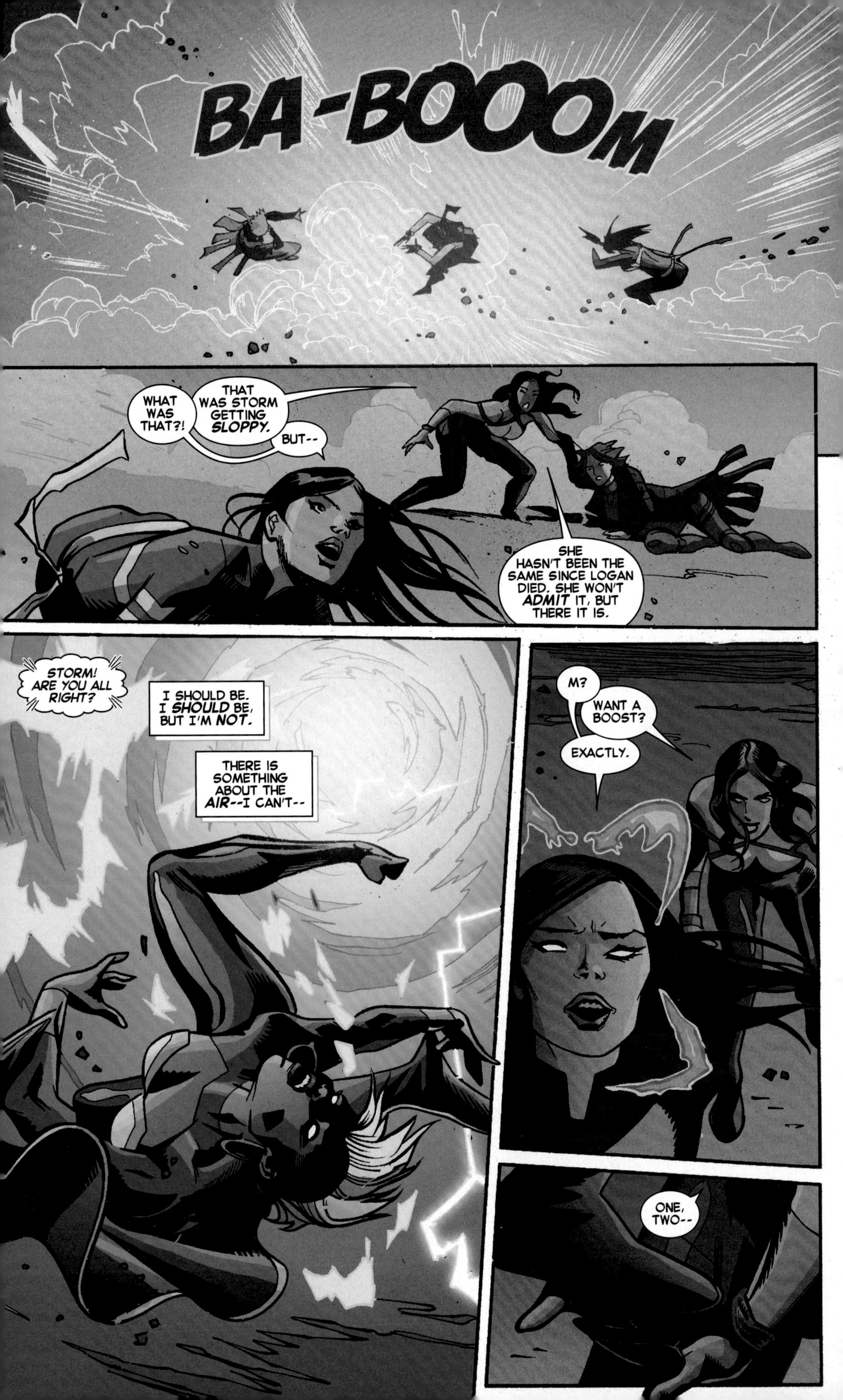
BA-BOOOM
WHAT WAS THAT?!
THAT WAS STORM GETTING SLOPPY.
BUT--
SHE HASN'T BEEN THE SAME SINCE LOGAN DIED. SHE WON'T ADMIT IT, BUT THERE IT IS.
STORM! ARE YOU ALL RIGHT?
I SHOULD BE. I SHOULD BE, BUT I'M NOT.
THERE IS SOMETHING ABOUT THE AIR--I CAN'T--
M?
WANT A BOOST?
EXACTLY.
ONE, TWO--

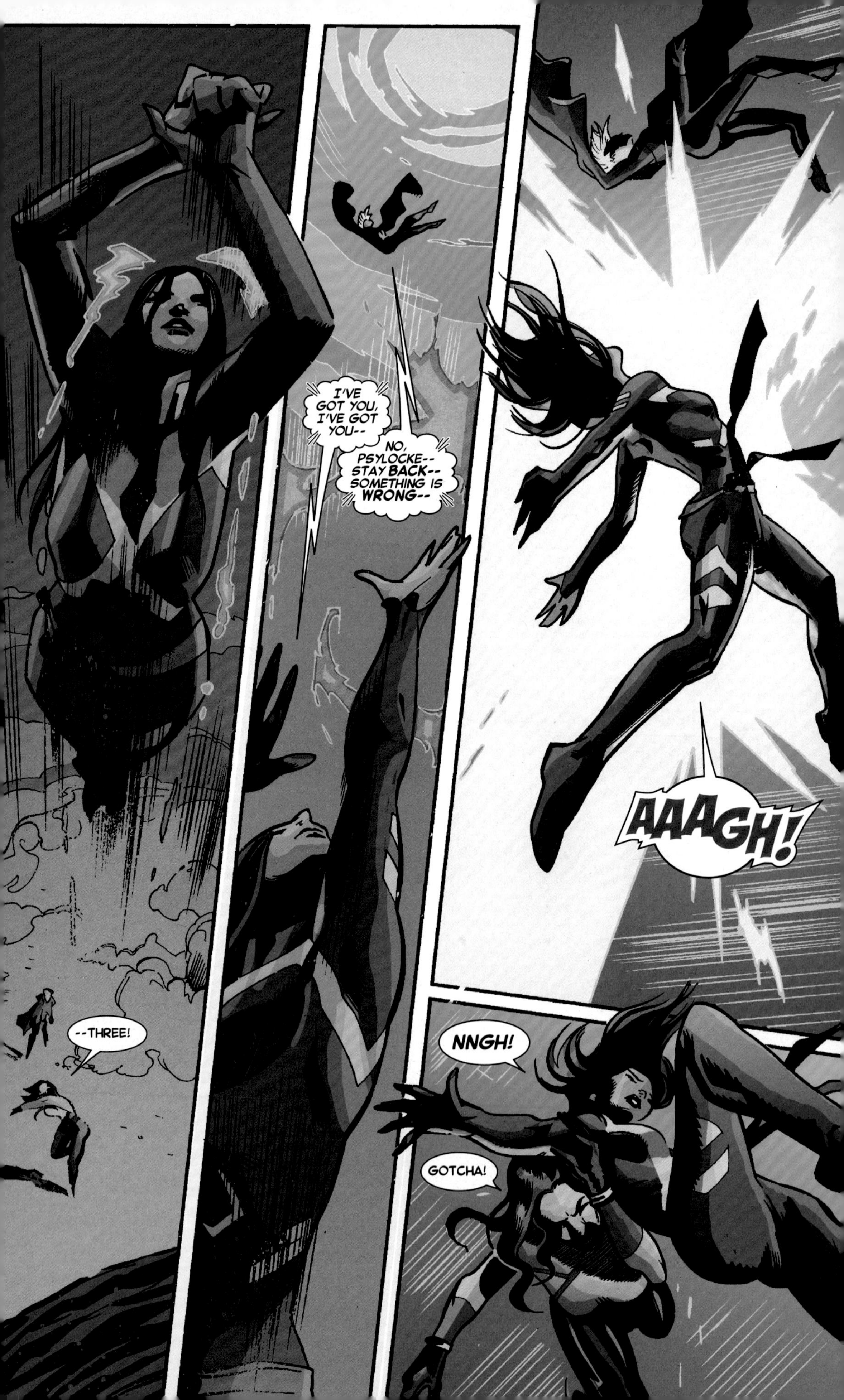
--THREE!
I'VE GOT YOU, I'VE GOT YOU--
NO, PSYLOCKE-- STAY BACK-- SOMETHING IS WRONG--
AAAGH!
NNGH!
GOTCHA!

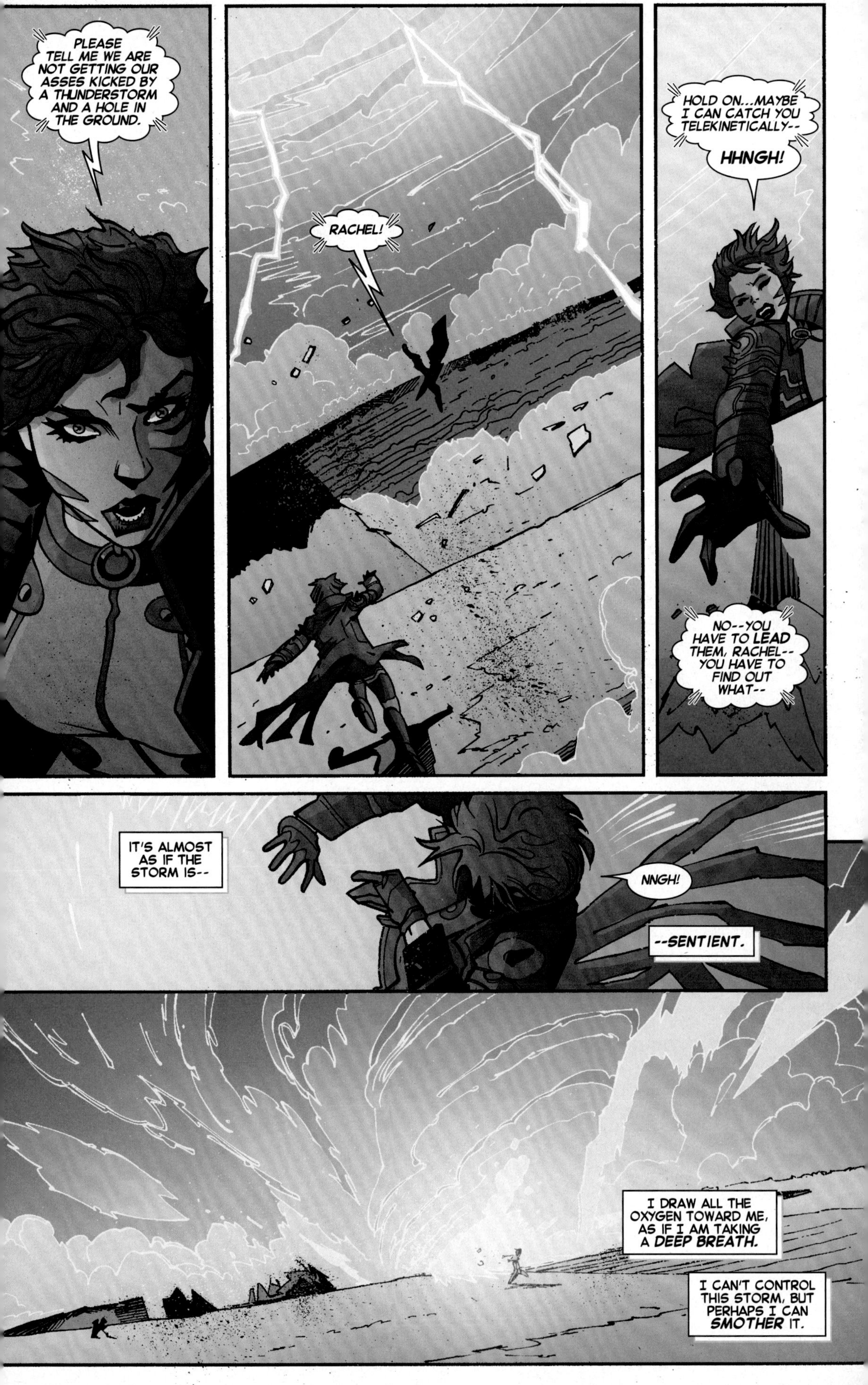
PLEASE TELL ME WE ARE NOT GETTING OUR ASSES KICKED BY A THUNDERSTORM AND A HOLE IN THE GROUND.
RACHEL!
HOLD ON...MAYBE I CAN CATCH YOU TELEKINETICALLY--
HHNGH!
NO--YOU HAVE TO LEAD THEM, RACHEL-- YOU HAVE TO FIND OUT WHAT--
IT'S ALMOST AS IF THE STORM IS--
NNGH!
--SENTIENT.
I DRAW ALL THE OXYGEN TOWARD ME, AS IF I AM TAKING A DEEP BREATH.
I CAN'T CONTROL THIS STORM, BUT PERHAPS I CAN SMOTHER IT.

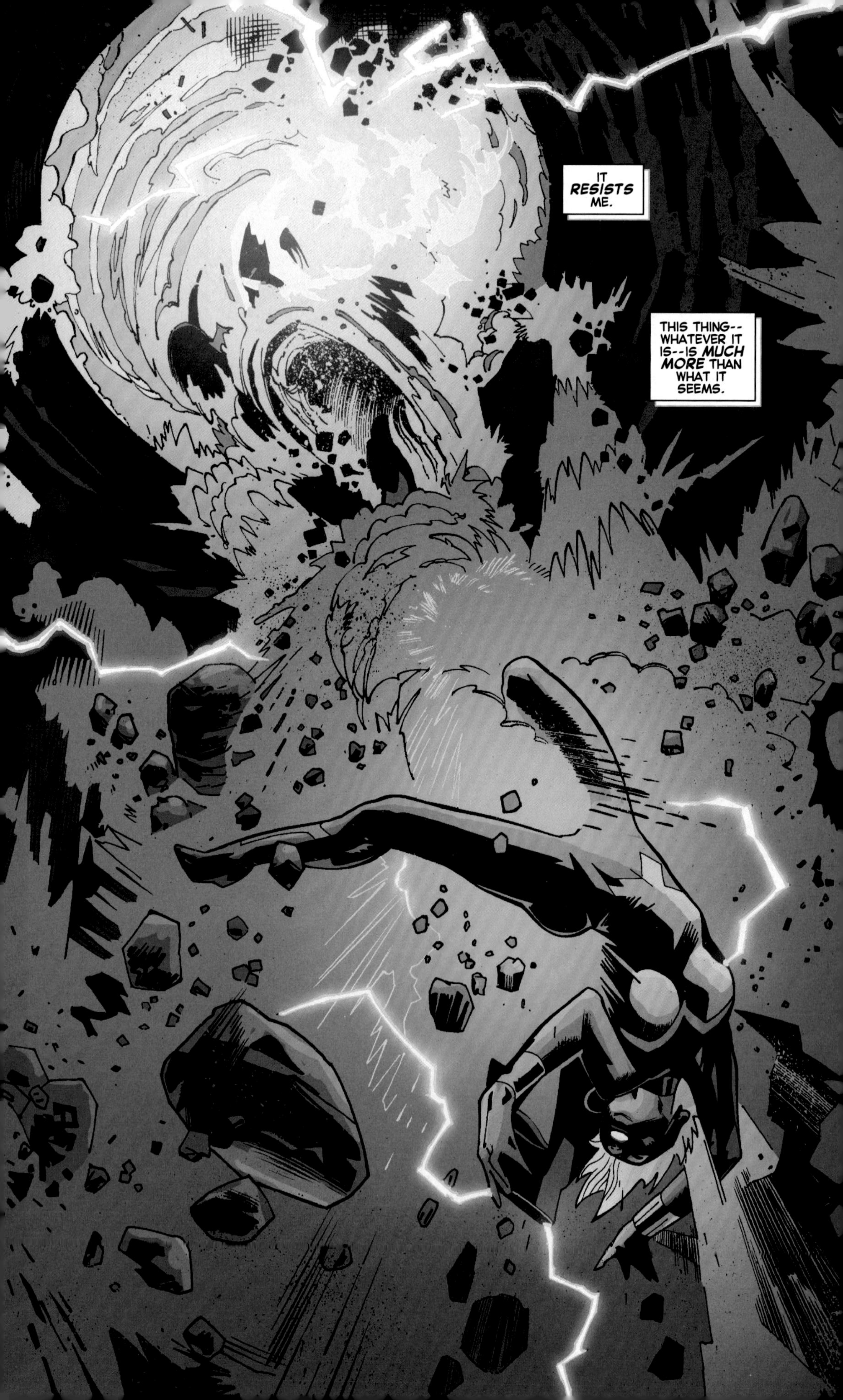
IT RESISTS ME.
THIS THING--WHATEVER IT IS--IS MUCH MORE THAN WHAT IT SEEMS.

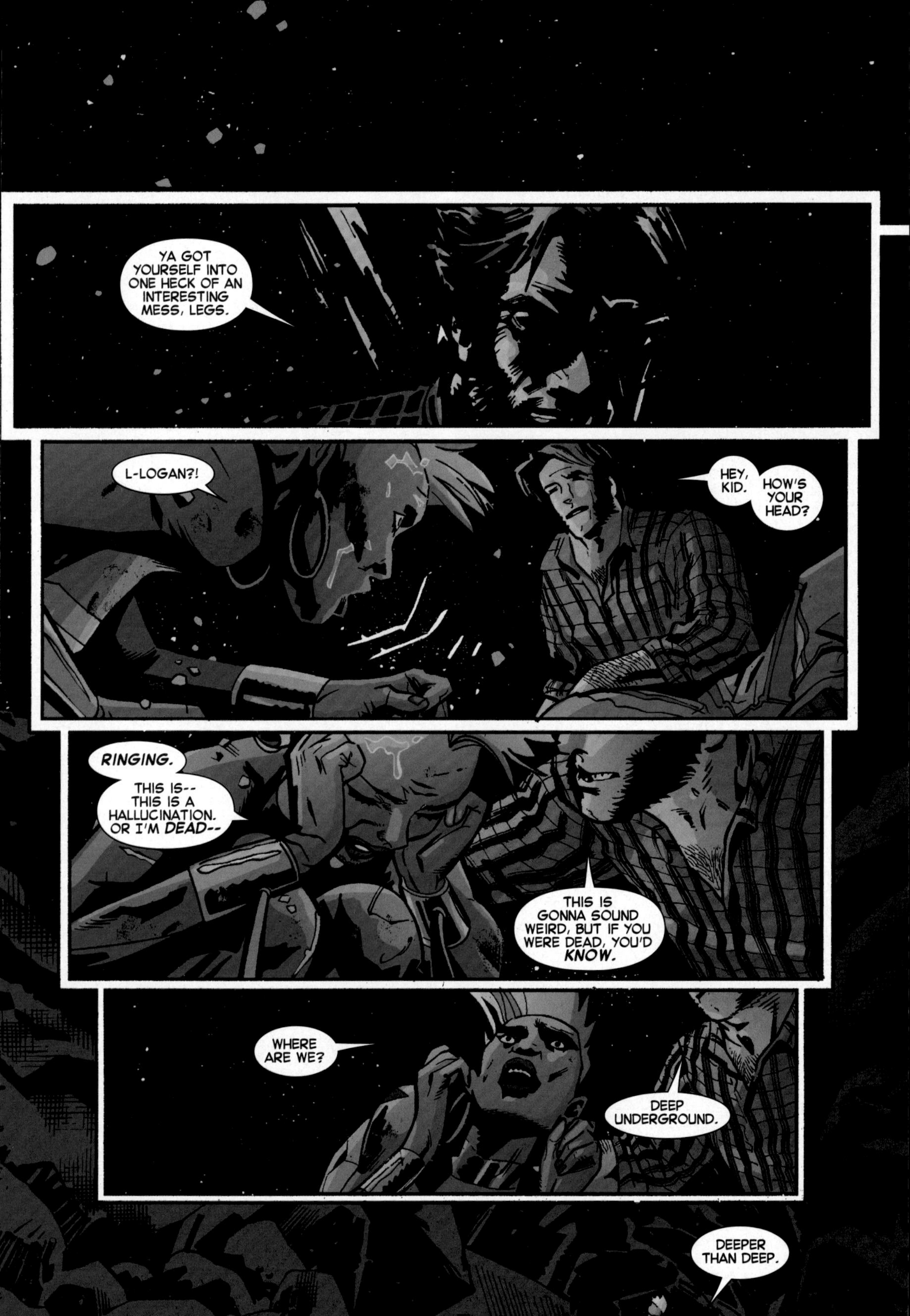
YA GOT YOURSELF INTO ONE HECK OF AN INTERESTING MESS, LEGS.
L-LOGAN?!
HEY, KID.
HOW'S YOUR HEAD?
RINGING.
THIS IS-- THIS IS A HALLUCINATION. OR I'M DEAD--
THIS IS GONNA SOUND WEIRD, BUT IF YOU WERE DEAD, YOU'D KNOW.
WHERE ARE WE?
DEEP UNDERGROUND.
DEEPER THAN DEEP.

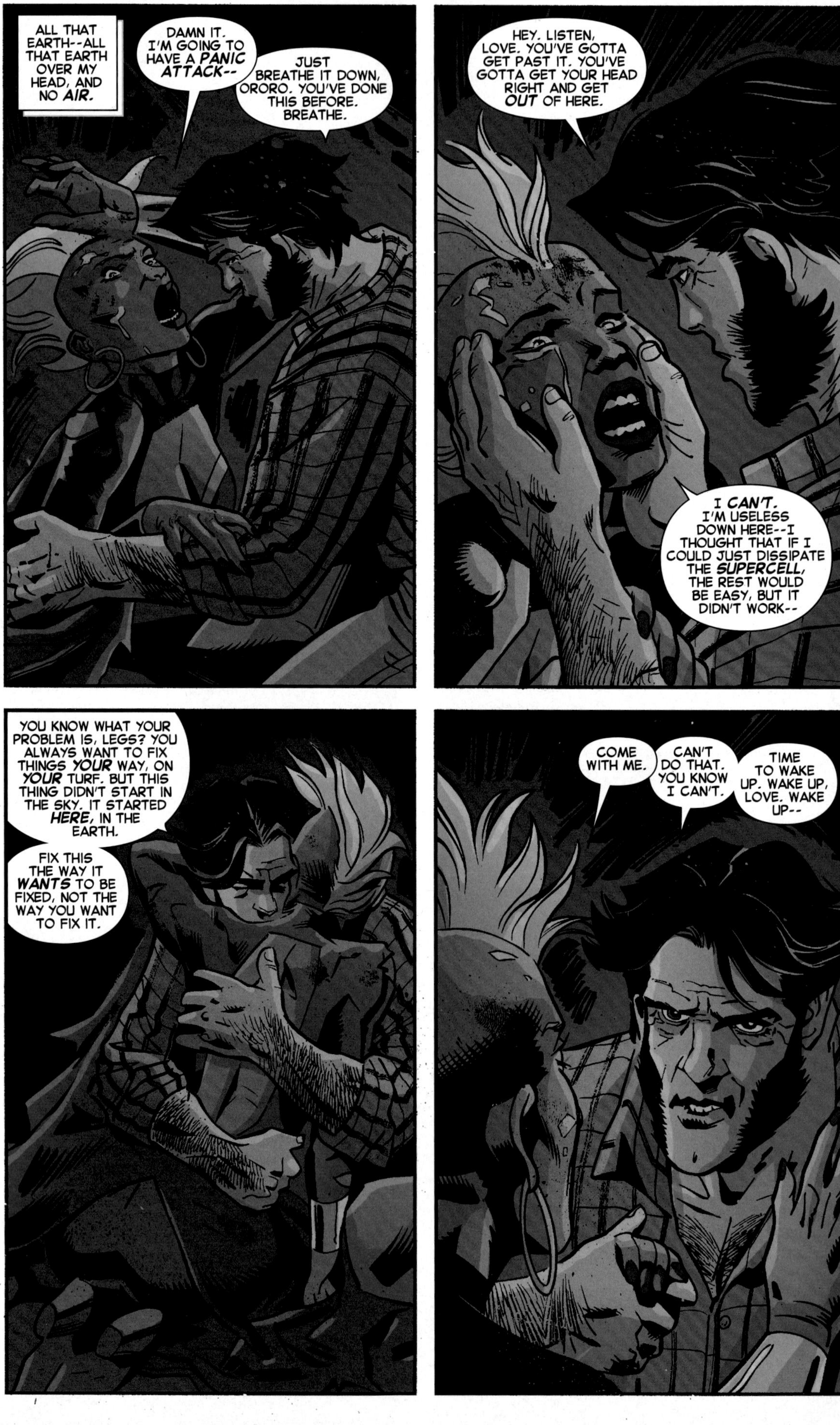
ALL THAT EARTH--ALL THAT EARTH OVER MY HEAD, AND NO AIR.
DAMN IT. I'M GOING TO HAVE A PANIC ATTACK--
JUST BREATHE IT DOWN, ORORO. YOU'VE DONE THIS BEFORE. BREATHE.
HEY. LISTEN, LOVE. YOU'VE GOTTA GET PAST IT. YOU'VE GOTTA GET YOUR HEAD RIGHT AND GET OUT OF HERE.
I CAN'T. I'M USELESS DOWN HERE--I THOUGHT THAT IF I COULD JUST DISSIPATE THE SUPERCELL, THE REST WOULD BE EASY, BUT IT DIDN'T WORK--
YOU KNOW WHAT YOUR PROBLEM IS, LEGS? YOU ALWAYS WANT TO FIX THINGS YOUR WAY, ON YOUR TURF. BUT THIS THING DIDN'T START IN THE SKY. IT STARTED HERE, IN THE EARTH.
FIX THIS THE WAY IT WANTS TO BE FIXED, NOT THE WAY YOU WANT TO FIX IT.
COME WITH ME.
CAN'T DO THAT. YOU KNOW I CAN'T.
TIME TO WAKE UP. WAKE UP, LOVE. WAKE UP--

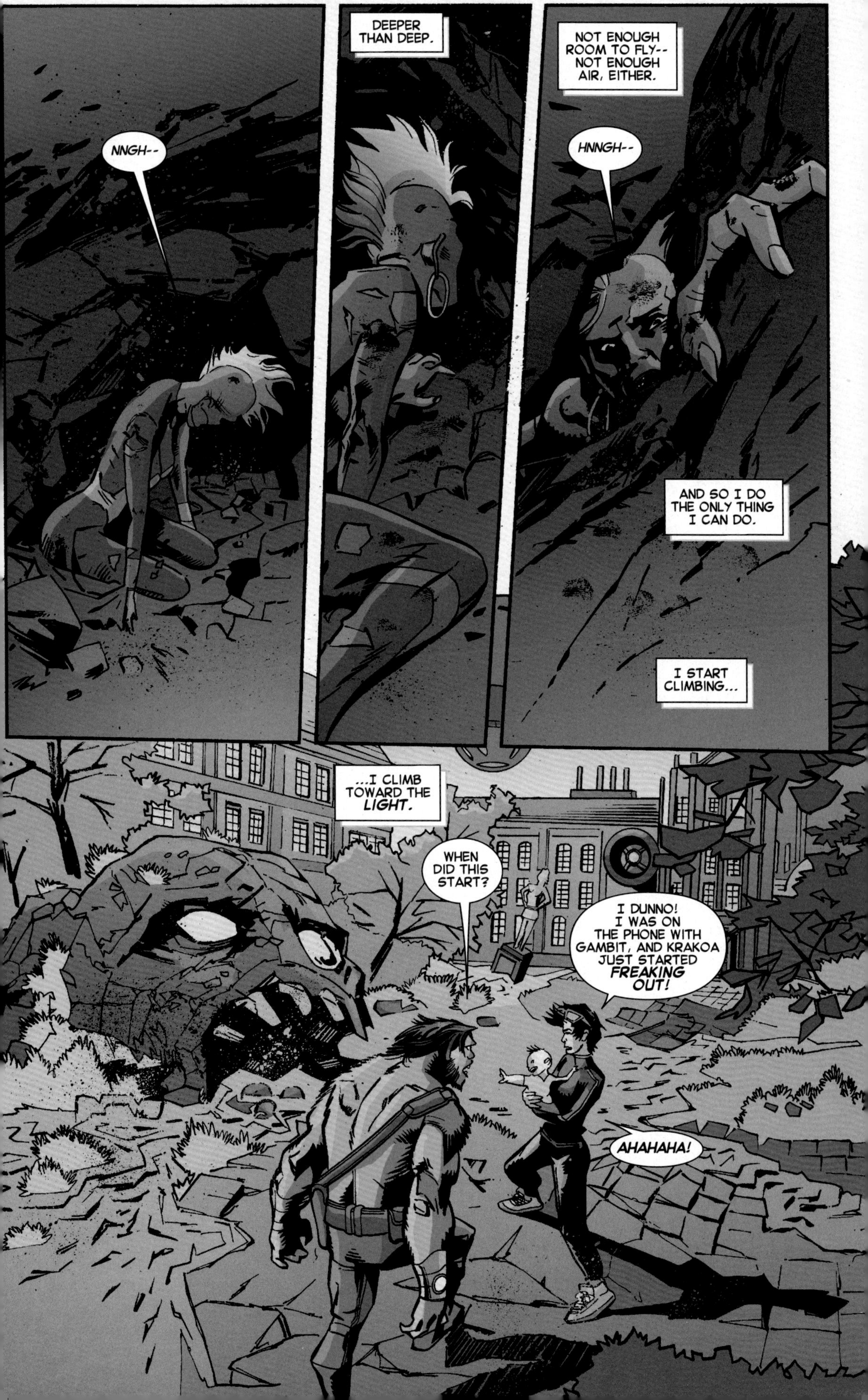
NNGH--
DEEPER THAN DEEP.
NOT ENOUGH ROOM TO FLY-- NOT ENOUGH AIR, EITHER.
HNNGH--
AND SO I DO THE ONLY THING I CAN DO.
I START CLIMBING...
...I CLIMB TOWARD THE LIGHT.
WHEN DID THIS START?
I DUNNO! I WAS ON THE PHONE WITH GAMBIT, AND KRAKOA JUST STARTED FREAKING OUT!
AHAHAHA!

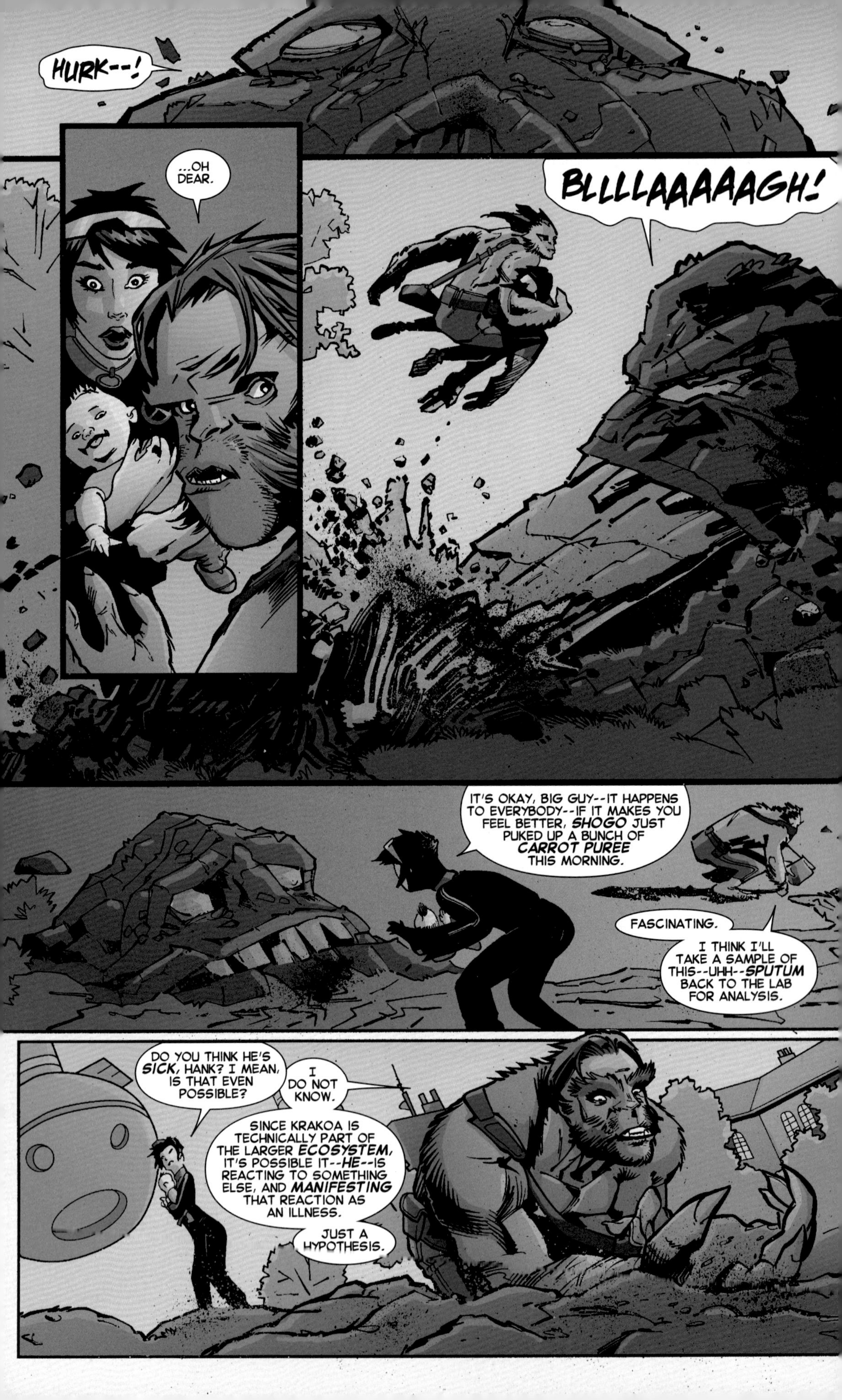
HURK--!
...OH DEAR.
BLLLLAAAAAGH!
IT'S OKAY, BIG GUY--IT HAPPENS TO EVERYBODY--IF IT MAKES YOU FEEL BETTER, SHOGO JUST PUKED UP A BUNCH OF CARROT PUREE THIS MORNING.
FASCINATING.
I THINK I'LL TAKE A SAMPLE OF THIS--UHH--SPUTUM BACK TO THE LAB FOR ANALYSIS.
DO YOU THINK HE'S SICK, HANK? I MEAN, IS THAT EVEN POSSIBLE?
I DO NOT KNOW.
SINCE KRAKOA IS TECHNICALLY PART OF THE LARGER ECOSYSTEM, IT'S POSSIBLE IT--HE--IS REACTING TO SOMETHING ELSE, AND MANIFESTING THAT REACTION AS AN ILLNESS.
JUST A HYPOTHESIS.

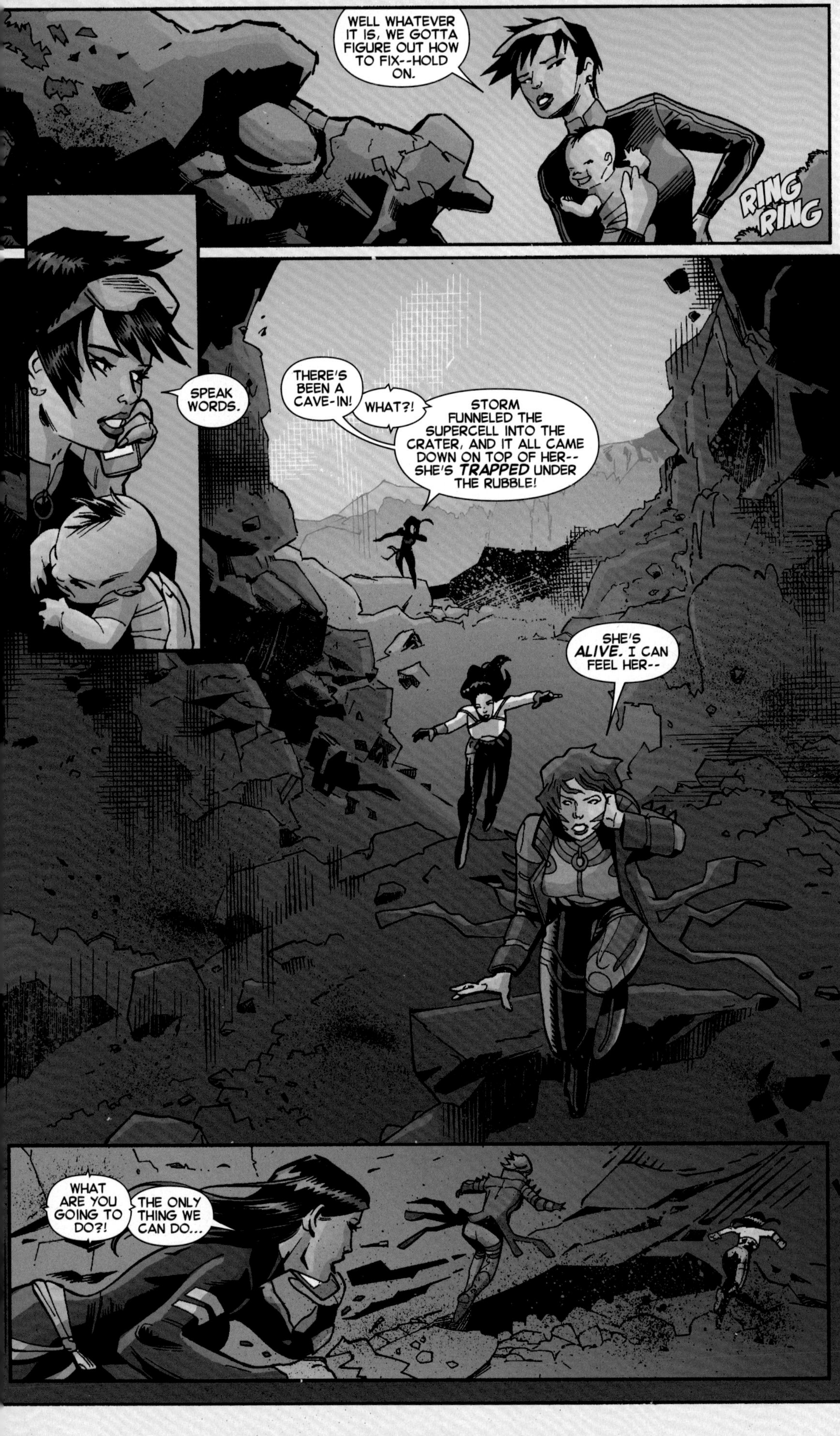

WELL WHATEVER IT IS, WE GOTTA FIGURE OUT HOW TO FIX--HOLD ON.
RING RING
SPEAK WORDS.
THERE'S BEEN A CAVE-IN!
WHAT?!
STORM FUNNELED THE SUPERCELL INTO THE CRATER, AND IT ALL CAME DOWN ON TOP OF HER--SHE'S *TRAPPED* UNDER THE RUBBLE!
SHE'S *ALIVE.* I CAN FEEL HER--
WHAT ARE YOU GOING TO DO?!
THE ONLY THING WE CAN DO...

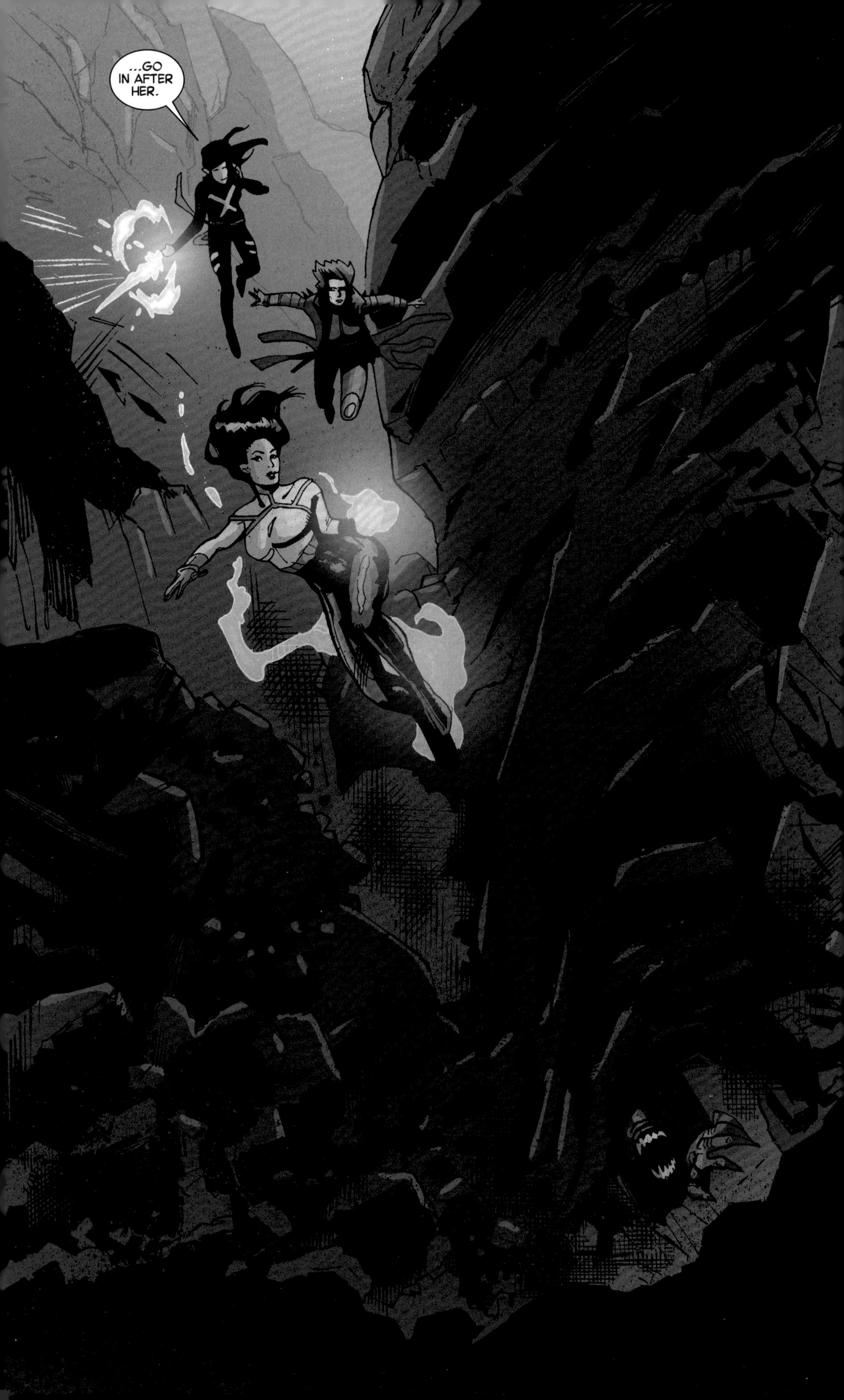
...GO IN AFTER HER.

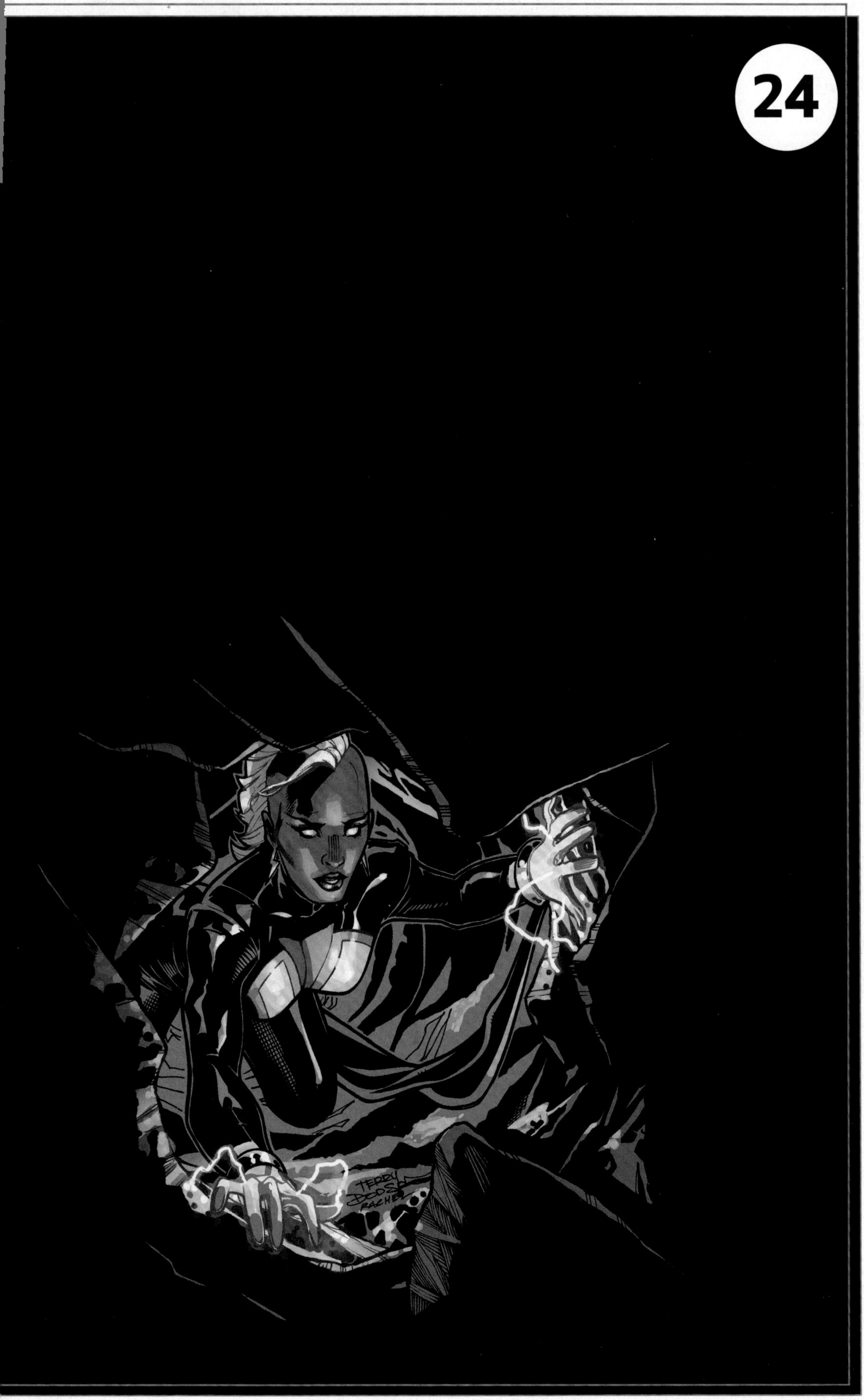
24

WHEN I THINK OF MYSELF AS *PSYLOCKE* INSTEAD OF BETSY, SOMETIMES I GET *OVERCONFIDENT.* SOMEBODY CALLED *PSYLOCKE* OBVIOUSLY KNOWS WHAT THE SCORE IS AT ALL TIMES.

AT THE BEGINNING, I ASSUMED THIS WOULD BE ONE OF THOSE *STRAIGHTFORWARD* MISSIONS.

WE GO IN, WE GET *STORM,* WE GET OUT. WHAT COULD BE EASIER.

HHNGH!

WOMP

YES, THERE HAD BEEN A GIANT, INEXPLICABLE *SUPERCELL,* A HOLE IN THE GROUND *OUTGASSING HYDROGEN,* BUT FOR US, THAT'S BASICALLY *TUESDAY.*

IT WAS ONLY AFTER WE'D CLIMBED DOWN FORTY FEET THAT WE REALIZED...

GUYS--

WE HAD *NO IDEA* WHAT WE WERE REALLY GETTING INTO.

UGH!

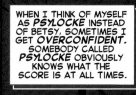

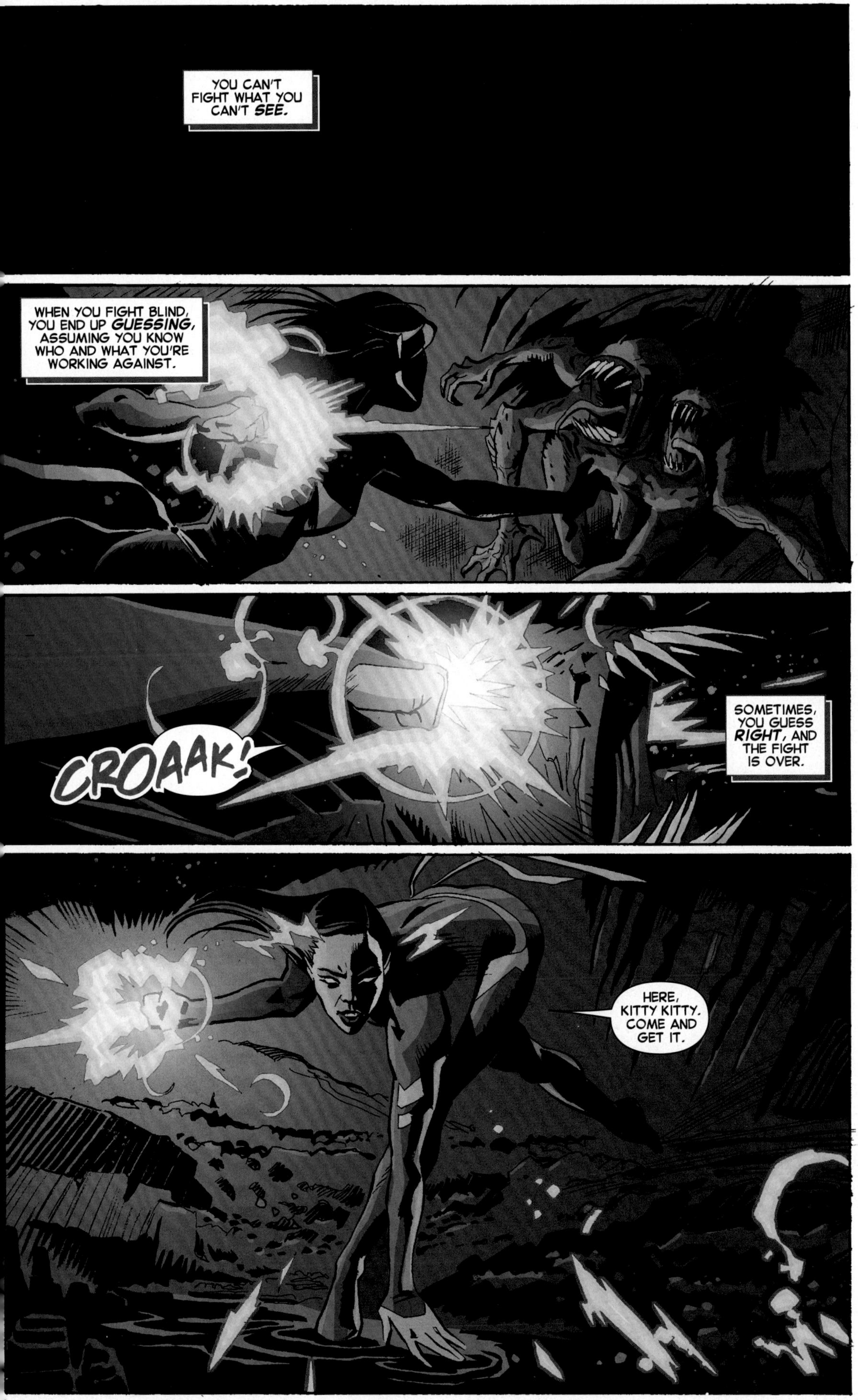
YOU CAN'T FIGHT WHAT YOU CAN'T *SEE.*
WHEN YOU FIGHT BLIND, YOU END UP *GUESSING*, ASSUMING YOU KNOW WHO AND WHAT YOU'RE WORKING AGAINST.
CROAAK!
SOMETIMES, YOU GUESS *RIGHT*, AND THE FIGHT IS OVER.
HERE, KITTY KITTY. COME AND GET IT.

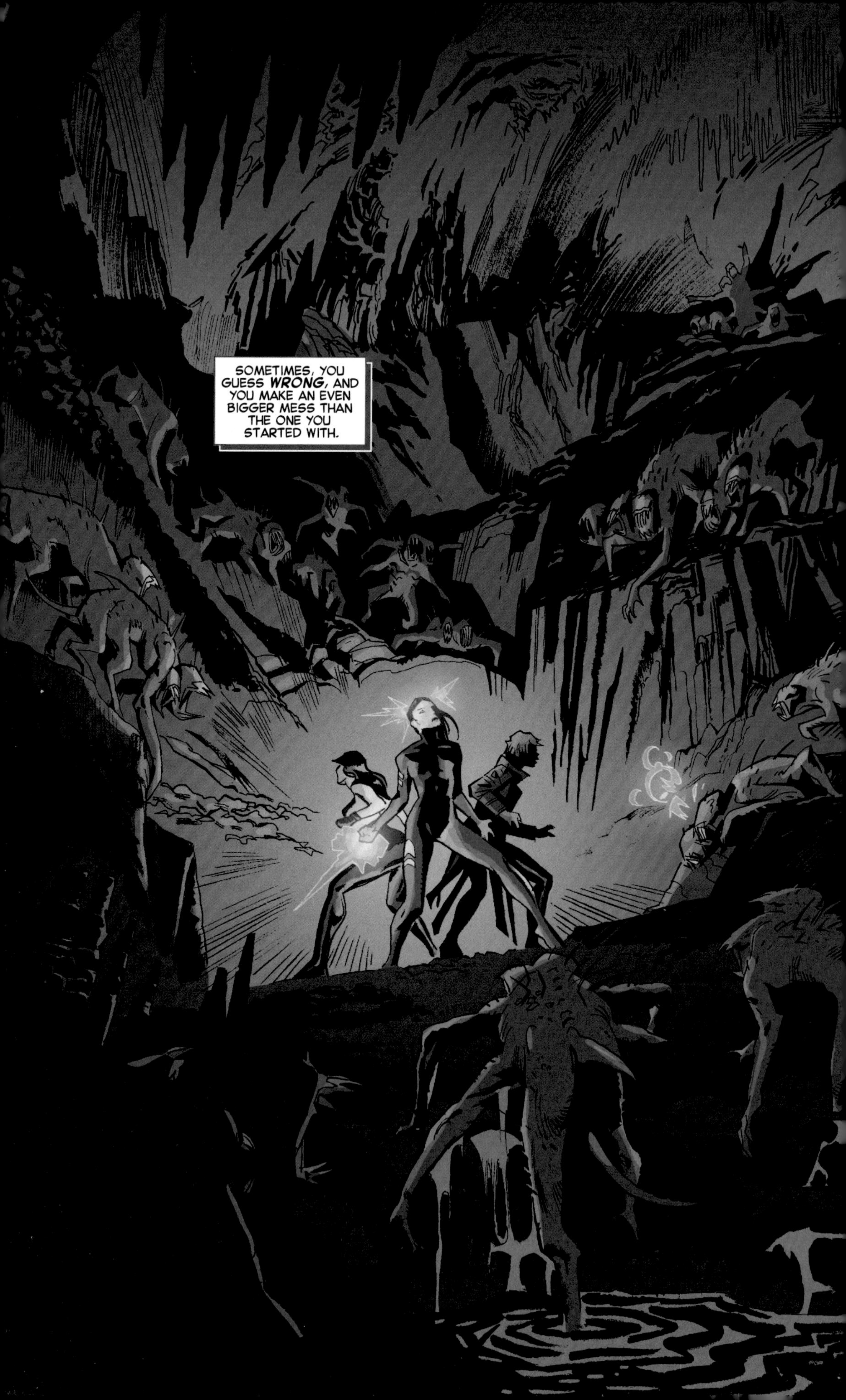
SOMETIMES, YOU GUESS **WRONG**, AND YOU MAKE AN EVEN BIGGER MESS THAN THE ONE YOU STARTED WITH.

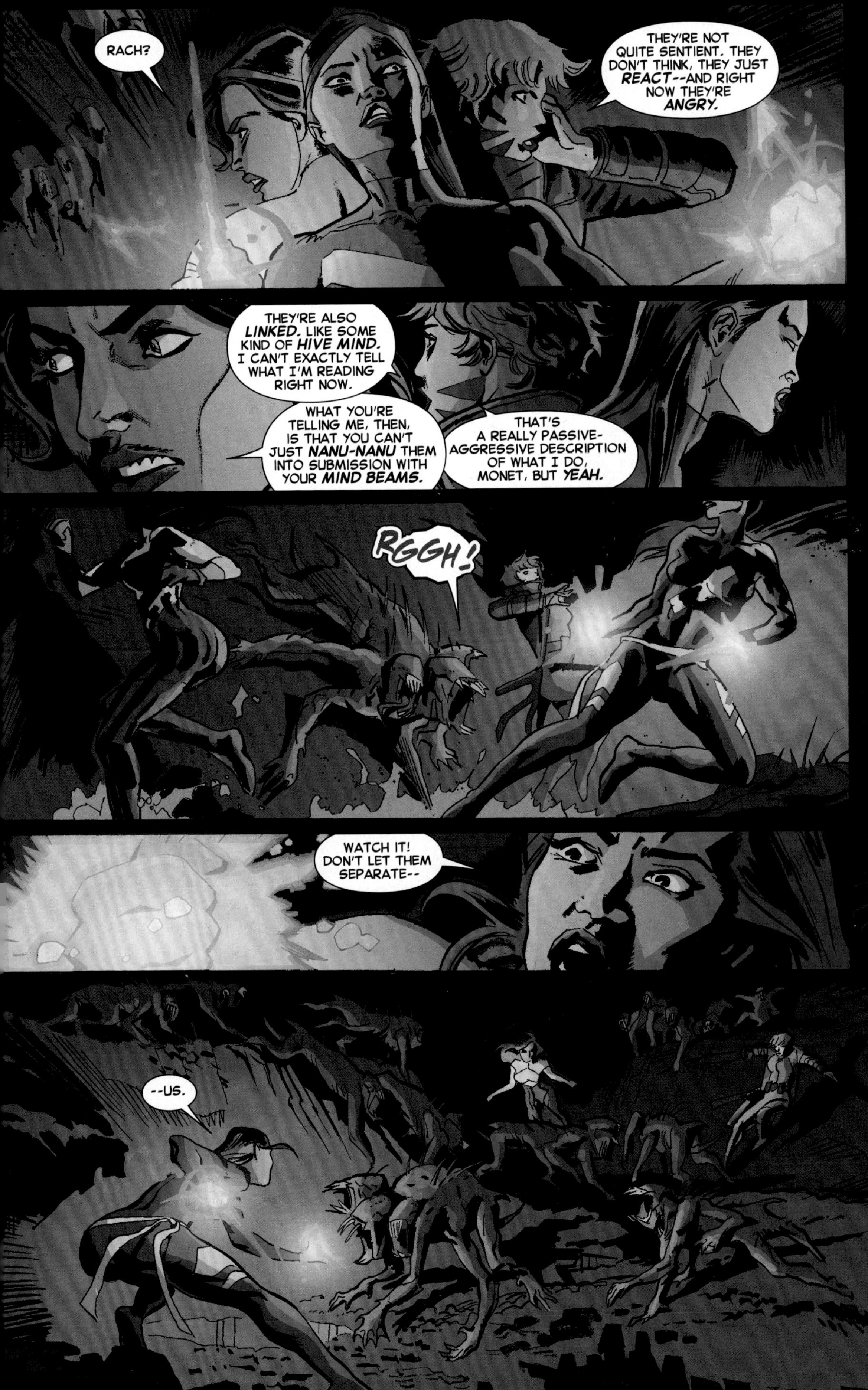
RACH?
THEY'RE NOT QUITE SENTIENT. THEY DON'T THINK, THEY JUST REACT--AND RIGHT NOW THEY'RE ANGRY.
THEY'RE ALSO LINKED. LIKE SOME KIND OF HIVE MIND. I CAN'T EXACTLY TELL WHAT I'M READING RIGHT NOW.
WHAT YOU'RE TELLING ME, THEN, IS THAT YOU CAN'T JUST NANU-NANU THEM INTO SUBMISSION WITH YOUR MIND BEAMS.
THAT'S A REALLY PASSIVE-AGGRESSIVE DESCRIPTION OF WHAT I DO, MONET, BUT YEAH.
RGGH!
WATCH IT! DON'T LET THEM SEPARATE--
--US.

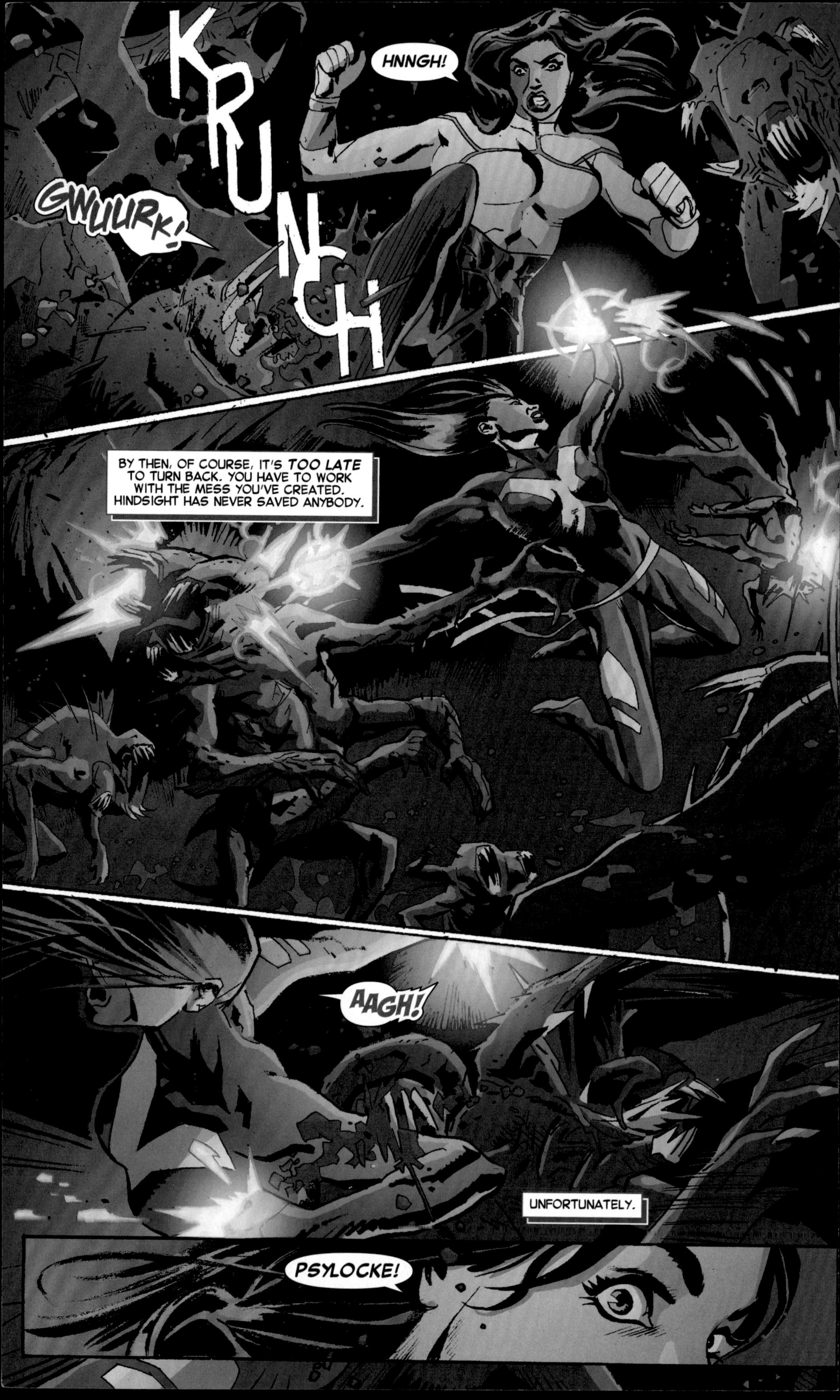
KRUNCH
HNNGH!
GWUUURK!
BY THEN, OF COURSE, IT'S *TOO LATE* TO TURN BACK. YOU HAVE TO WORK WITH THE MESS YOU'VE CREATED. HINDSIGHT HAS NEVER SAVED ANYBODY.
AAGH!
UNFORTUNATELY.
PSYLOCKE!

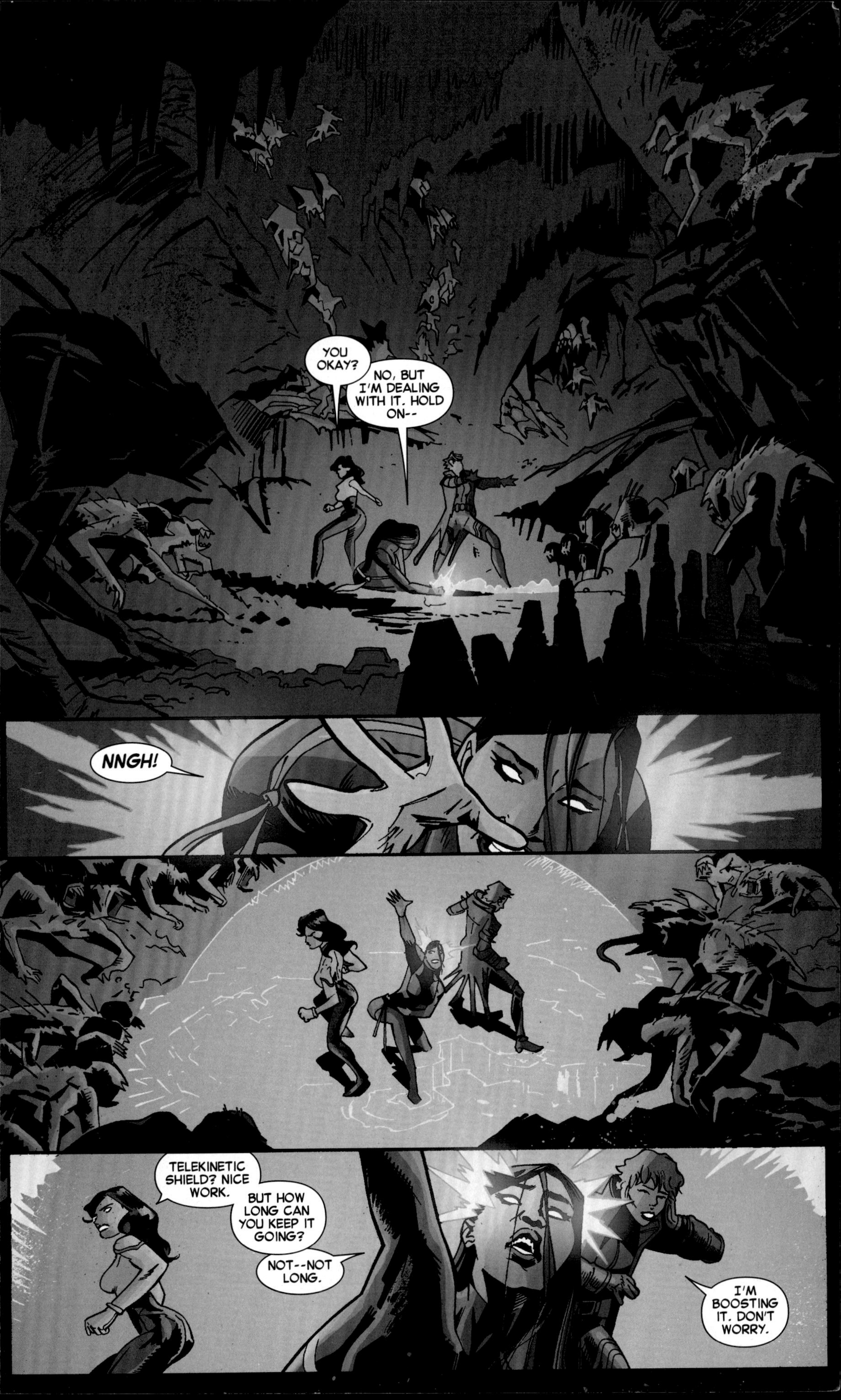
YOU OKAY?
NO, BUT I'M DEALING WITH IT. HOLD ON--
NNGH!
TELEKINETIC SHIELD? NICE WORK.
BUT HOW LONG CAN YOU KEEP IT GOING?
NOT--NOT LONG.
I'M BOOSTING IT. DON'T WORRY.

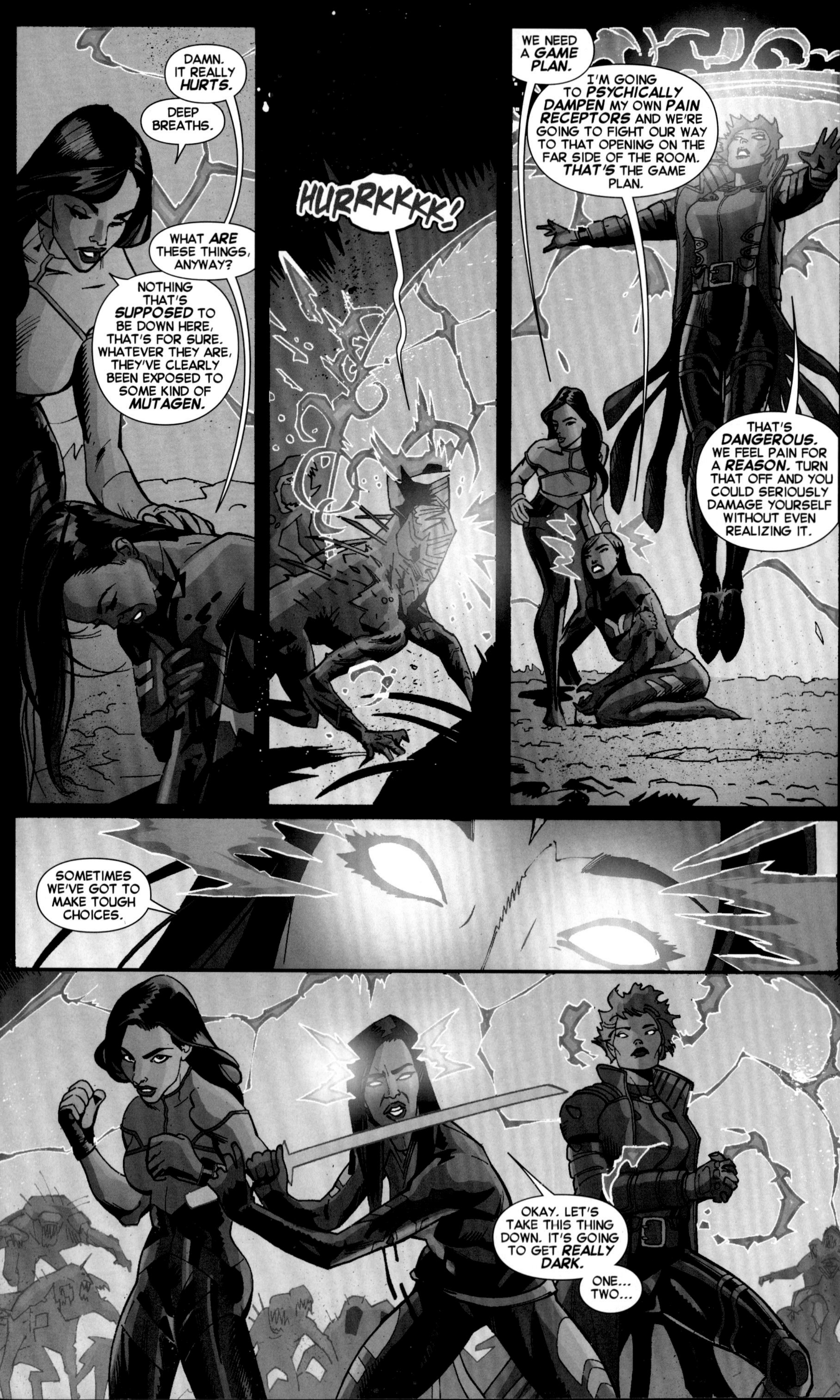
DAMN. IT REALLY HURTS.
DEEP BREATHS.
WHAT ARE THESE THINGS, ANYWAY?
NOTHING THAT'S SUPPOSED TO BE DOWN HERE, THAT'S FOR SURE. WHATEVER THEY ARE, THEY'VE CLEARLY BEEN EXPOSED TO SOME KIND OF MUTAGEN.
HURRKKKK!
WE NEED A GAME PLAN.
I'M GOING TO PSYCHICALLY DAMPEN MY OWN PAIN RECEPTORS AND WE'RE GOING TO FIGHT OUR WAY TO THAT OPENING ON THE FAR SIDE OF THE ROOM. THAT'S THE GAME PLAN.
THAT'S DANGEROUS. WE FEEL PAIN FOR A REASON. TURN THAT OFF AND YOU COULD SERIOUSLY DAMAGE YOURSELF WITHOUT EVEN REALIZING IT.
SOMETIMES WE'VE GOT TO MAKE TOUGH CHOICES.
OKAY. LET'S TAKE THIS THING DOWN. IT'S GOING TO GET REALLY DARK.
ONE... TWO...

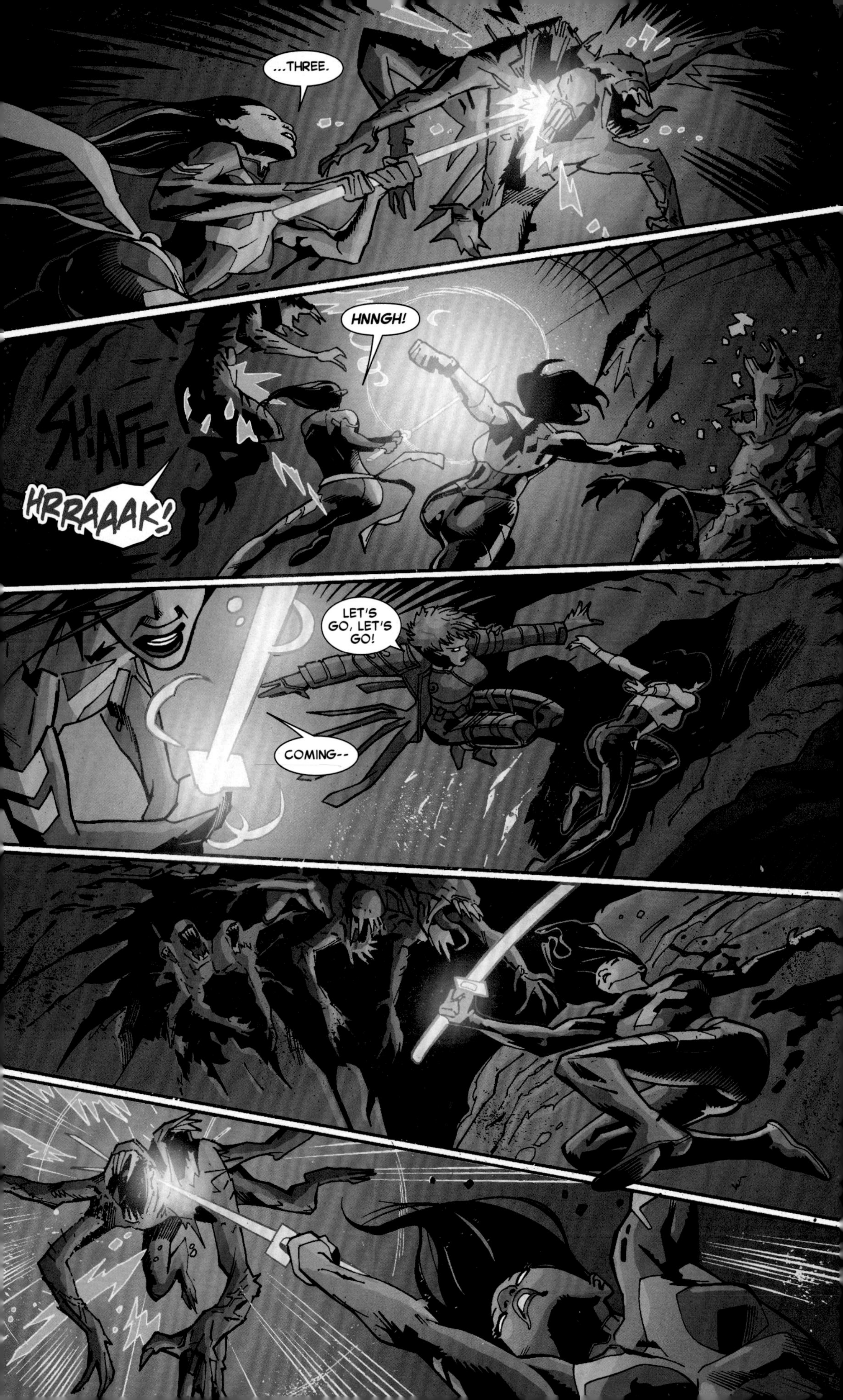
...THREE.
HNNGH!
SHAFF
HRRAAAK!
LET'S GO, LET'S GO!
COMING--

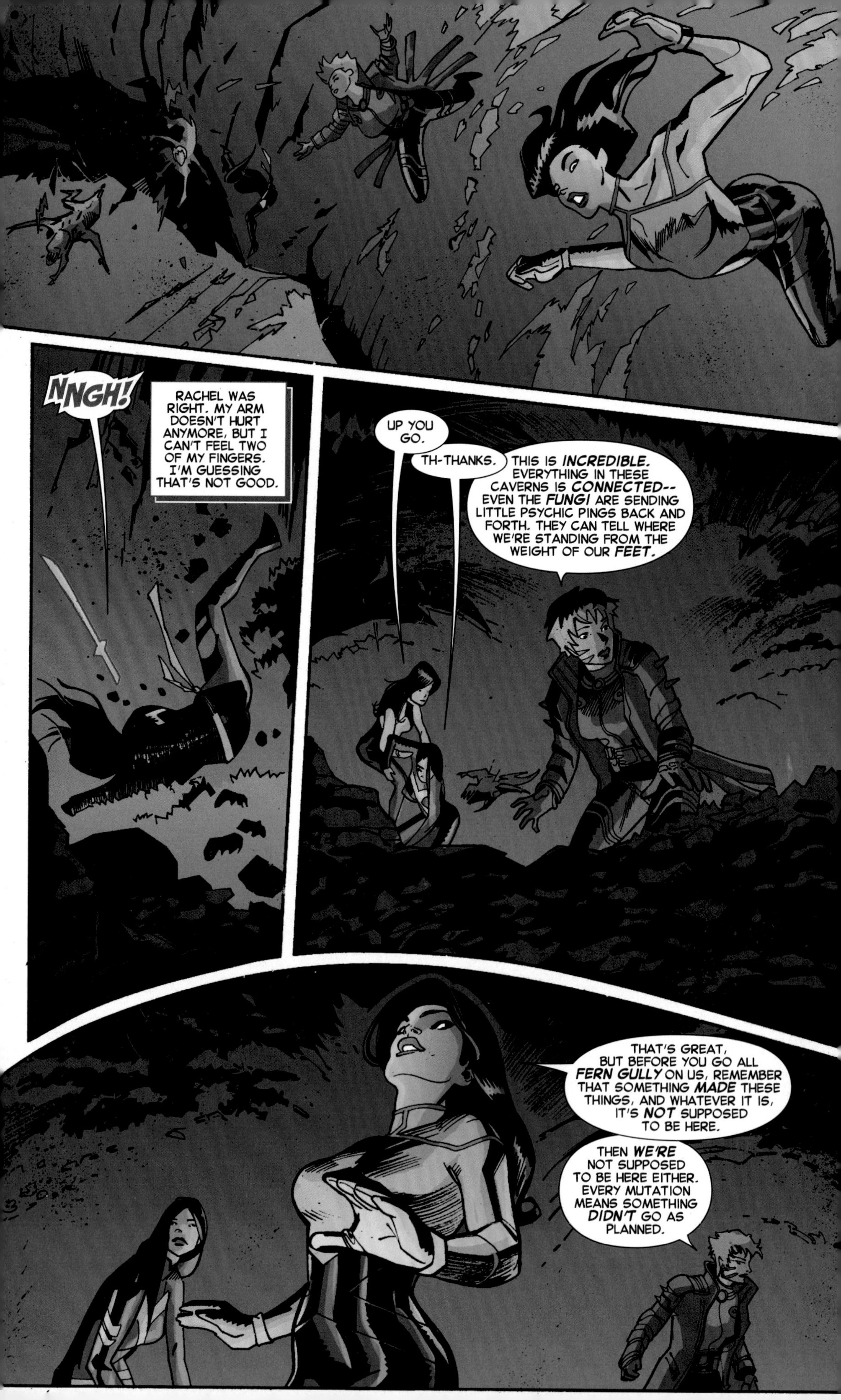
NNGH!
RACHEL WAS RIGHT. MY ARM DOESN'T HURT ANYMORE, BUT I CAN'T FEEL TWO OF MY FINGERS. I'M GUESSING THAT'S NOT GOOD.
UP YOU GO.
TH-THANKS.
THIS IS INCREDIBLE. EVERYTHING IN THESE CAVERNS IS CONNECTED-- EVEN THE FUNGI ARE SENDING LITTLE PSYCHIC PINGS BACK AND FORTH. THEY CAN TELL WHERE WE'RE STANDING FROM THE WEIGHT OF OUR FEET.
THAT'S GREAT, BUT BEFORE YOU GO ALL FERN GULLY ON US, REMEMBER THAT SOMETHING MADE THESE THINGS, AND WHATEVER IT IS, IT'S NOT SUPPOSED TO BE HERE.
THEN WE'RE NOT SUPPOSED TO BE HERE EITHER. EVERY MUTATION MEANS SOMETHING DIDN'T GO AS PLANNED.

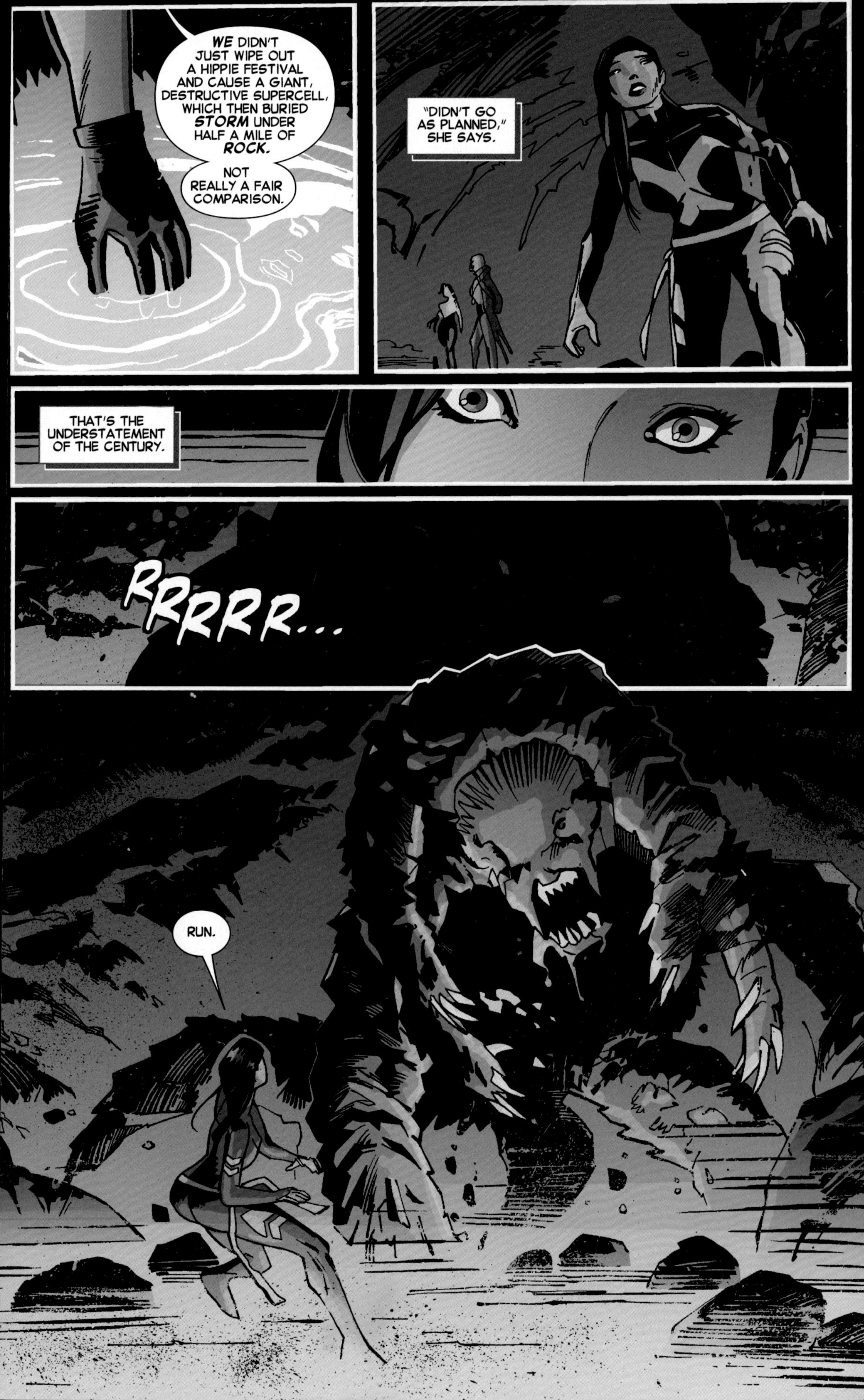
WE DIDN'T JUST WIPE OUT A HIPPIE FESTIVAL AND CAUSE A GIANT, DESTRUCTIVE SUPERCELL, WHICH THEN BURIED STORM UNDER HALF A MILE OF ROCK.
NOT REALLY A FAIR COMPARISON.
"DIDN'T GO AS PLANNED," SHE SAYS.
THAT'S THE UNDERSTATEMENT OF THE CENTURY.
RRRRRR...
RUN.

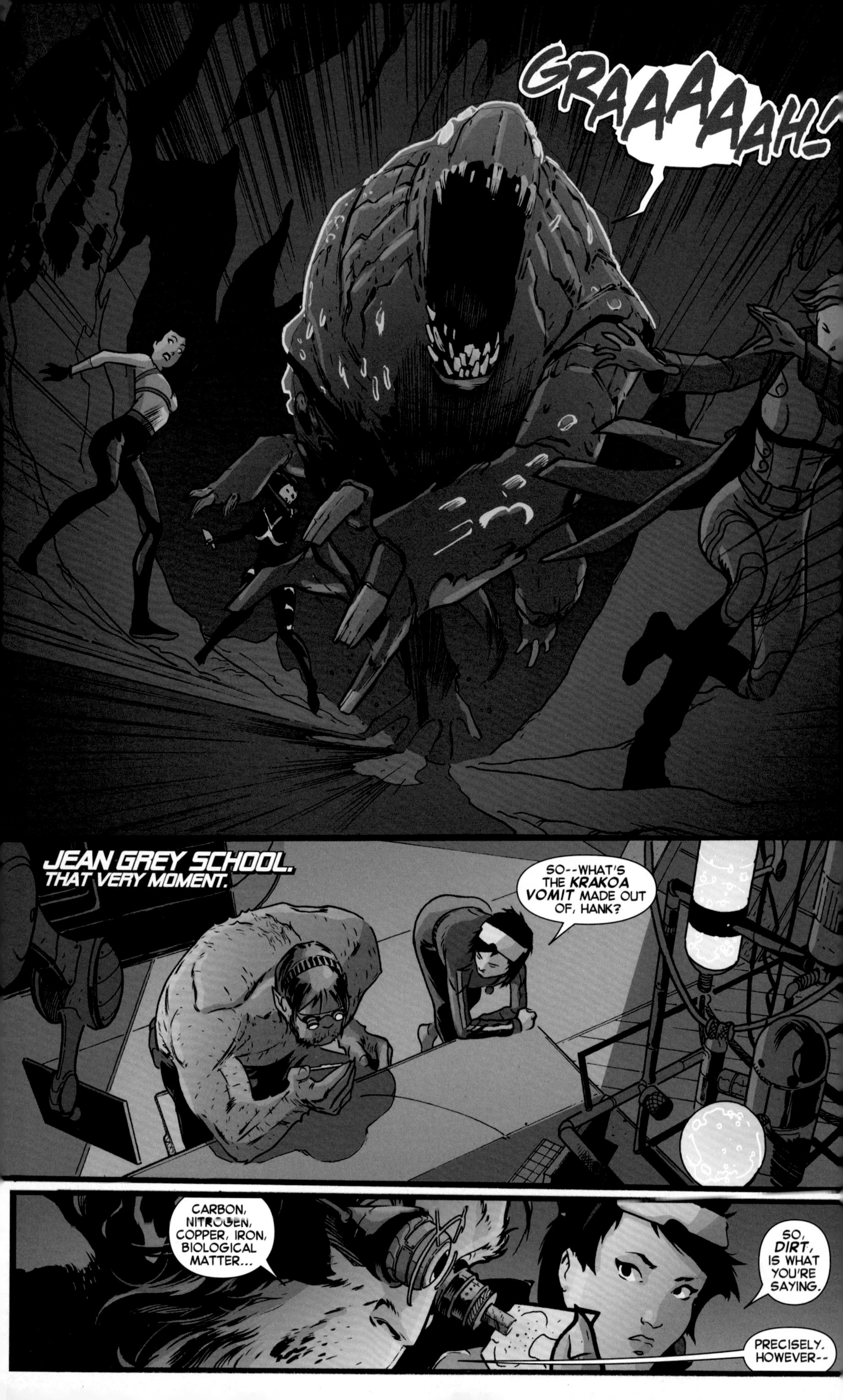
GRAAAAAAH!
JEAN GREY SCHOOL.
THAT VERY MOMENT.
SO--WHAT'S THE KRAKOA VOMIT MADE OUT OF, HANK?
CARBON, NITROGEN, COPPER, IRON, BIOLOGICAL MATTER...
SO, DIRT, IS WHAT YOU'RE SAYING.
PRECISELY. HOWEVER--

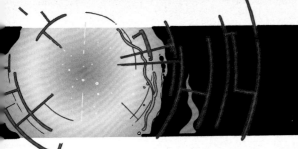

"THERE ARE TWO THINGS THAT PERPLEX ME. ONE, THE SAMPLE IS ABOUT NINETY DEGREES FAHRENHEIT. COLD FOR A HUMAN, BUT *VERY WARM* FOR DIRT.

"TWO, THERE IS A CERTAIN AMOUNT OF *HYDROGEN GAS* TRAPPED INSIDE IT. *INTERSTELLAR* HYDROGEN."

YOU MEAN WHATEVER IS MAKING KRAKOA SICK CAME FROM *OUTER SPACE?*

POSSIBLY. IT COULD BE A *COINCIDENCE*--ALL HYDROGEN ORIGINATED IN SPACE, AFTER ALL. A CERTAIN AMOUNT OF ATMOSPHERIC EXCHANGE IS NORMAL.

YEAH, WELL, YOU KNOW WHAT A BUNCH OF YEARS ON THE X-MEN HAS TAUGHT ME?

THE COMPLETE IRRELEVANCE OF THE TERM "COINCIDENCE"?

QUITE SO, MY GOOD MAN.

KEEP AN EYE ON SHOGO FOR ME?

WHERE ARE YOU GOING, JUBILEE?

UTAH! I GOTTA TEST A THEORY!

I JUST HOPE I'M RIGHT...

AND IF I AM, THAT WE FIGURE EVERYTHING OUT IN TIME TO HELP STORM...

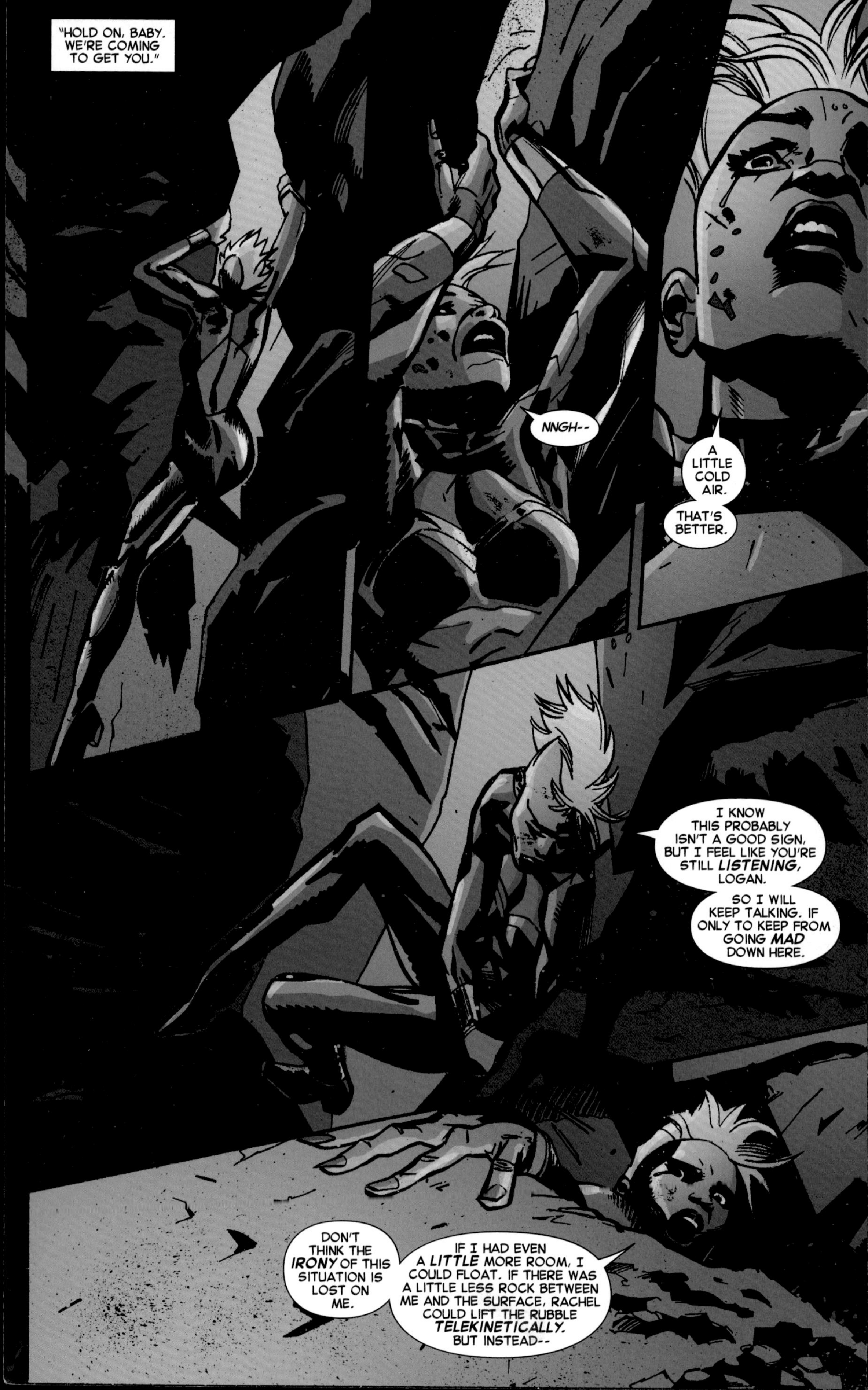
"HOLD ON, BABY. WE'RE COMING TO GET YOU."
NNGH--
A LITTLE COLD AIR.
THAT'S BETTER.
I KNOW THIS PROBABLY ISN'T A GOOD SIGN, BUT I FEEL LIKE YOU'RE STILL LISTENING, LOGAN.
SO I WILL KEEP TALKING. IF ONLY TO KEEP FROM GOING MAD DOWN HERE.
DON'T THINK THE IRONY OF THIS SITUATION IS LOST ON ME.
IF I HAD EVEN A LITTLE MORE ROOM, I COULD FLOAT. IF THERE WAS A LITTLE LESS ROCK BETWEEN ME AND THE SURFACE, RACHEL COULD LIFT THE RUBBLE TELEKINETICALLY. BUT INSTEAD--

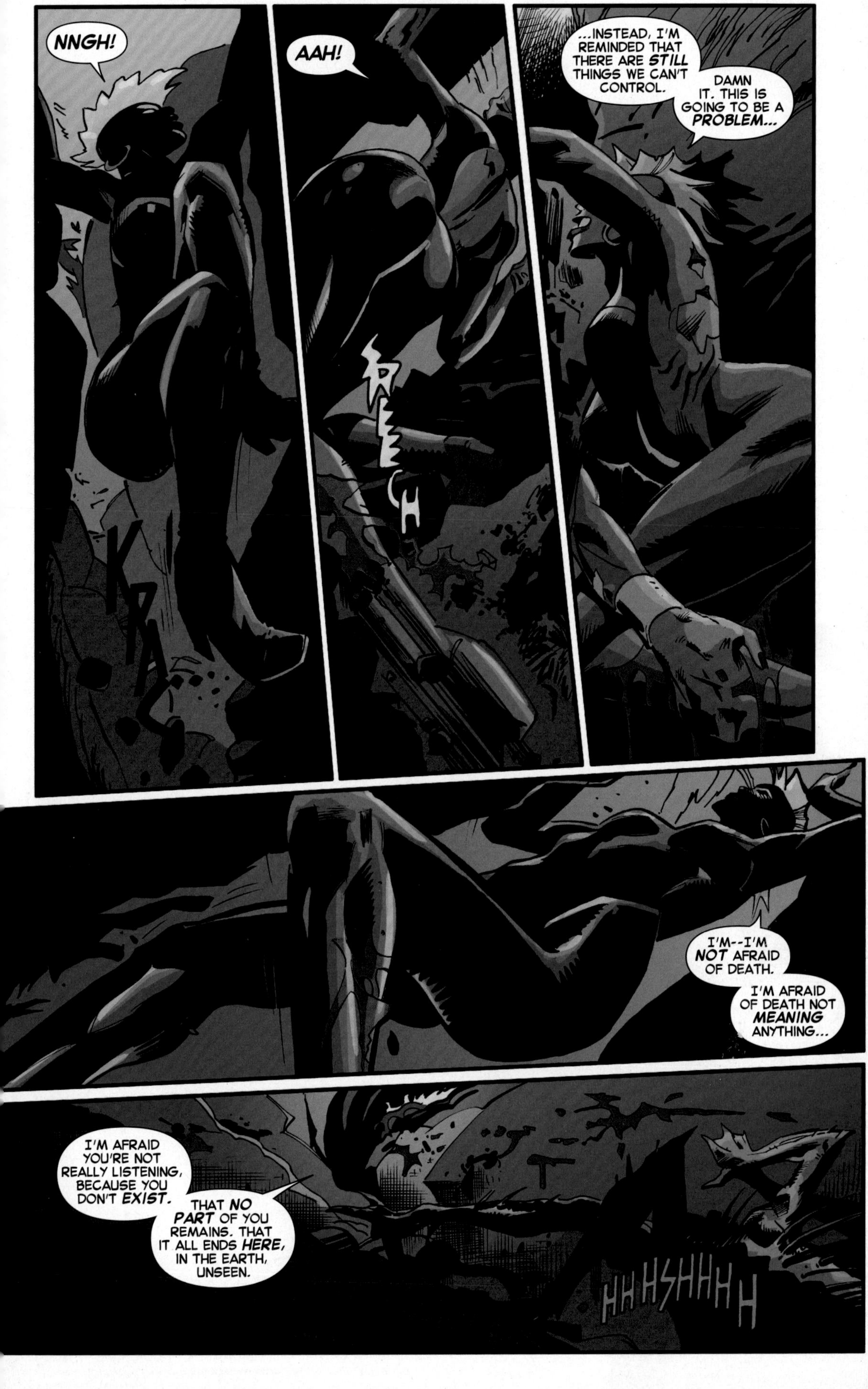
NNGH!
KRAK
AAH!
SPLUNCH
...INSTEAD, I'M REMINDED THAT THERE ARE STILL THINGS WE CAN'T CONTROL.
DAMN IT. THIS IS GOING TO BE A PROBLEM...
I'M--I'M NOT AFRAID OF DEATH.
I'M AFRAID OF DEATH NOT MEANING ANYTHING...
I'M AFRAID YOU'RE NOT REALLY LISTENING, BECAUSE YOU DON'T EXIST.
THAT NO PART OF YOU REMAINS. THAT IT ALL ENDS HERE, IN THE EARTH, UNSEEN.
HHHSHHHH

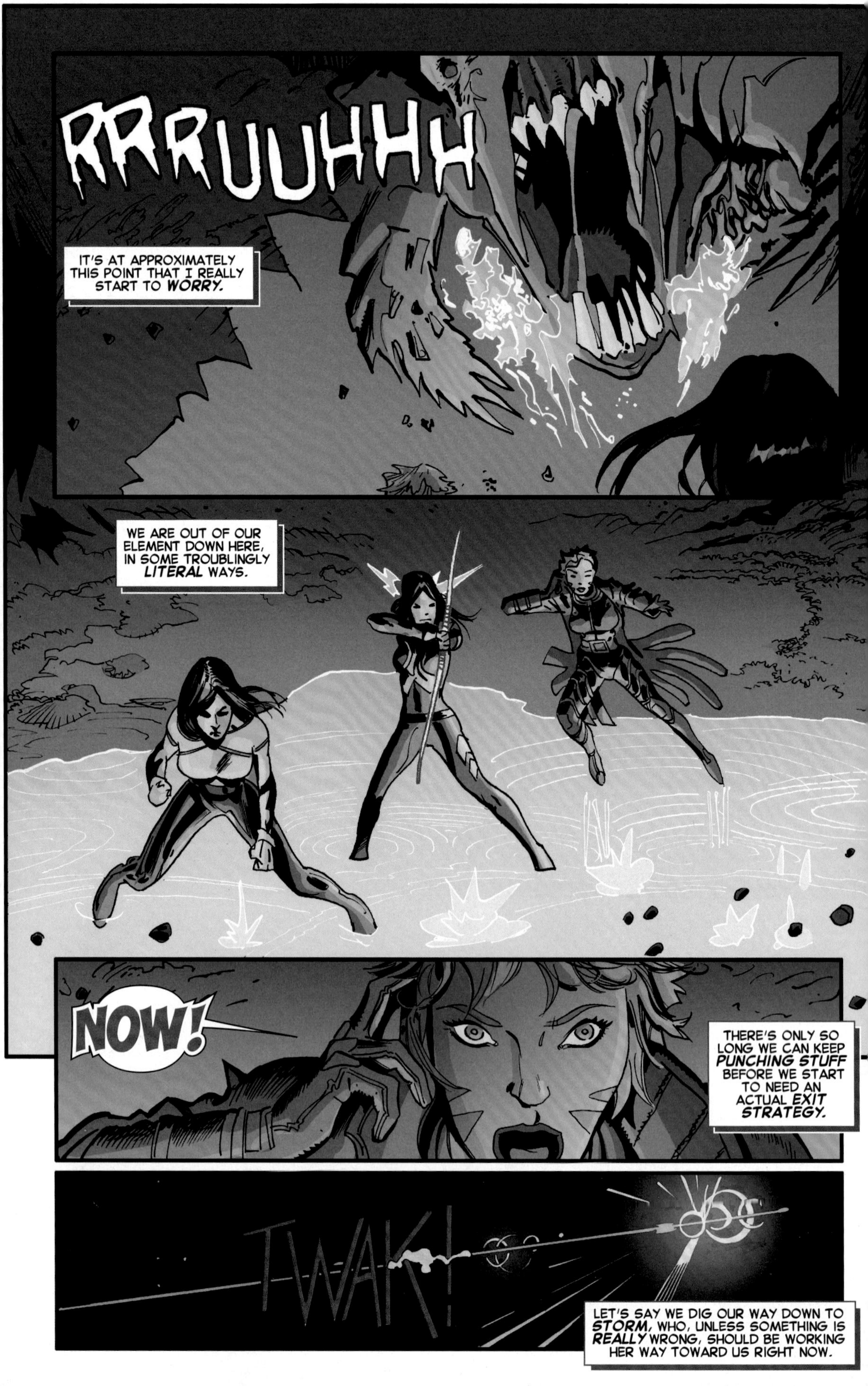
RRRUUHHH
IT'S AT APPROXIMATELY THIS POINT THAT I REALLY START TO WORRY.
WE ARE OUT OF OUR ELEMENT DOWN HERE, IN SOME TROUBLINGLY LITERAL WAYS.
NOW!
THERE'S ONLY SO LONG WE CAN KEEP PUNCHING STUFF BEFORE WE START TO NEED AN ACTUAL EXIT STRATEGY.
TWAK!
LET'S SAY WE DIG OUR WAY DOWN TO STORM, WHO, UNLESS SOMETHING IS REALLY WRONG, SHOULD BE WORKING HER WAY TOWARD US RIGHT NOW.

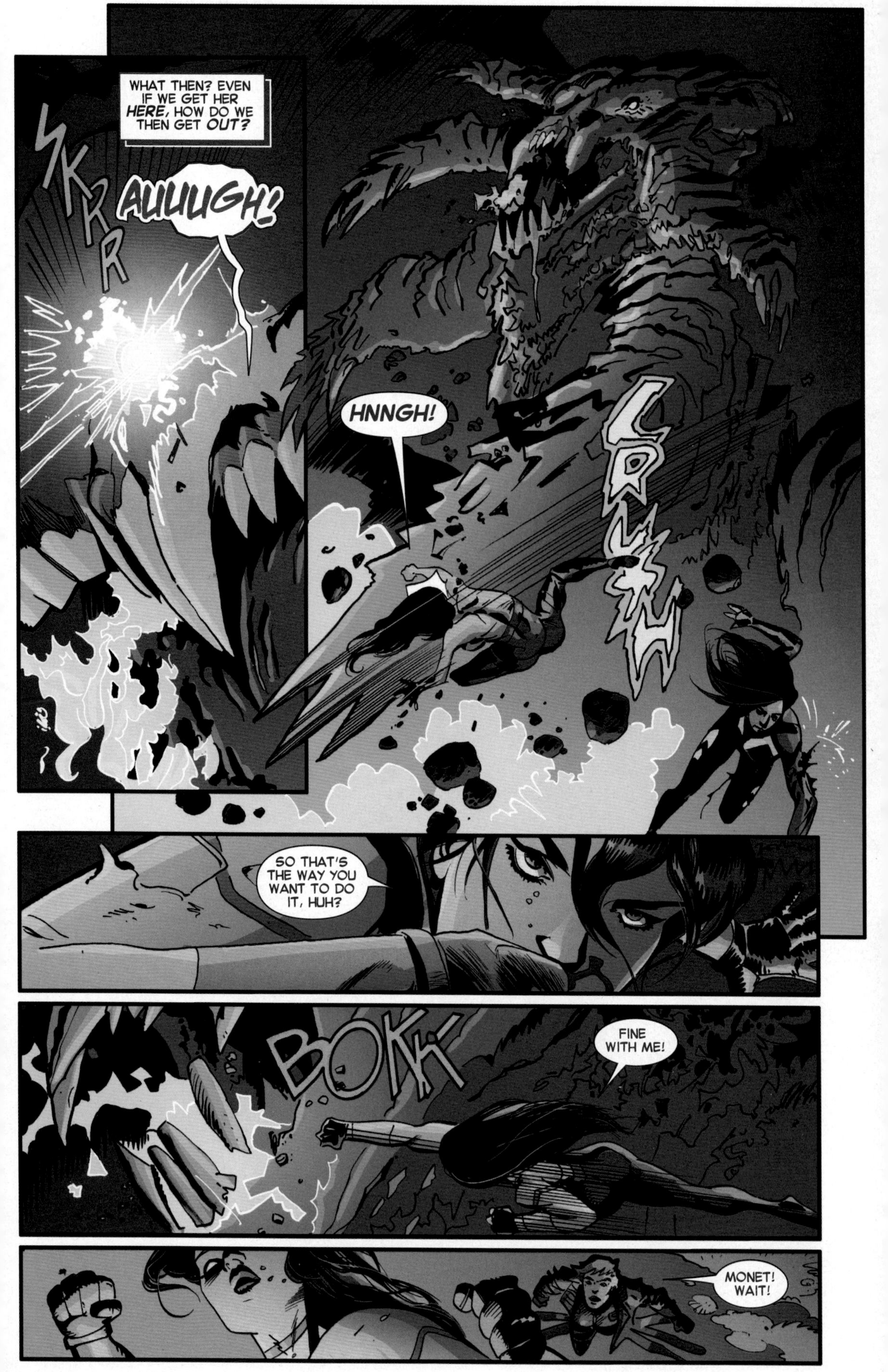
WHAT THEN? EVEN IF WE GET HER HERE, HOW DO WE THEN GET OUT?
SKKRR
AUUUGH!
HNNGH!
SO THAT'S THE WAY YOU WANT TO DO IT, HUH?
BOKK
FINE WITH ME!
MONET! WAIT!

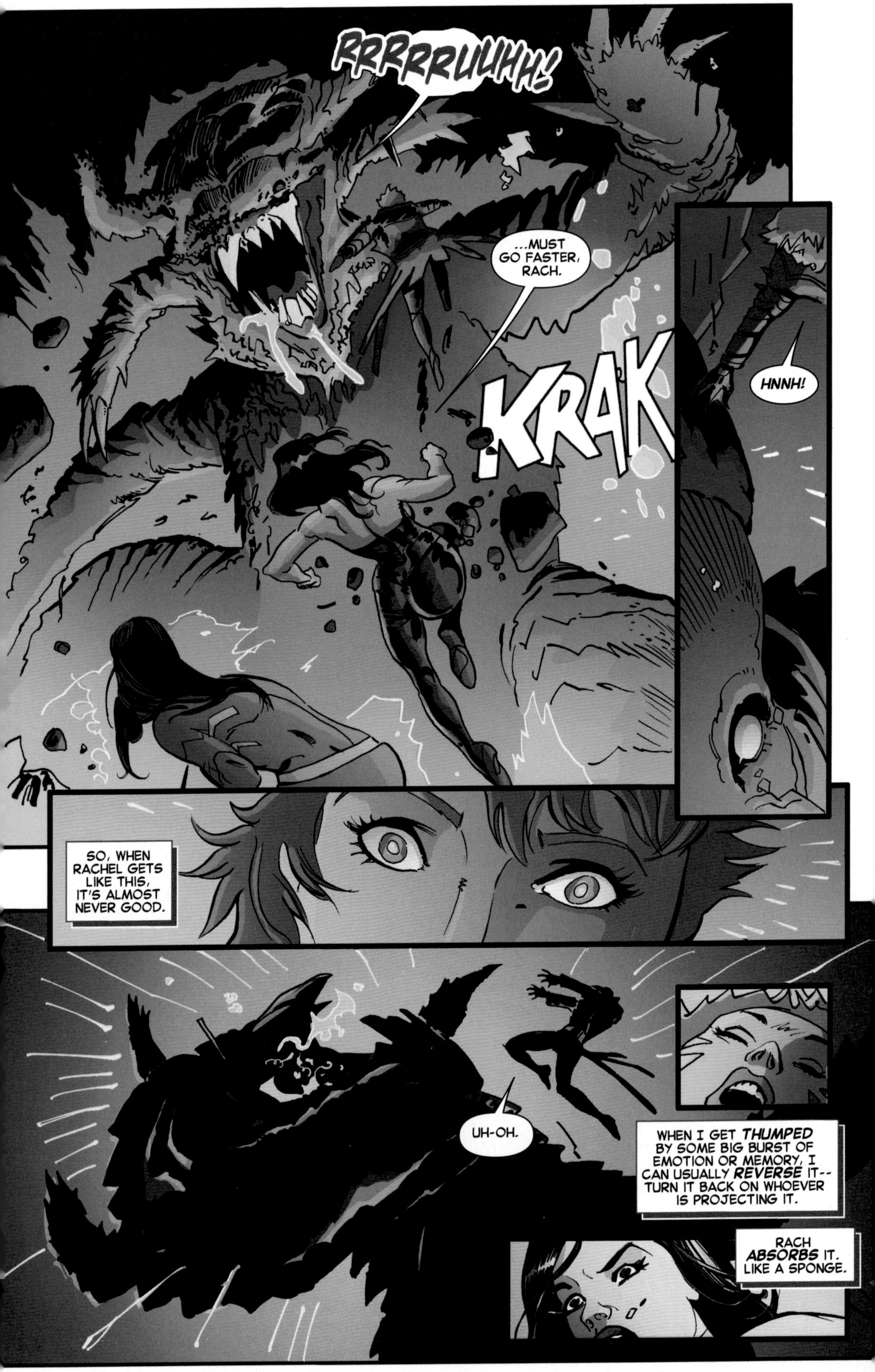
RRRRRUUHH!
...MUST GO FASTER, RACH.
KRAK
HNNH!
SO, WHEN RACHEL GETS LIKE THIS, IT'S ALMOST NEVER GOOD.
UH-OH.
WHEN I GET THUMPED BY SOME BIG BURST OF EMOTION OR MEMORY, I CAN USUALLY REVERSE IT-- TURN IT BACK ON WHOEVER IS PROJECTING IT.
RACH ABSORBS IT. LIKE A SPONGE.

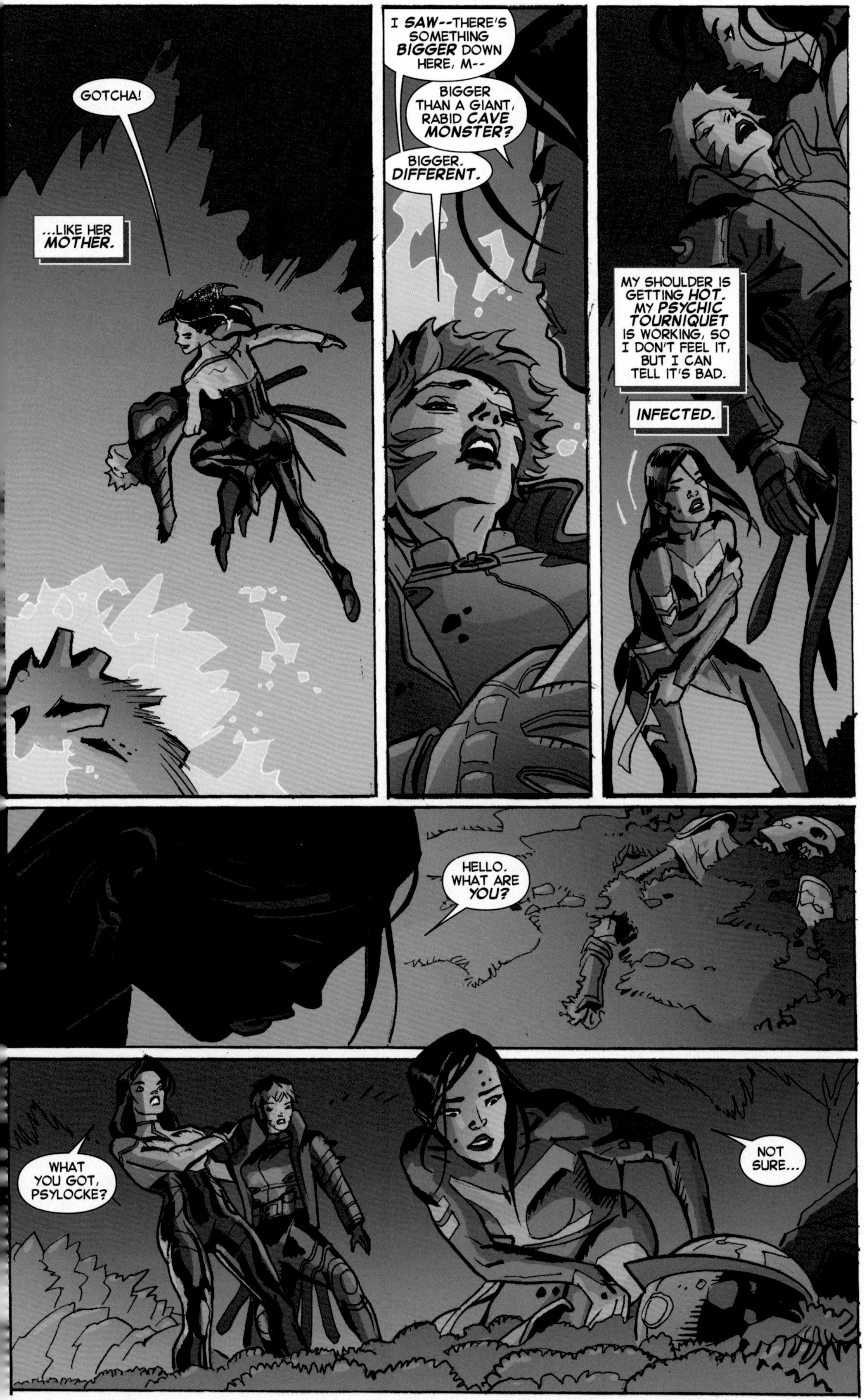
GOTCHA!
...LIKE HER MOTHER.
I SAW--THERE'S SOMETHING BIGGER DOWN HERE, M--
BIGGER THAN A GIANT, RABID CAVE MONSTER?
BIGGER. DIFFERENT.
MY SHOULDER IS GETTING HOT. MY PSYCHIC TOURNIQUET IS WORKING, SO I DON'T FEEL IT, BUT I CAN TELL IT'S BAD.
INFECTED.
HELLO. WHAT ARE YOU?
WHAT YOU GOT, PSYLOCKE?
NOT SURE...

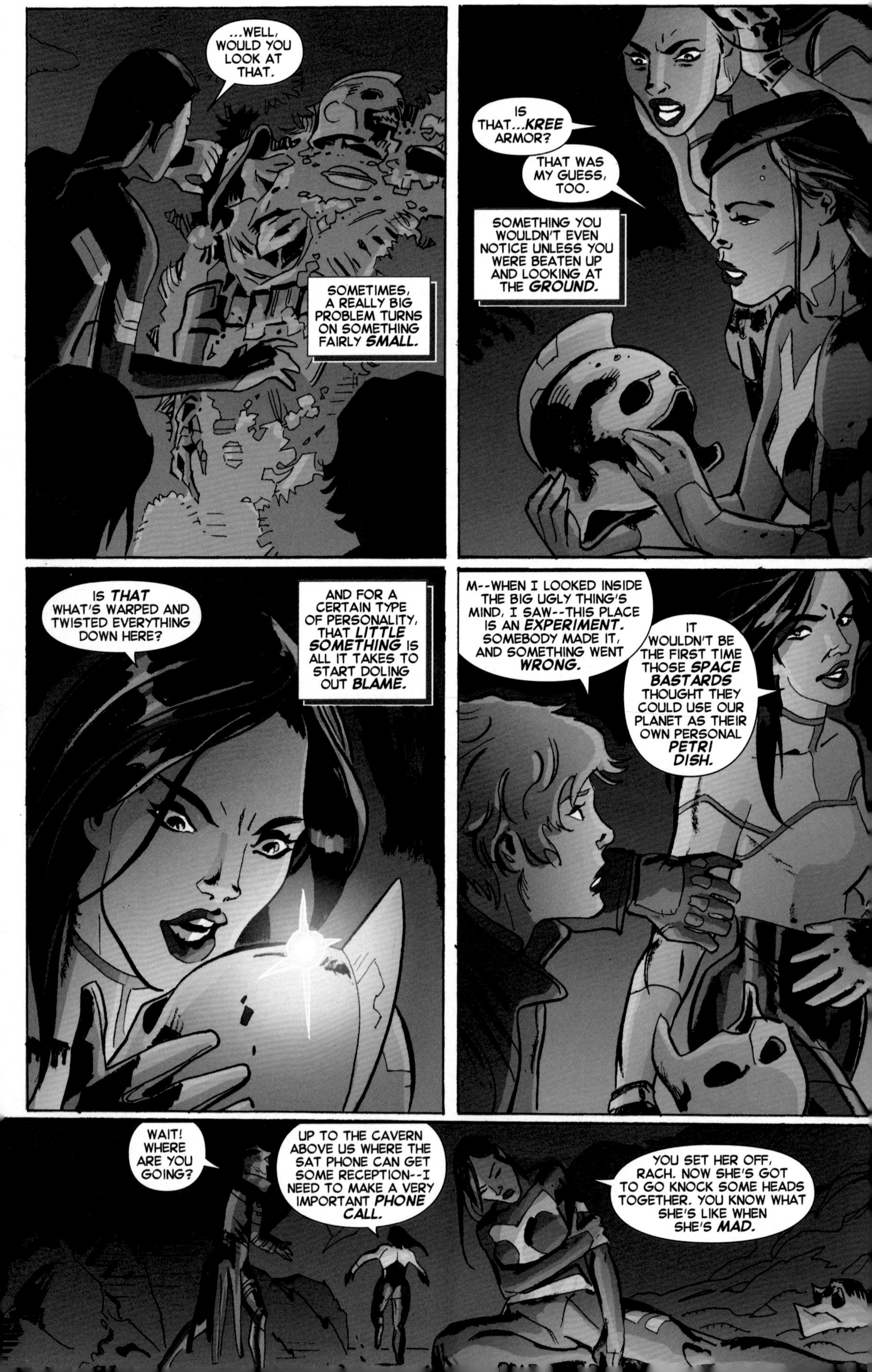
...WELL, WOULD YOU LOOK AT THAT.
SOMETIMES, A REALLY BIG PROBLEM TURNS ON SOMETHING FAIRLY SMALL.
IS THAT...KREE ARMOR?
THAT WAS MY GUESS, TOO.
SOMETHING YOU WOULDN'T EVEN NOTICE UNLESS YOU WERE BEATEN UP AND LOOKING AT THE GROUND.
IS THAT WHAT'S WARPED AND TWISTED EVERYTHING DOWN HERE?
AND FOR A CERTAIN TYPE OF PERSONALITY, THAT LITTLE SOMETHING IS ALL IT TAKES TO START DOLING OUT BLAME.
M--WHEN I LOOKED INSIDE THE BIG UGLY THING'S MIND, I SAW--THIS PLACE IS AN EXPERIMENT. SOMEBODY MADE IT, AND SOMETHING WENT WRONG.
IT WOULDN'T BE THE FIRST TIME THOSE SPACE BASTARDS THOUGHT THEY COULD USE OUR PLANET AS THEIR OWN PERSONAL PETRI DISH.
WAIT! WHERE ARE YOU GOING?
UP TO THE CAVERN ABOVE US WHERE THE SAT PHONE CAN GET SOME RECEPTION--I NEED TO MAKE A VERY IMPORTANT PHONE CALL.
YOU SET HER OFF, RACH. NOW SHE'S GOT TO GO KNOCK SOME HEADS TOGETHER. YOU KNOW WHAT SHE'S LIKE WHEN SHE'S MAD.

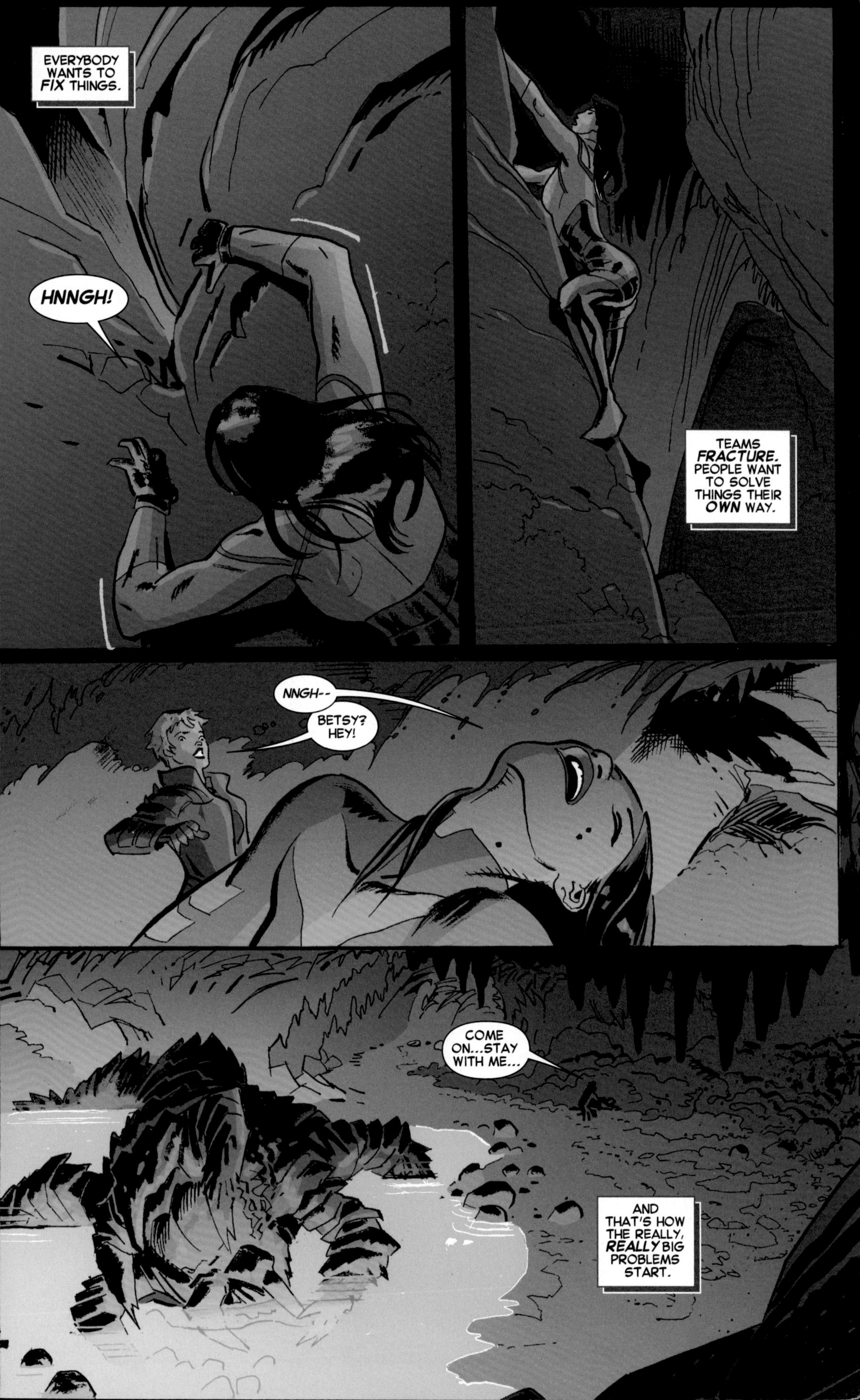

EVERYBODY WANTS TO *FIX* THINGS.
HNNGH!
TEAMS *FRACTURE.* PEOPLE WANT TO SOLVE THINGS THEIR *OWN* WAY.
NNGH--
BETSY? HEY!
COME ON...STAY WITH ME...
AND THAT'S HOW THE REALLY, *REALLY* BIG PROBLEMS START.

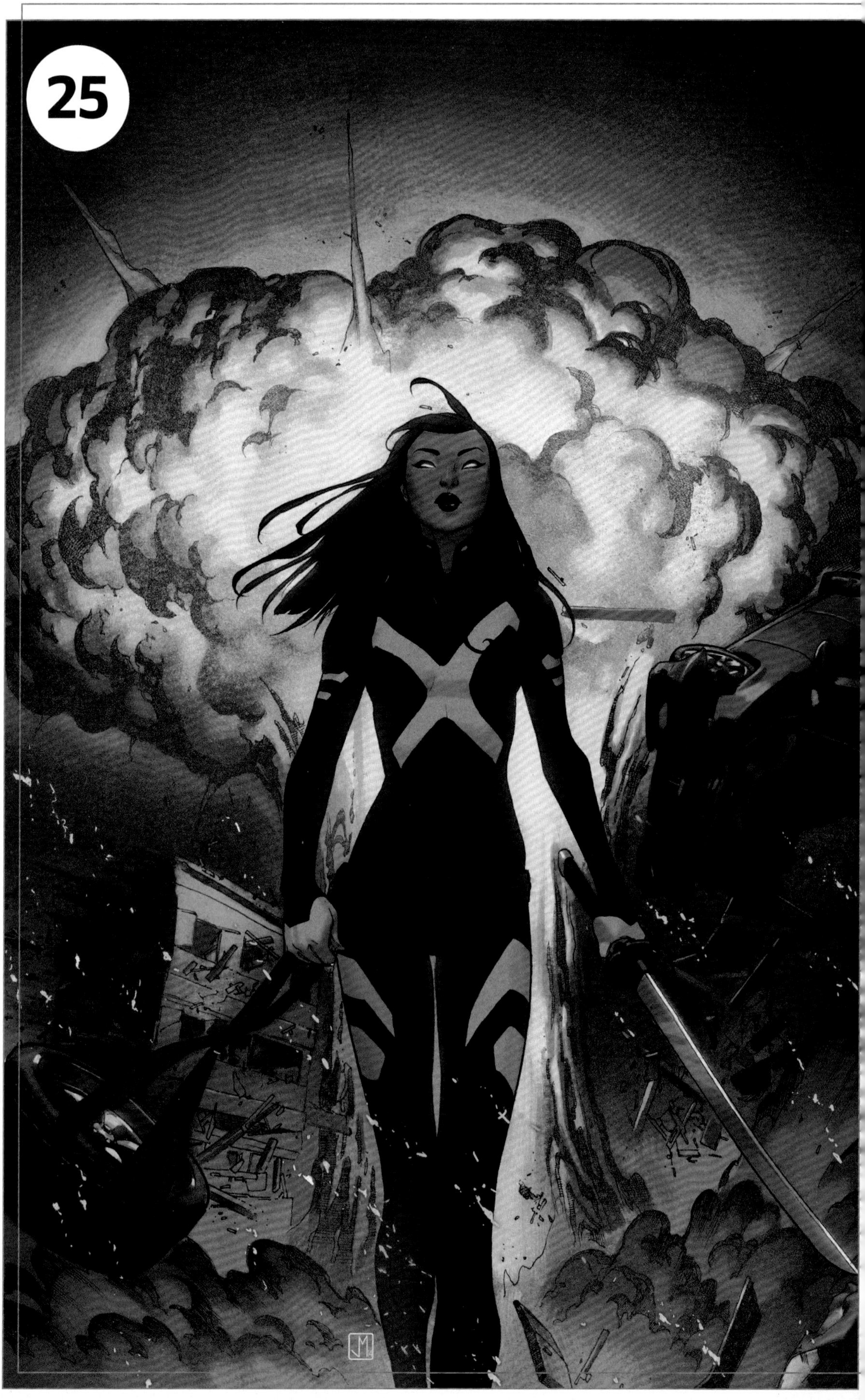
25

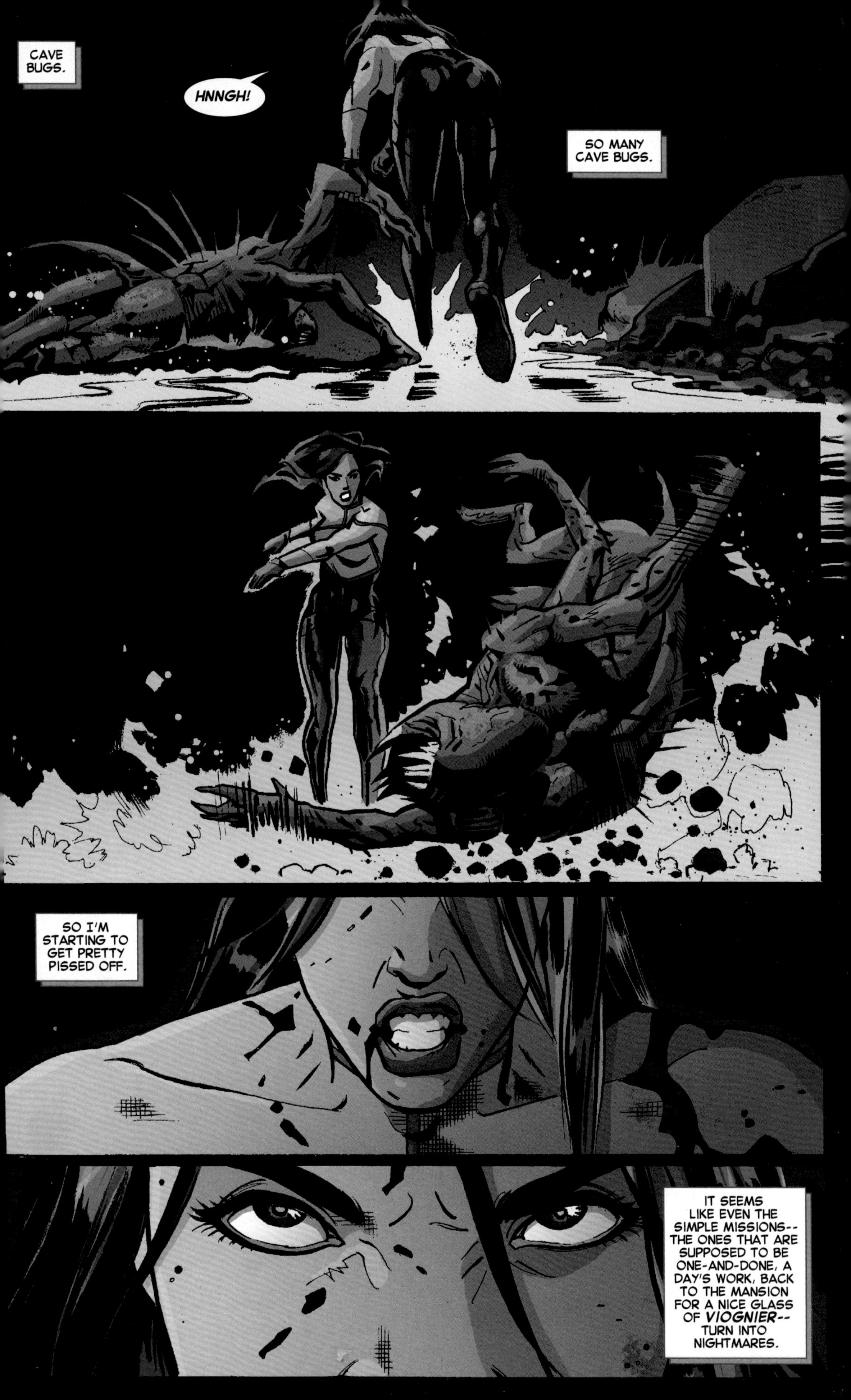
CAVE BUGS.
HNNGH!
SO MANY CAVE BUGS.
SO I'M STARTING TO GET PRETTY PISSED OFF.
IT SEEMS LIKE EVEN THE SIMPLE MISSIONS-- THE ONES THAT ARE SUPPOSED TO BE ONE-AND-DONE, A DAY'S WORK, BACK TO THE MANSION FOR A NICE GLASS OF VIOGNIER-- TURN INTO NIGHTMARES.

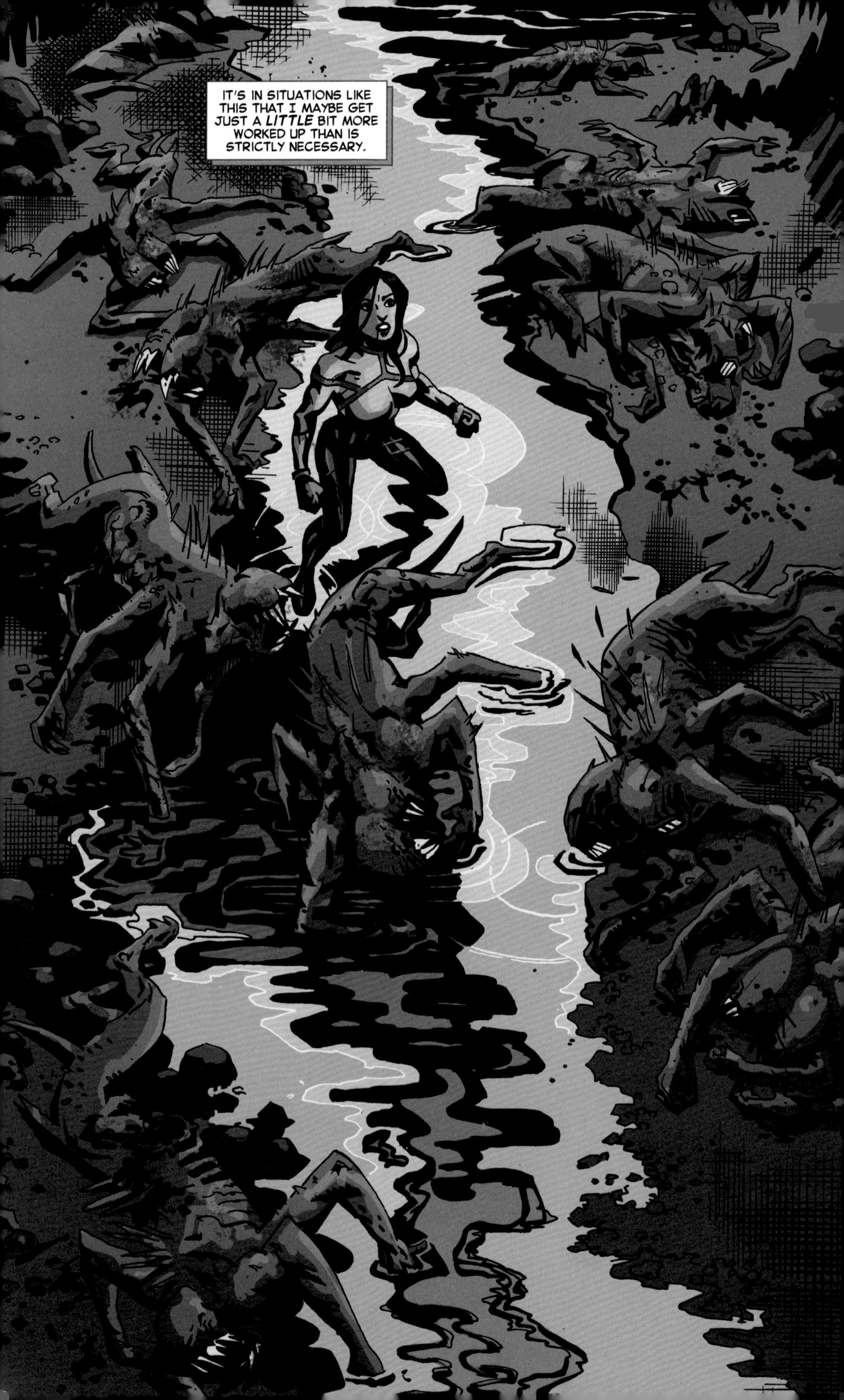
IT'S IN SITUATIONS LIKE THIS THAT I MAYBE GET JUST A *LITTLE* BIT MORE WORKED UP THAN IS STRICTLY NECESSARY.

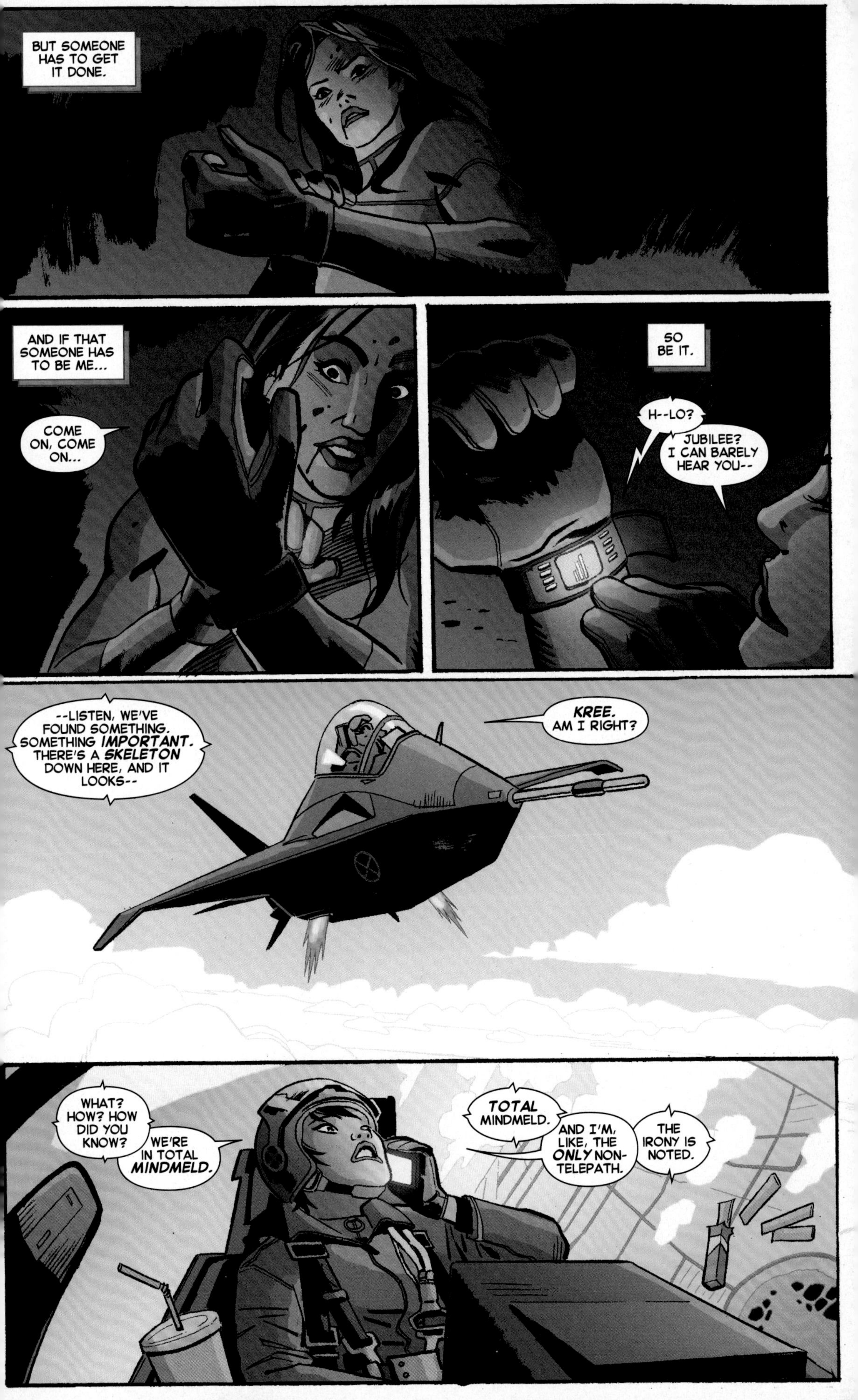
BUT SOMEONE HAS TO GET IT DONE.
AND IF THAT SOMEONE HAS TO BE ME...
COME ON, COME ON...
SO BE IT.
H--LO?
JUBILEE? I CAN BARELY HEAR YOU--
--LISTEN, WE'VE FOUND SOMETHING. SOMETHING *IMPORTANT.* THERE'S A *SKELETON* DOWN HERE, AND IT LOOKS--
KREE. AM I RIGHT?
WHAT? HOW? HOW DID YOU KNOW?
WE'RE IN TOTAL *MINDMELD.*
TOTAL MINDMELD.
AND I'M, LIKE, THE *ONLY* NON-TELEPATH.
THE IRONY IS NOTED.

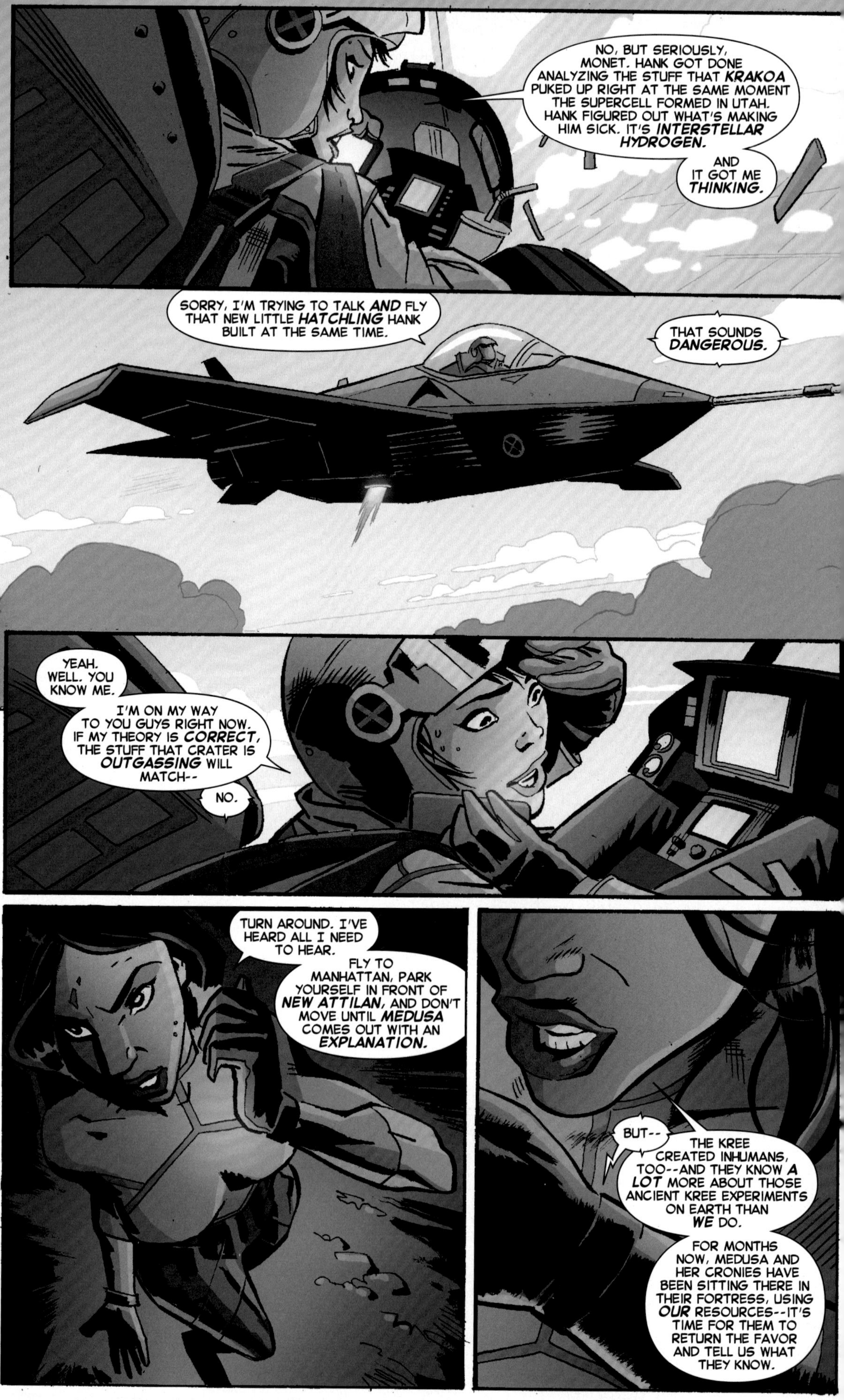
NO, BUT SERIOUSLY, MONET. HANK GOT DONE ANALYZING THE STUFF THAT KRAKOA PUKED UP RIGHT AT THE SAME MOMENT THE SUPERCELL FORMED IN UTAH. HANK FIGURED OUT WHAT'S MAKING HIM SICK. IT'S INTERSTELLAR HYDROGEN.
AND IT GOT ME THINKING.
SORRY, I'M TRYING TO TALK AND FLY THAT NEW LITTLE HATCHLING HANK BUILT AT THE SAME TIME.
THAT SOUNDS DANGEROUS.
YEAH. WELL. YOU KNOW ME.
I'M ON MY WAY TO YOU GUYS RIGHT NOW. IF MY THEORY IS CORRECT, THE STUFF THAT CRATER IS OUTGASSING WILL MATCH--
NO.
TURN AROUND. I'VE HEARD ALL I NEED TO HEAR.
FLY TO MANHATTAN, PARK YOURSELF IN FRONT OF NEW ATTILAN, AND DON'T MOVE UNTIL MEDUSA COMES OUT WITH AN EXPLANATION.
BUT--
THE KREE CREATED INHUMANS, TOO--AND THEY KNOW A LOT MORE ABOUT THOSE ANCIENT KREE EXPERIMENTS ON EARTH THAN WE DO.
FOR MONTHS NOW, MEDUSA AND HER CRONIES HAVE BEEN SITTING THERE IN THEIR FORTRESS, USING OUR RESOURCES--IT'S TIME FOR THEM TO RETURN THE FAVOR AND TELL US WHAT THEY KNOW.

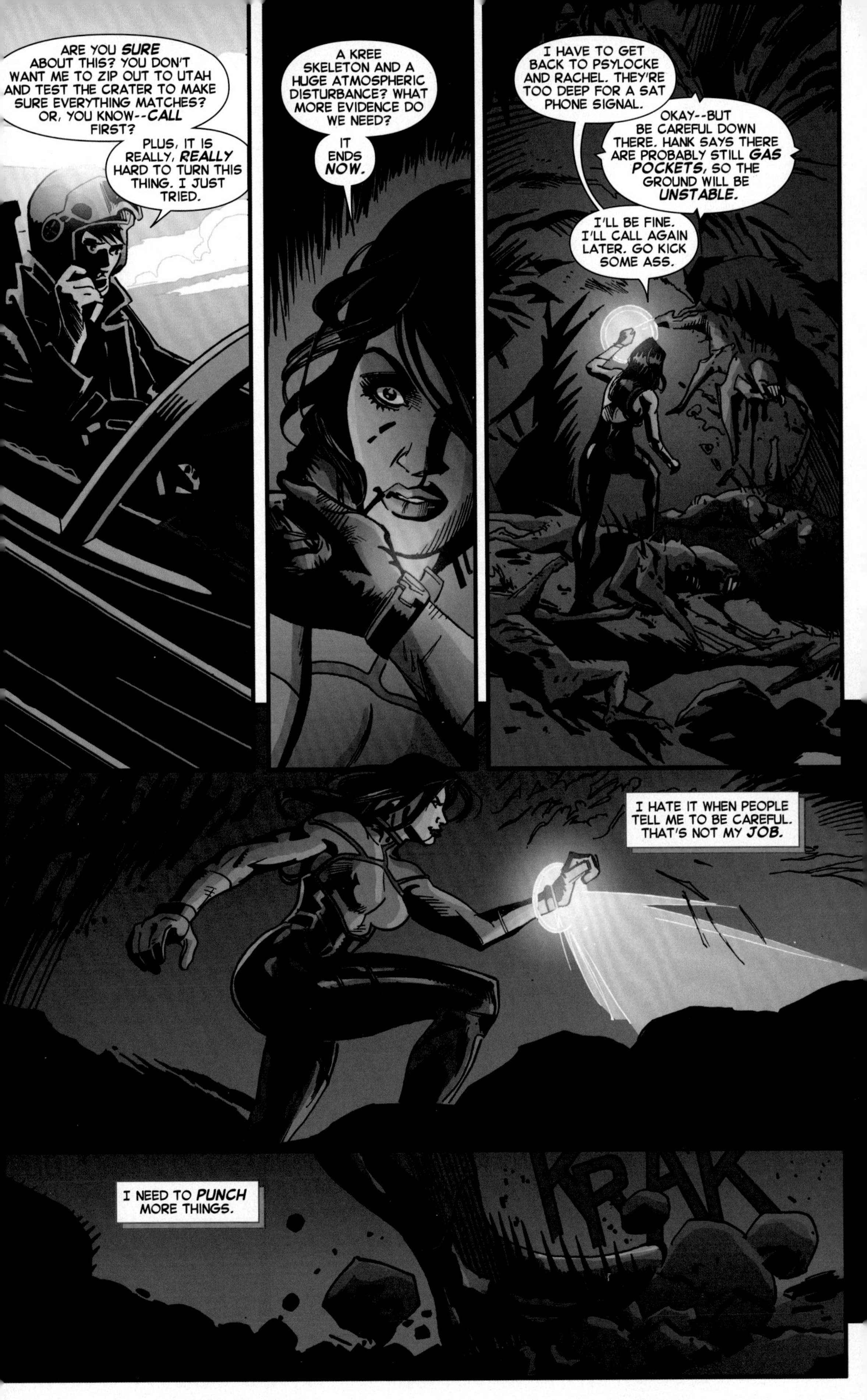
ARE YOU SURE ABOUT THIS? YOU DON'T WANT ME TO ZIP OUT TO UTAH AND TEST THE CRATER TO MAKE SURE EVERYTHING MATCHES? OR, YOU KNOW--CALL FIRST?
PLUS, IT IS REALLY, REALLY HARD TO TURN THIS THING. I JUST TRIED.
A KREE SKELETON AND A HUGE ATMOSPHERIC DISTURBANCE? WHAT MORE EVIDENCE DO WE NEED?
IT ENDS NOW.
I HAVE TO GET BACK TO PSYLOCKE AND RACHEL. THEY'RE TOO DEEP FOR A SAT PHONE SIGNAL.
OKAY--BUT BE CAREFUL DOWN THERE. HANK SAYS THERE ARE PROBABLY STILL GAS POCKETS, SO THE GROUND WILL BE UNSTABLE.
I'LL BE FINE. I'LL CALL AGAIN LATER. GO KICK SOME ASS.
I HATE IT WHEN PEOPLE TELL ME TO BE CAREFUL. THAT'S NOT MY JOB.
I NEED TO PUNCH MORE THINGS.
KRAK

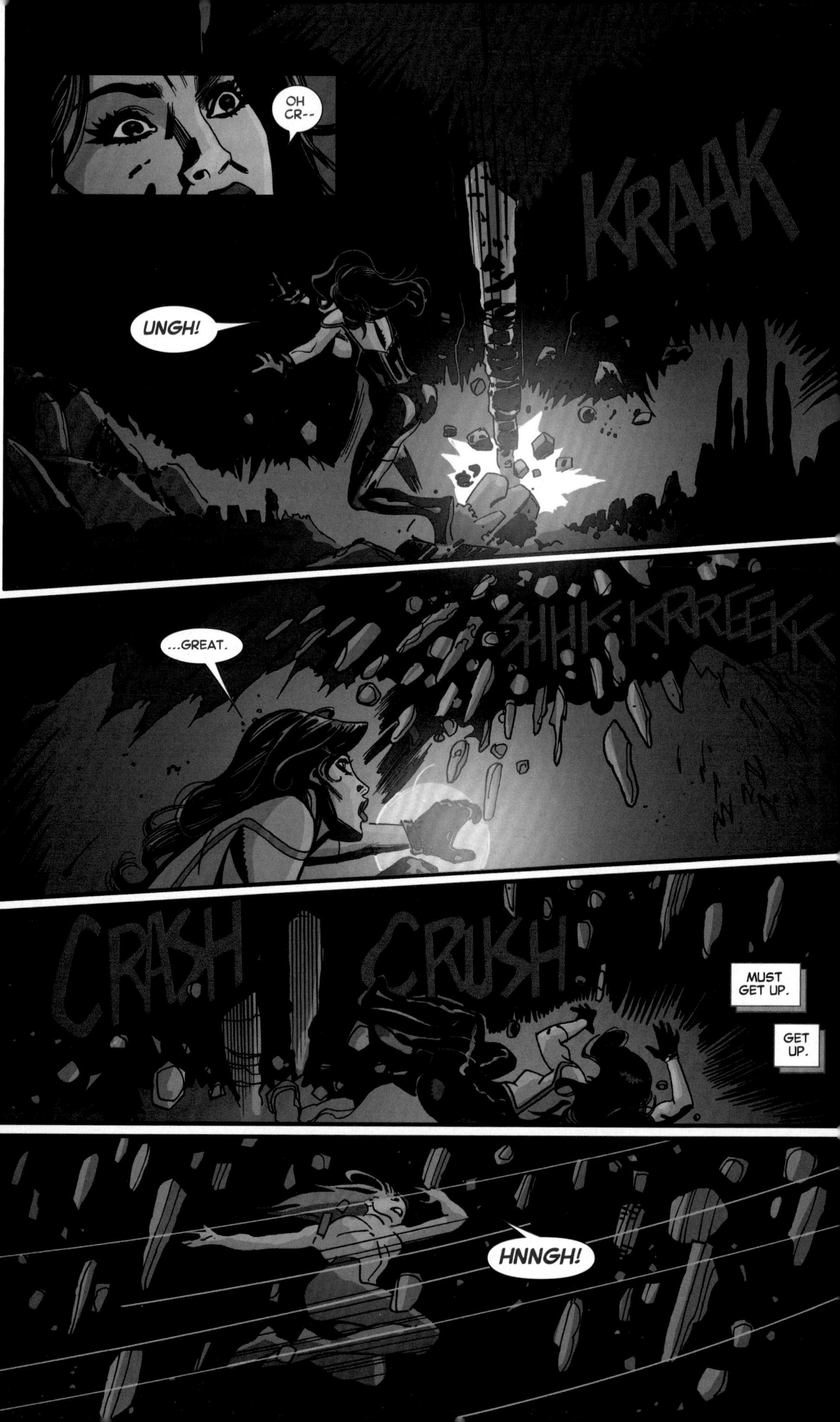
OH CR--
KRAAK
UNGH!
...GREAT.
SHHK KRRREEKK
CRASH
CRUSH
MUST GET UP.
GET UP.
HNNGH!

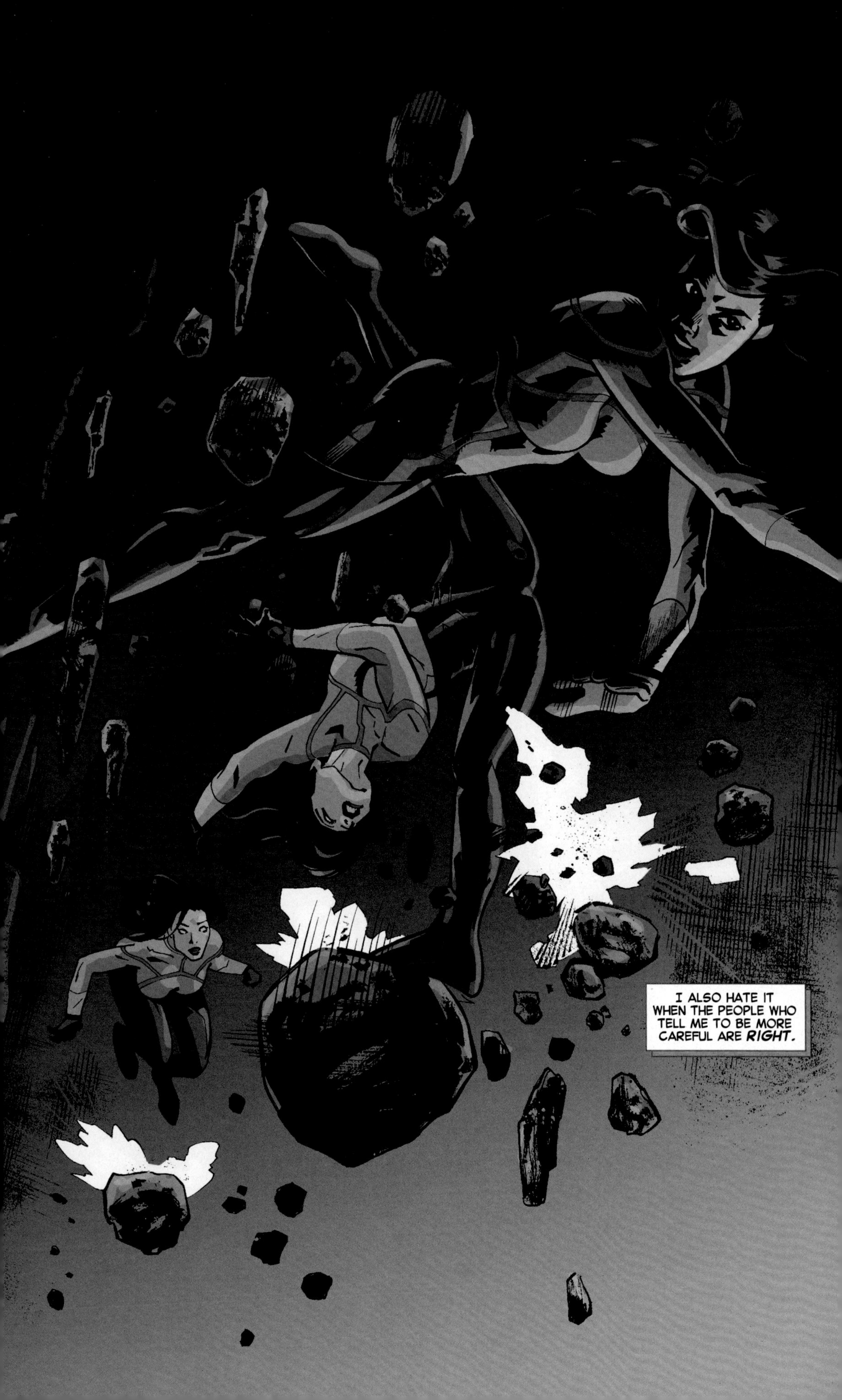
I ALSO HATE IT WHEN THE PEOPLE WHO TELL ME TO BE MORE CAREFUL ARE RIGHT.

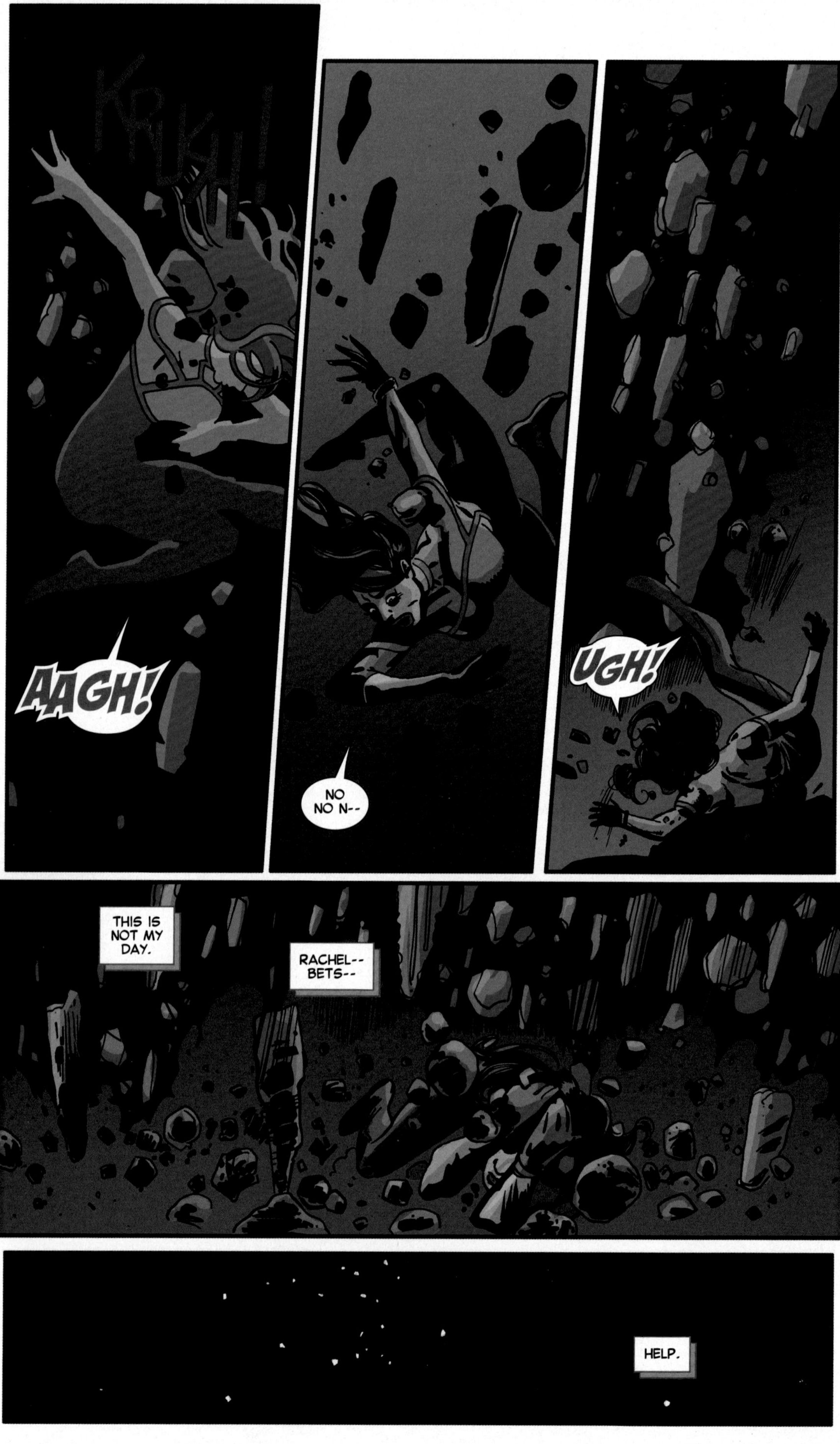
KRUKH!
AAGH!
NO NO N--
UGH!
THIS IS NOT MY DAY.
RACHEL-- BETS--
HELP.

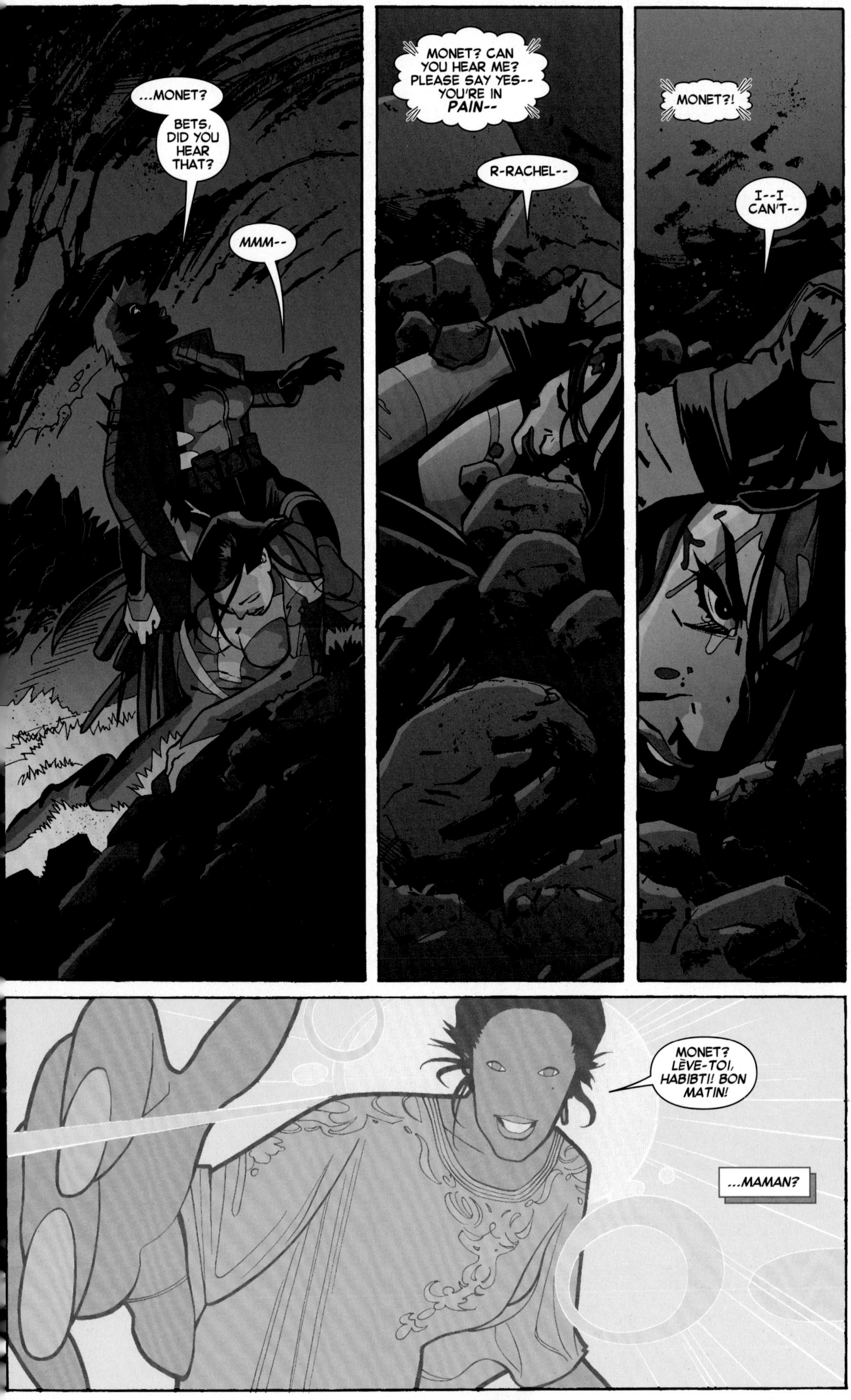
...MONET?
BETS, DID YOU HEAR THAT?
MMM--
MONET? CAN YOU HEAR ME? PLEASE SAY YES-- YOU'RE IN *PAIN--*
R-RACHEL--
MONET?!
I--I CAN'T--
MONET? LÈVE-TOI, HABIBTI! BON MATIN!
...MAMAN?

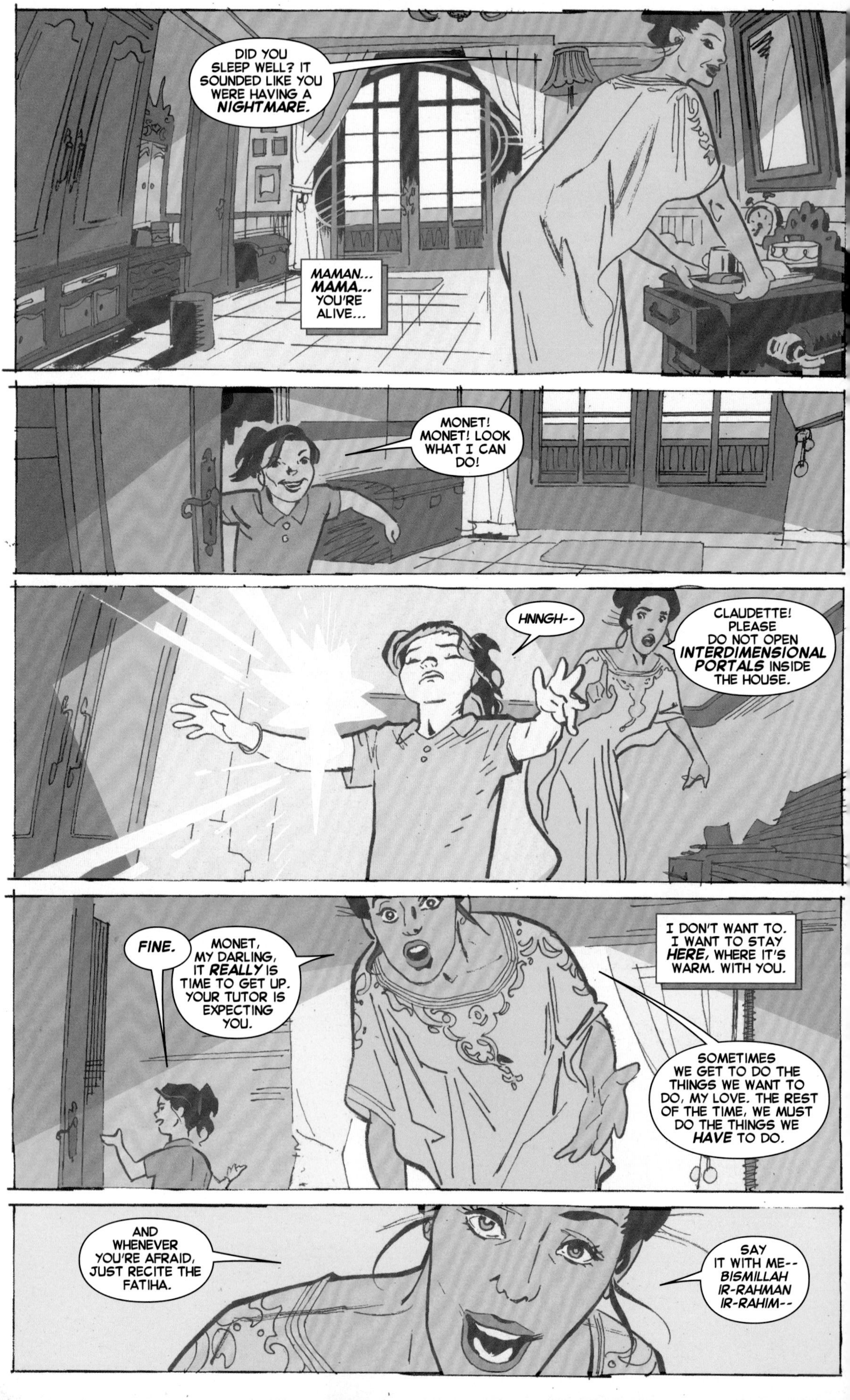
DID YOU SLEEP WELL? IT SOUNDED LIKE YOU WERE HAVING A NIGHTMARE.
MAMAN... MAMA... YOU'RE ALIVE...
MONET! MONET! LOOK WHAT I CAN DO!
HNNGH--
CLAUDETTE! PLEASE DO NOT OPEN INTERDIMENSIONAL PORTALS INSIDE THE HOUSE.
FINE.
MONET, MY DARLING, IT REALLY IS TIME TO GET UP. YOUR TUTOR IS EXPECTING YOU.
I DON'T WANT TO. I WANT TO STAY HERE, WHERE IT'S WARM. WITH YOU.
SOMETIMES WE GET TO DO THE THINGS WE WANT TO DO, MY LOVE. THE REST OF THE TIME, WE MUST DO THE THINGS WE HAVE TO DO.
AND WHENEVER YOU'RE AFRAID, JUST RECITE THE FATIHA.
SAY IT WITH ME-- BISMILLAH IR-RAHMAN IR-RAHIM--

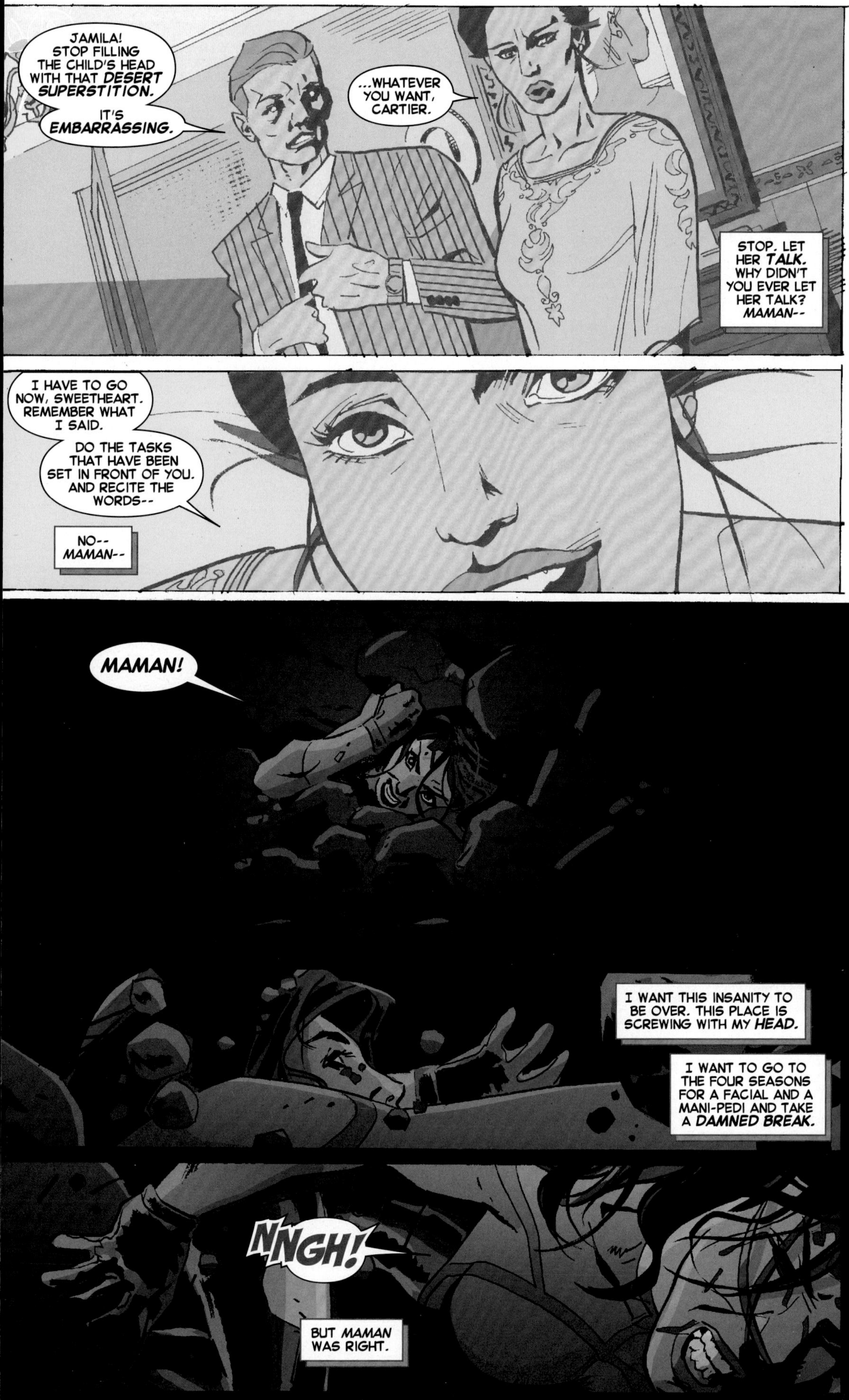
JAMILA! STOP FILLING THE CHILD'S HEAD WITH THAT DESERT SUPERSTITION.
IT'S EMBARRASSING.
...WHATEVER YOU WANT, CARTIER.
STOP. LET HER TALK. WHY DIDN'T YOU EVER LET HER TALK? MAMAN--
I HAVE TO GO NOW, SWEETHEART. REMEMBER WHAT I SAID.
DO THE TASKS THAT HAVE BEEN SET IN FRONT OF YOU. AND RECITE THE WORDS--
NO-- MAMAN--
MAMAN!
I WANT THIS INSANITY TO BE OVER. THIS PLACE IS SCREWING WITH MY HEAD.
I WANT TO GO TO THE FOUR SEASONS FOR A FACIAL AND A MANI-PEDI AND TAKE A DAMNED BREAK.
NNGH!
BUT MAMAN WAS RIGHT.

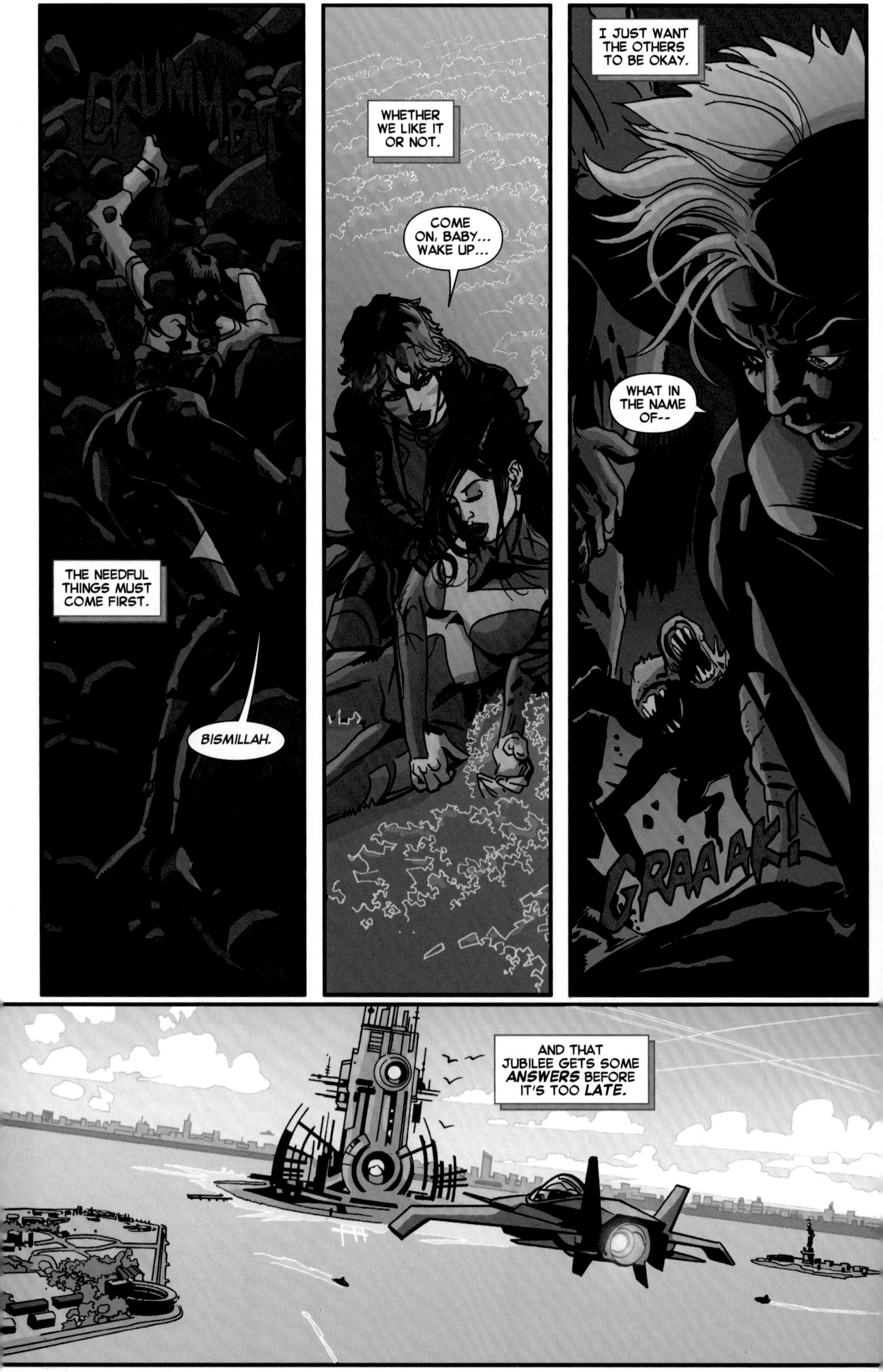
CRUMMBLE
THE NEEDFUL THINGS MUST COME FIRST.
BISMILLAH.
WHETHER WE LIKE IT OR NOT.
COME ON, BABY... WAKE UP...
I JUST WANT THE OTHERS TO BE OKAY.
WHAT IN THE NAME OF--
GRAAAK!
AND THAT JUBILEE GETS SOME ANSWERS BEFORE IT'S TOO LATE.

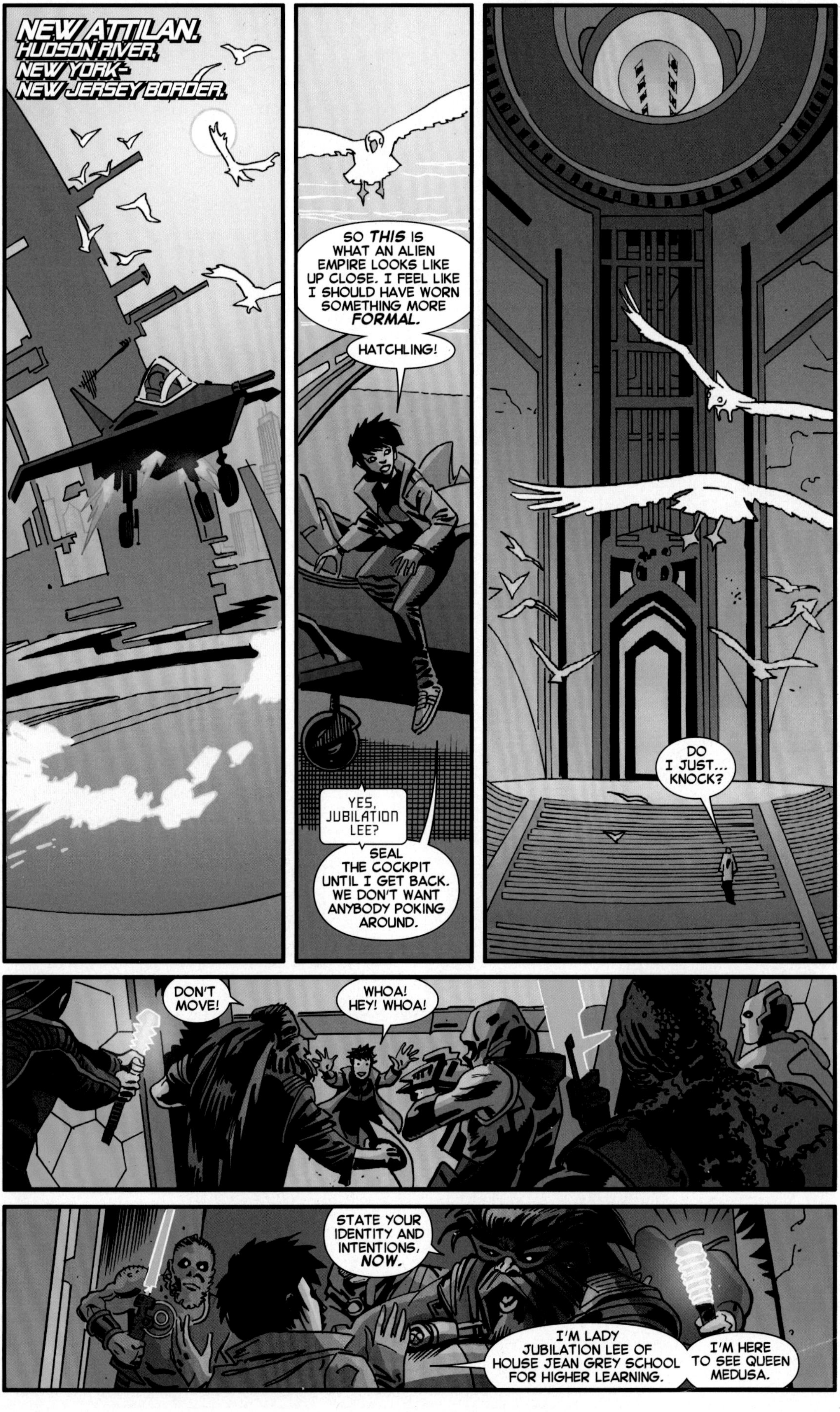
NEW ATTILAN. HUDSON RIVER, NEW YORK-NEW JERSEY BORDER.
SO THIS IS WHAT AN ALIEN EMPIRE LOOKS LIKE UP CLOSE. I FEEL LIKE I SHOULD HAVE WORN SOMETHING MORE FORMAL.
HATCHLING!
YES, JUBILATION LEE?
SEAL THE COCKPIT UNTIL I GET BACK. WE DON'T WANT ANYBODY POKING AROUND.
DO I JUST... KNOCK?
DON'T MOVE!
WHOA! HEY! WHOA!
STATE YOUR IDENTITY AND INTENTIONS, NOW.
I'M LADY JUBILATION LEE OF HOUSE JEAN GREY SCHOOL FOR HIGHER LEARNING.
I'M HERE TO SEE QUEEN MEDUSA.

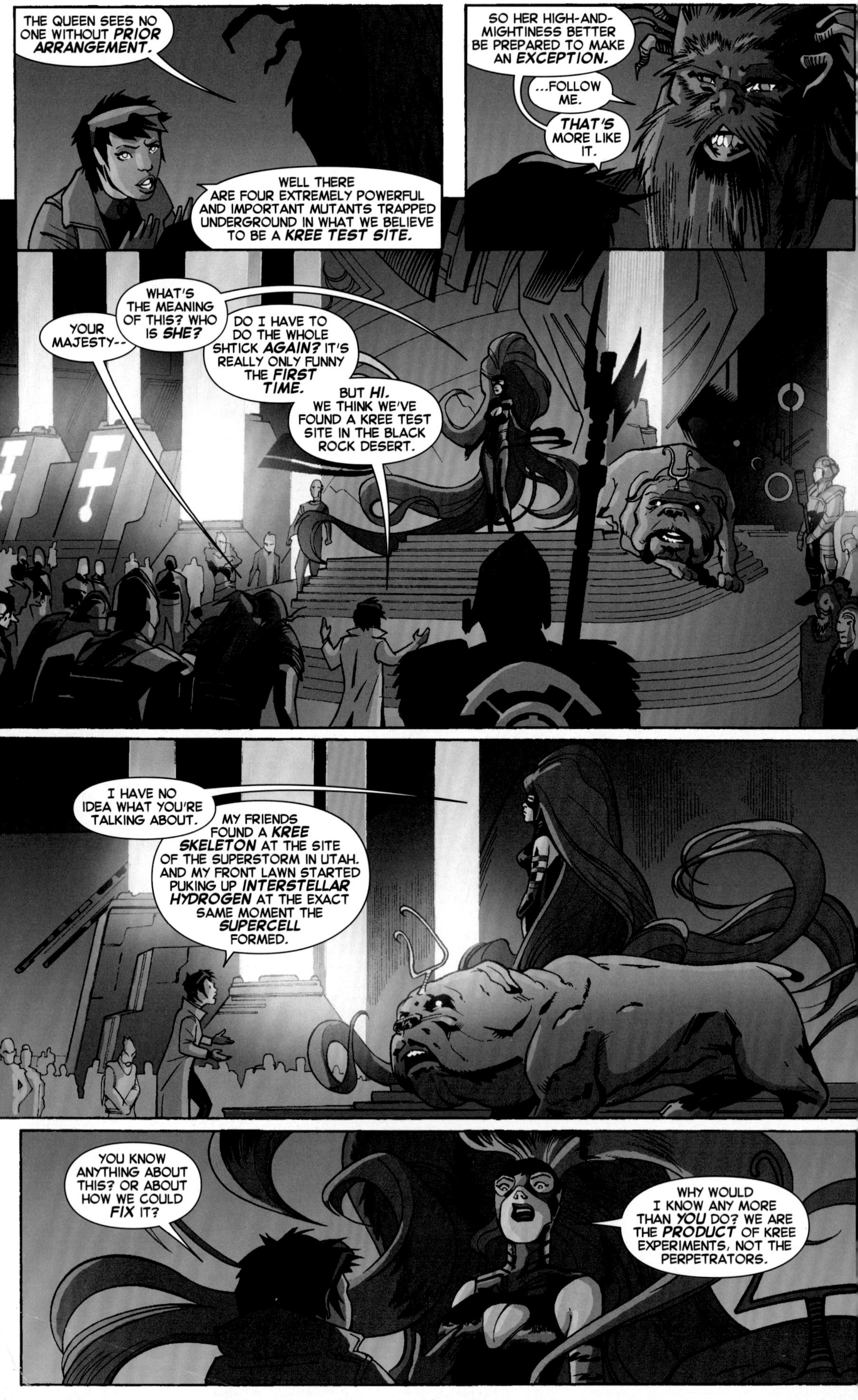
THE QUEEN SEES NO ONE WITHOUT PRIOR ARRANGEMENT.
WELL THERE ARE FOUR EXTREMELY POWERFUL AND IMPORTANT MUTANTS TRAPPED UNDERGROUND IN WHAT WE BELIEVE TO BE A KREE TEST SITE.
SO HER HIGH-AND-MIGHTINESS BETTER BE PREPARED TO MAKE AN EXCEPTION.
...FOLLOW ME.
THAT'S MORE LIKE IT.
YOUR MAJESTY--
WHAT'S THE MEANING OF THIS? WHO IS SHE?
DO I HAVE TO DO THE WHOLE SHTICK AGAIN? IT'S REALLY ONLY FUNNY THE FIRST TIME.
BUT HI. WE THINK WE'VE FOUND A KREE TEST SITE IN THE BLACK ROCK DESERT.
I HAVE NO IDEA WHAT YOU'RE TALKING ABOUT.
MY FRIENDS FOUND A KREE SKELETON AT THE SITE OF THE SUPERSTORM IN UTAH. AND MY FRONT LAWN STARTED PUKING UP INTERSTELLAR HYDROGEN AT THE EXACT SAME MOMENT THE SUPERCELL FORMED.
YOU KNOW ANYTHING ABOUT THIS? OR ABOUT HOW WE COULD FIX IT?
WHY WOULD I KNOW ANY MORE THAN YOU DO? WE ARE THE PRODUCT OF KREE EXPERIMENTS, NOT THE PERPETRATORS.

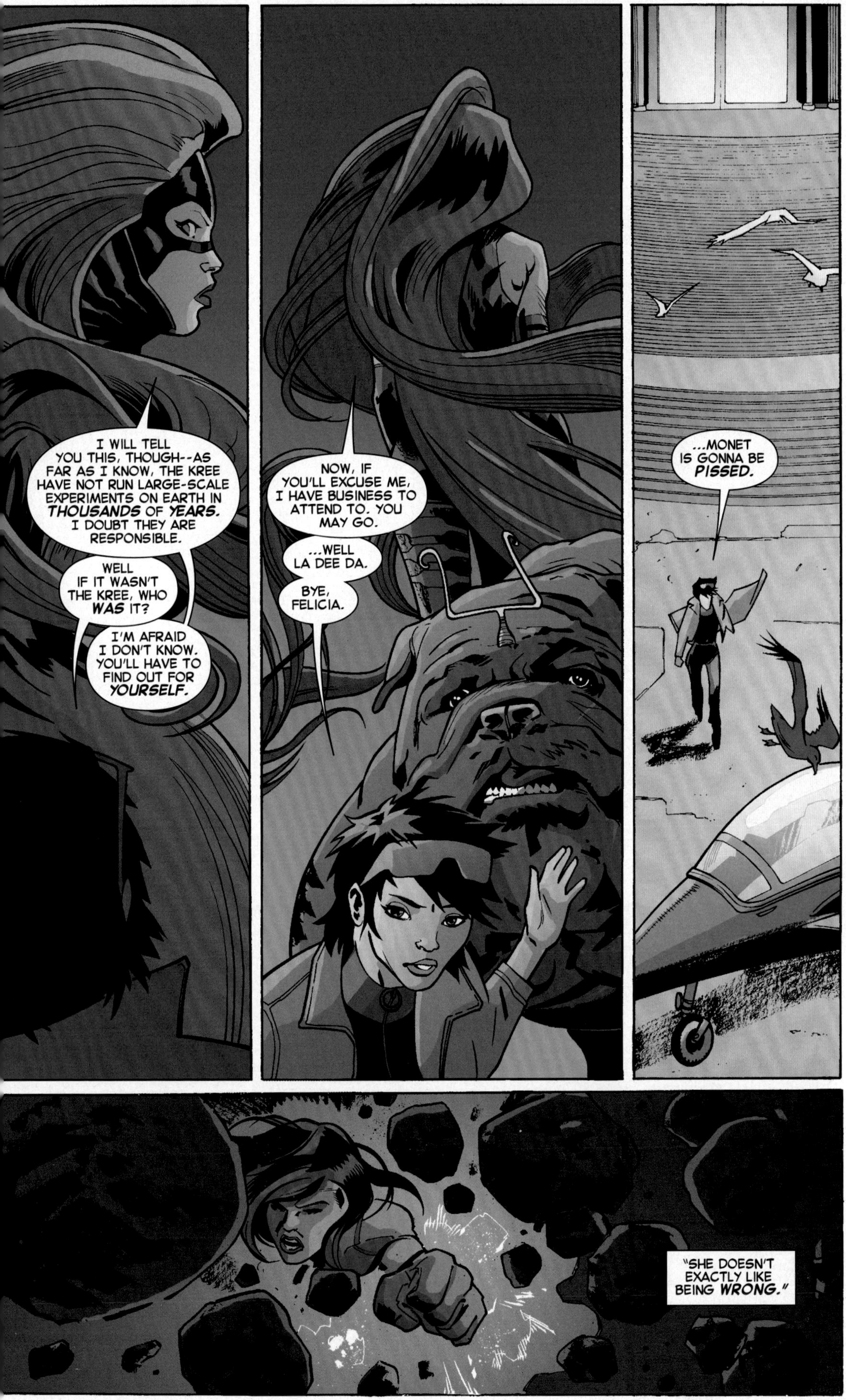

I WILL TELL YOU THIS, THOUGH--AS FAR AS I KNOW, THE KREE HAVE NOT RUN LARGE-SCALE EXPERIMENTS ON EARTH IN *THOUSANDS* OF *YEARS.* I DOUBT THEY ARE RESPONSIBLE.
WELL IF IT WASN'T THE KREE, WHO *WAS* IT?
I'M AFRAID I DON'T KNOW. YOU'LL HAVE TO FIND OUT FOR *YOURSELF.*
NOW, IF YOU'LL EXCUSE ME, I HAVE BUSINESS TO ATTEND TO. YOU MAY GO.
...WELL LA DEE DA.
BYE, FELICIA.
...MONET IS GONNA BE *PISSED.*
"SHE DOESN'T EXACTLY LIKE BEING *WRONG.*"

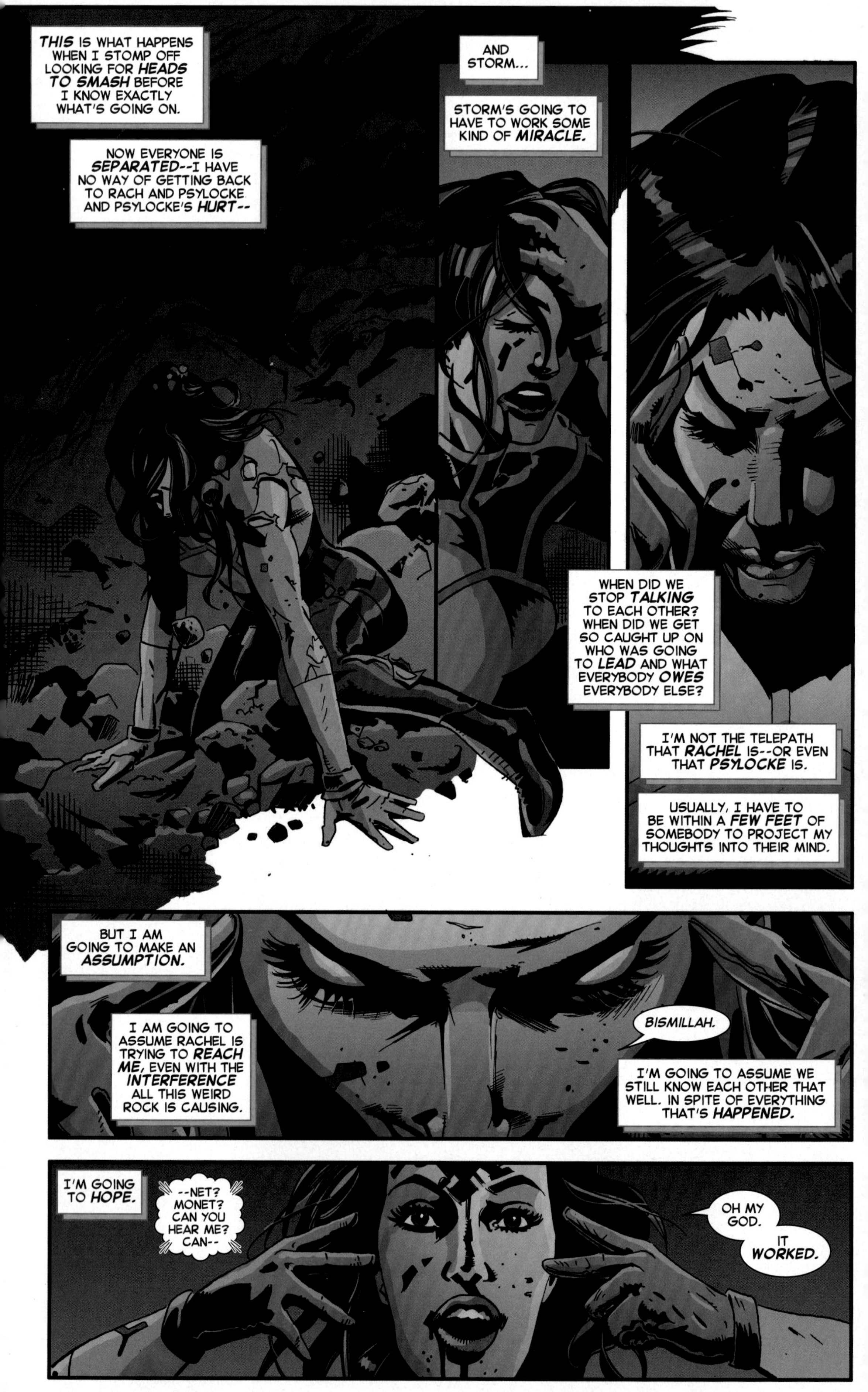
THIS IS WHAT HAPPENS WHEN I STOMP OFF LOOKING FOR HEADS TO SMASH BEFORE I KNOW EXACTLY WHAT'S GOING ON.
NOW EVERYONE IS SEPARATED--I HAVE NO WAY OF GETTING BACK TO RACH AND PSYLOCKE AND PSYLOCKE'S HURT--
AND STORM...
STORM'S GOING TO HAVE TO WORK SOME KIND OF MIRACLE.
WHEN DID WE STOP TALKING TO EACH OTHER? WHEN DID WE GET SO CAUGHT UP ON WHO WAS GOING TO LEAD AND WHAT EVERYBODY OWES EVERYBODY ELSE?
I'M NOT THE TELEPATH THAT RACHEL IS--OR EVEN THAT PSYLOCKE IS.
USUALLY, I HAVE TO BE WITHIN A FEW FEET OF SOMEBODY TO PROJECT MY THOUGHTS INTO THEIR MIND.
BUT I AM GOING TO MAKE AN ASSUMPTION.
I AM GOING TO ASSUME RACHEL IS TRYING TO REACH ME, EVEN WITH THE INTERFERENCE ALL THIS WEIRD ROCK IS CAUSING.
BISMILLAH.
I'M GOING TO ASSUME WE STILL KNOW EACH OTHER THAT WELL. IN SPITE OF EVERYTHING THAT'S HAPPENED.
I'M GOING TO HOPE.
--NET? MONET? CAN YOU HEAR ME? CAN--
OH MY GOD.
IT WORKED.

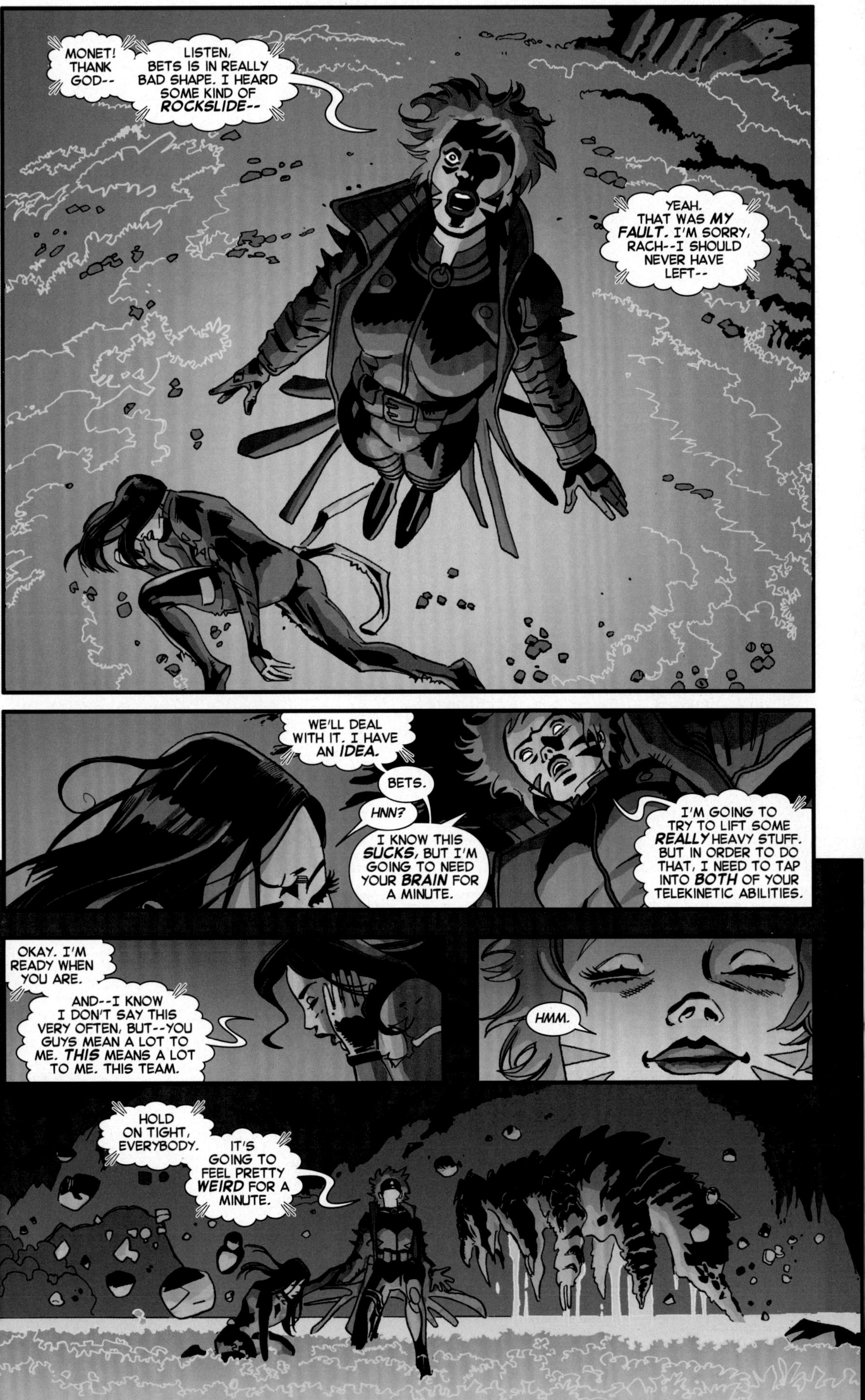
MONET! THANK GOD--
LISTEN, BETS IS IN REALLY BAD SHAPE. I HEARD SOME KIND OF ROCKSLIDE--
YEAH. THAT WAS MY FAULT. I'M SORRY, RACH--I SHOULD NEVER HAVE LEFT--
WE'LL DEAL WITH IT. I HAVE AN IDEA.
BETS.
HNN?
I KNOW THIS SUCKS, BUT I'M GOING TO NEED YOUR BRAIN FOR A MINUTE.
I'M GOING TO TRY TO LIFT SOME REALLY HEAVY STUFF. BUT IN ORDER TO DO THAT, I NEED TO TAP INTO BOTH OF YOUR TELEKINETIC ABILITIES.
OKAY. I'M READY WHEN YOU ARE.
AND--I KNOW I DON'T SAY THIS VERY OFTEN, BUT--YOU GUYS MEAN A LOT TO ME. THIS MEANS A LOT TO ME. THIS TEAM.
HMM.
HOLD ON TIGHT, EVERYBODY.
IT'S GOING TO FEEL PRETTY WEIRD FOR A MINUTE.

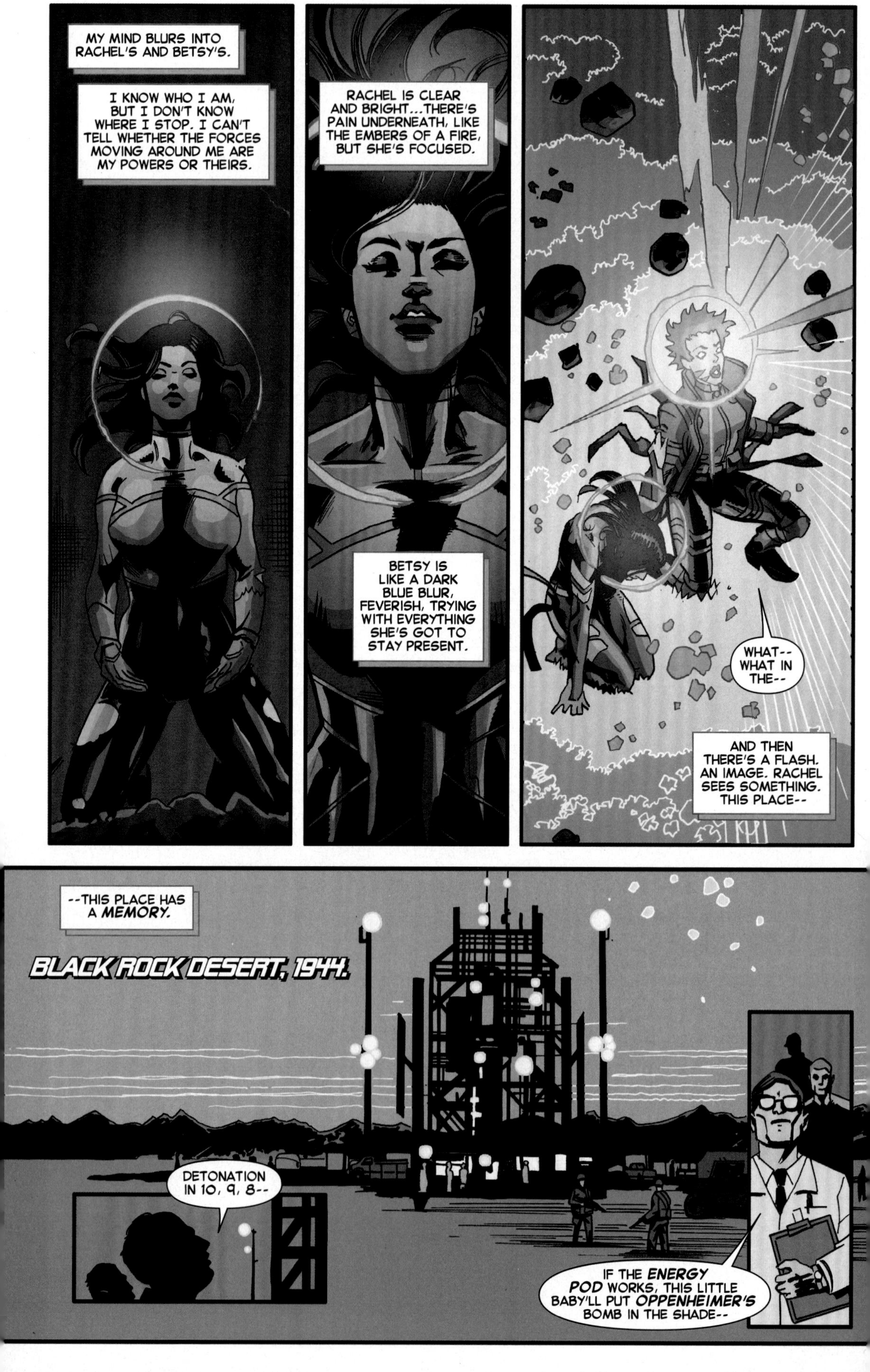
MY MIND BLURS INTO RACHEL'S AND BETSY'S.
I KNOW WHO I AM, BUT I DON'T KNOW WHERE I STOP. I CAN'T TELL WHETHER THE FORCES MOVING AROUND ME ARE MY POWERS OR THEIRS.
RACHEL IS CLEAR AND BRIGHT...THERE'S PAIN UNDERNEATH, LIKE THE EMBERS OF A FIRE, BUT SHE'S FOCUSED.
BETSY IS LIKE A DARK BLUE BLUR, FEVERISH, TRYING WITH EVERYTHING SHE'S GOT TO STAY PRESENT.
WHAT-- WHAT IN THE--
AND THEN THERE'S A FLASH. AN IMAGE. RACHEL SEES SOMETHING. THIS PLACE--
--THIS PLACE HAS A MEMORY.
BLACK ROCK DESERT, 1944.
DETONATION IN 10, 9, 8--
IF THE ENERGY POD WORKS, THIS LITTLE BABY'LL PUT OPPENHEIMER'S BOMB IN THE SHADE--

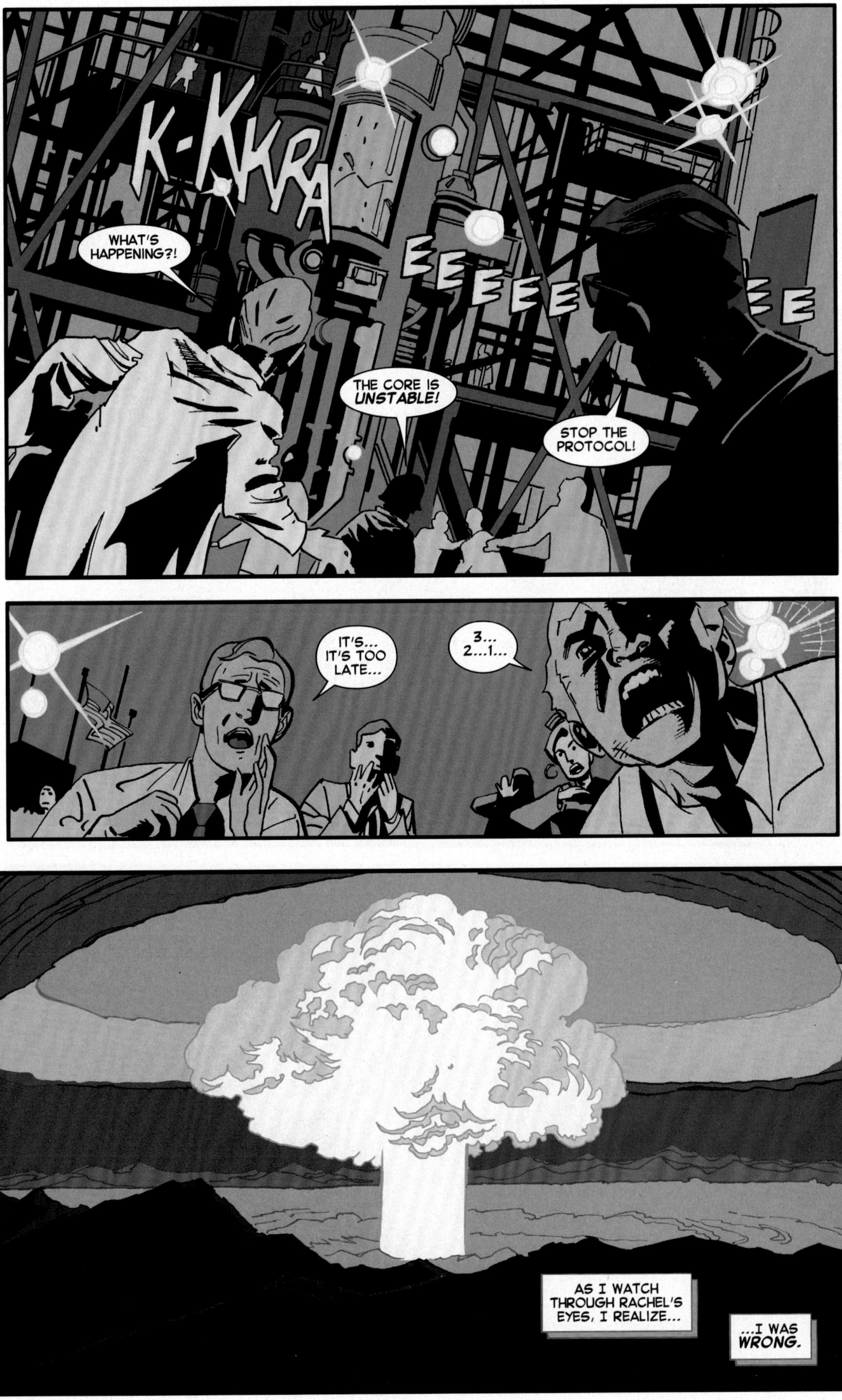
K-KKRA
WHAT'S HAPPENING?!
EEEEEEE
THE CORE IS UNSTABLE!
STOP THE PROTOCOL!
IT'S... IT'S TOO LATE...
3... 2...1...
AS I WATCH THROUGH RACHEL'S EYES, I REALIZE...
...I WAS WRONG.

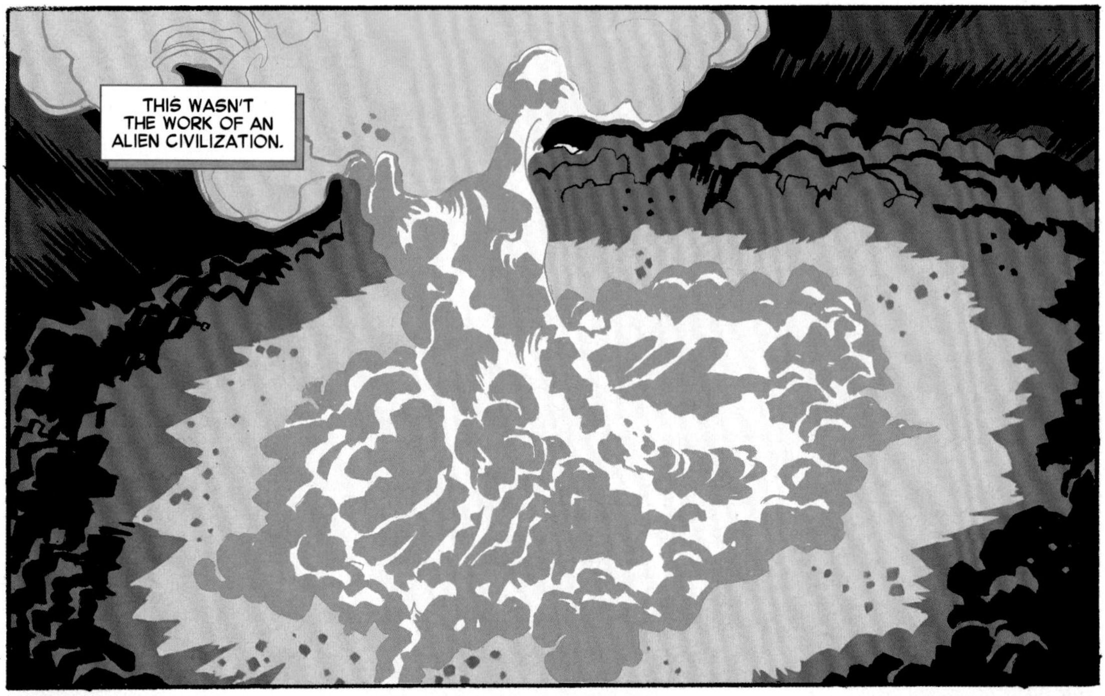
THIS WASN'T THE WORK OF AN ALIEN CIVILIZATION.

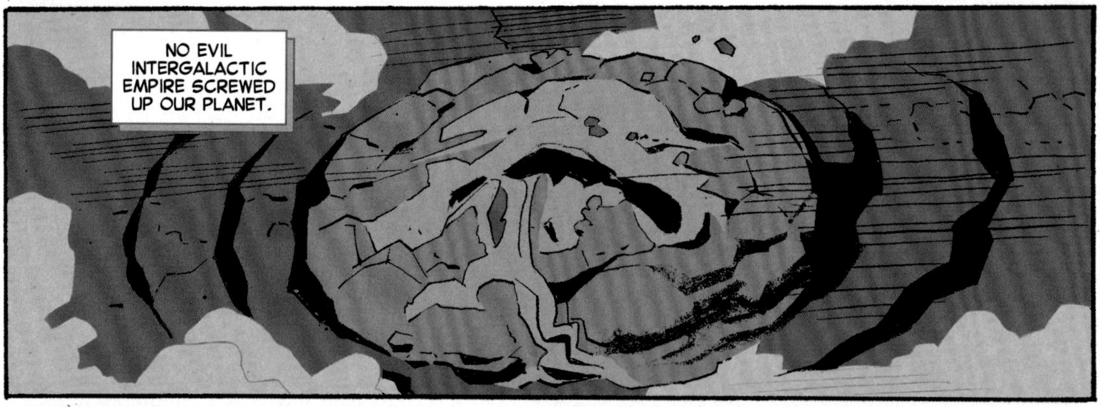
NO EVIL INTERGALACTIC EMPIRE SCREWED UP OUR PLANET.

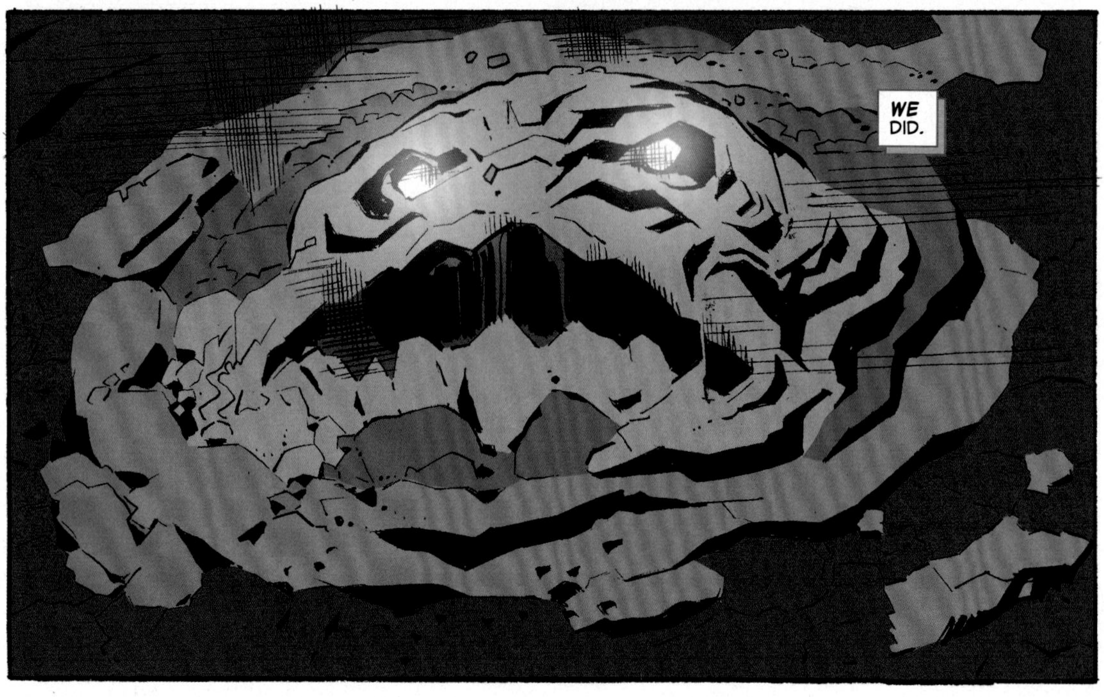
WE DID.

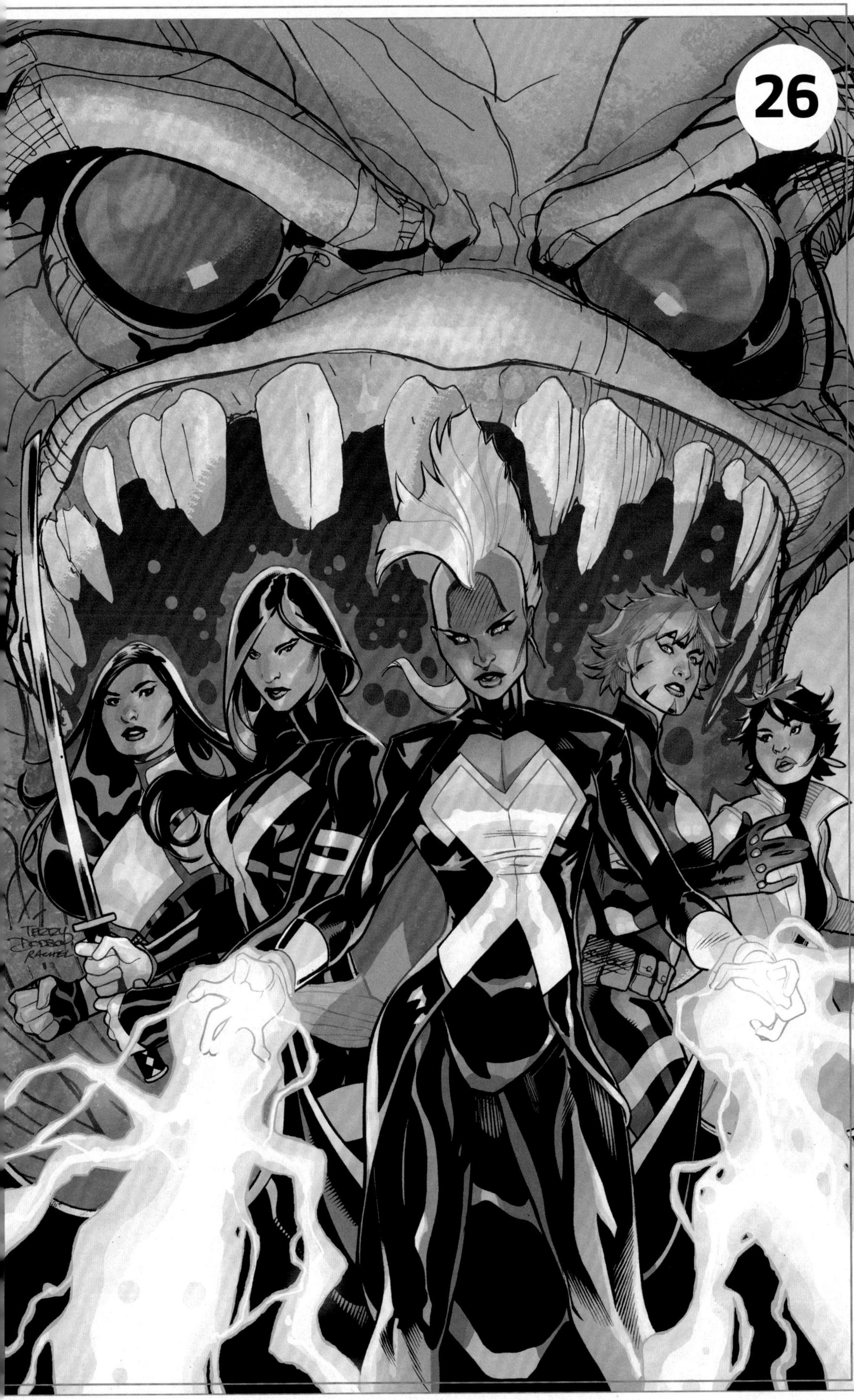
26

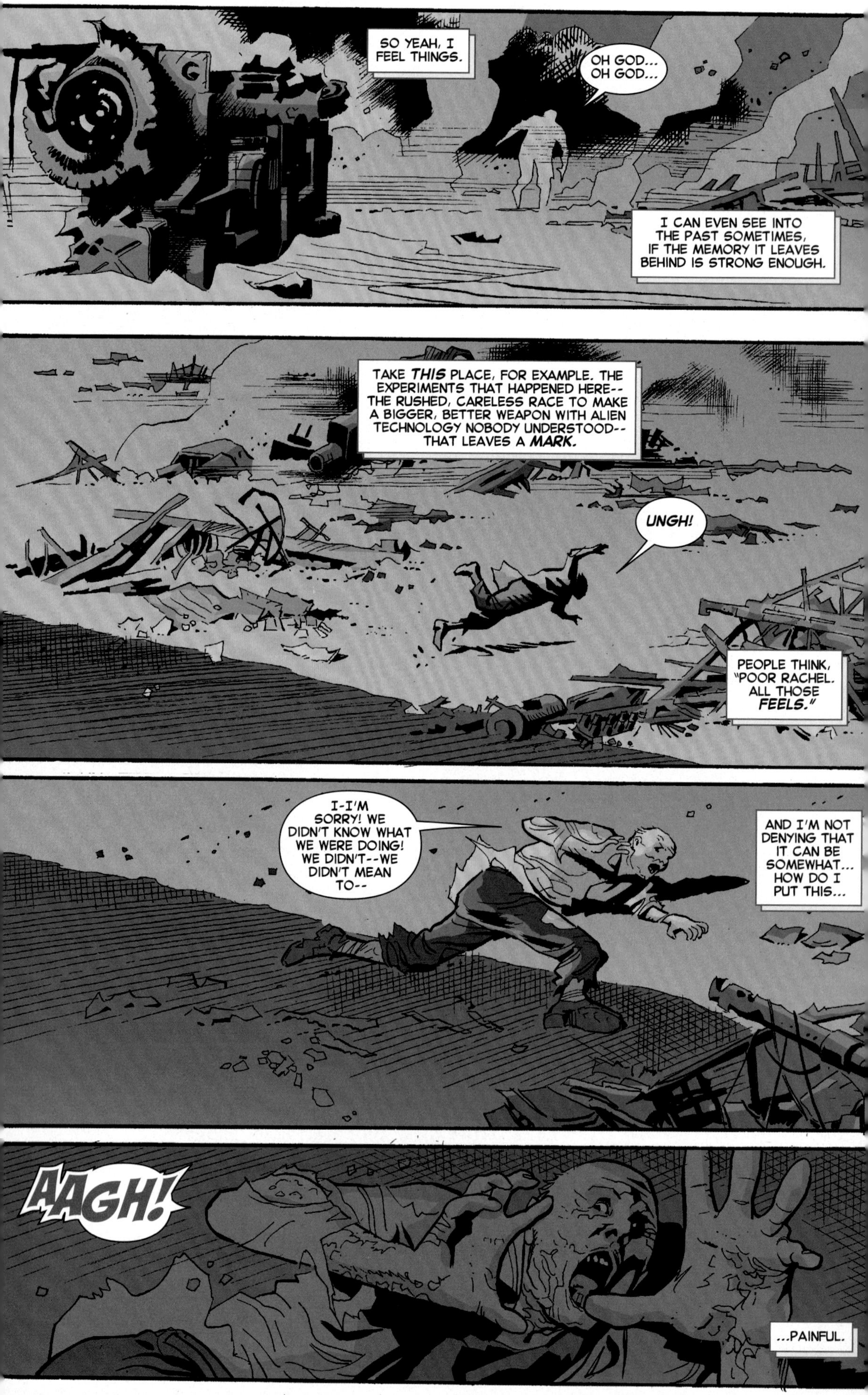
SO YEAH, I FEEL THINGS.
OH GOD... OH GOD...
I CAN EVEN SEE INTO THE PAST SOMETIMES, IF THE MEMORY IT LEAVES BEHIND IS STRONG ENOUGH.
TAKE *THIS* PLACE, FOR EXAMPLE. THE EXPERIMENTS THAT HAPPENED HERE-- THE RUSHED, CARELESS RACE TO MAKE A BIGGER, BETTER WEAPON WITH ALIEN TECHNOLOGY NOBODY UNDERSTOOD-- THAT LEAVES A *MARK.*
UNGH!
PEOPLE THINK, "POOR RACHEL. ALL THOSE *FEELS.*"
I-I'M SORRY! WE DIDN'T KNOW WHAT WE WERE DOING! WE DIDN'T--WE DIDN'T MEAN TO--
AND I'M NOT DENYING THAT IT CAN BE SOMEWHAT... HOW DO I PUT THIS...
AAGH!
...PAINFUL.

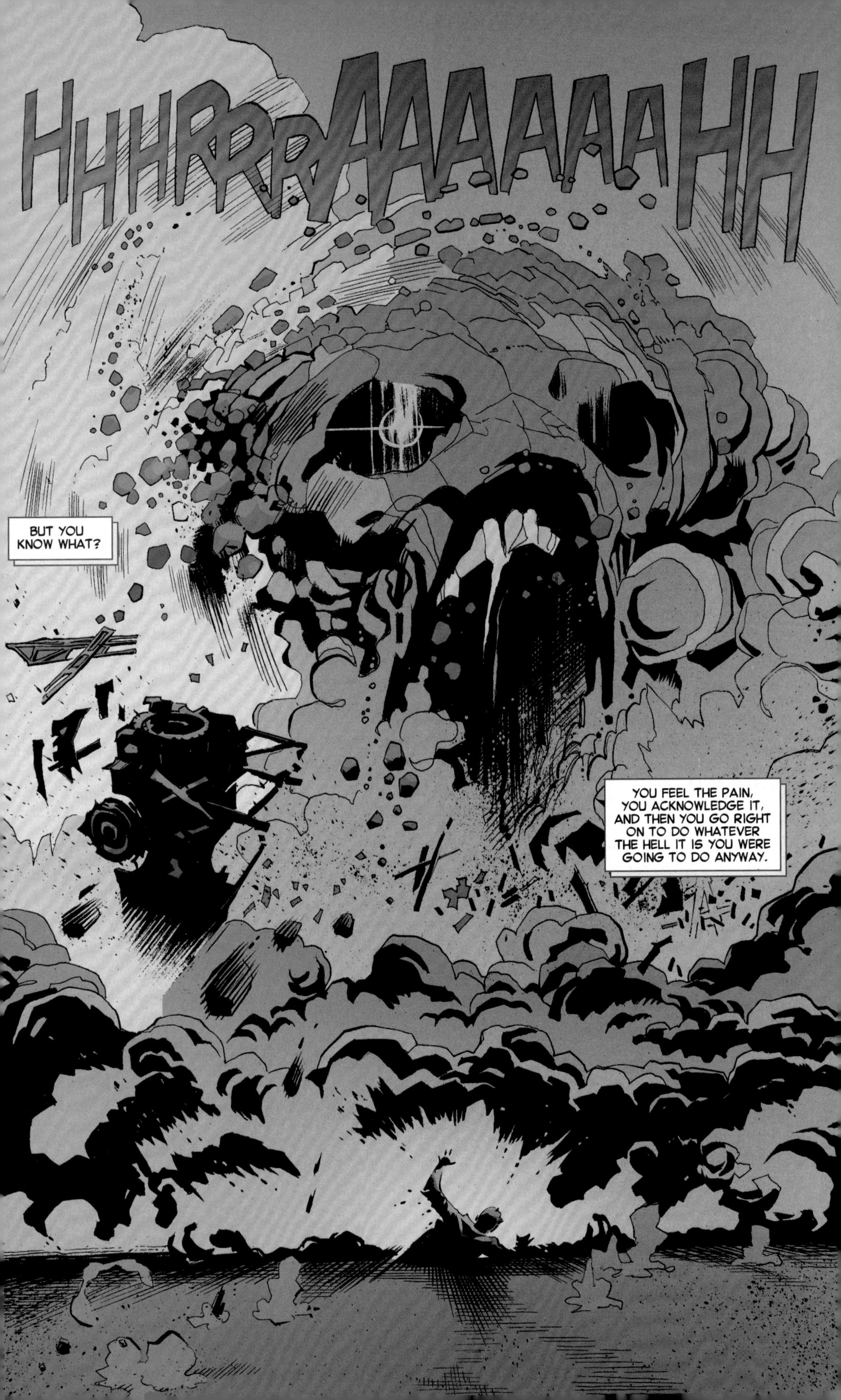
HHHRRRAAAAAAAHH
BUT YOU KNOW WHAT?
YOU FEEL THE PAIN, YOU ACKNOWLEDGE IT, AND THEN YOU GO RIGHT ON TO DO WHATEVER THE HELL IT IS YOU WERE GOING TO DO ANYWAY.

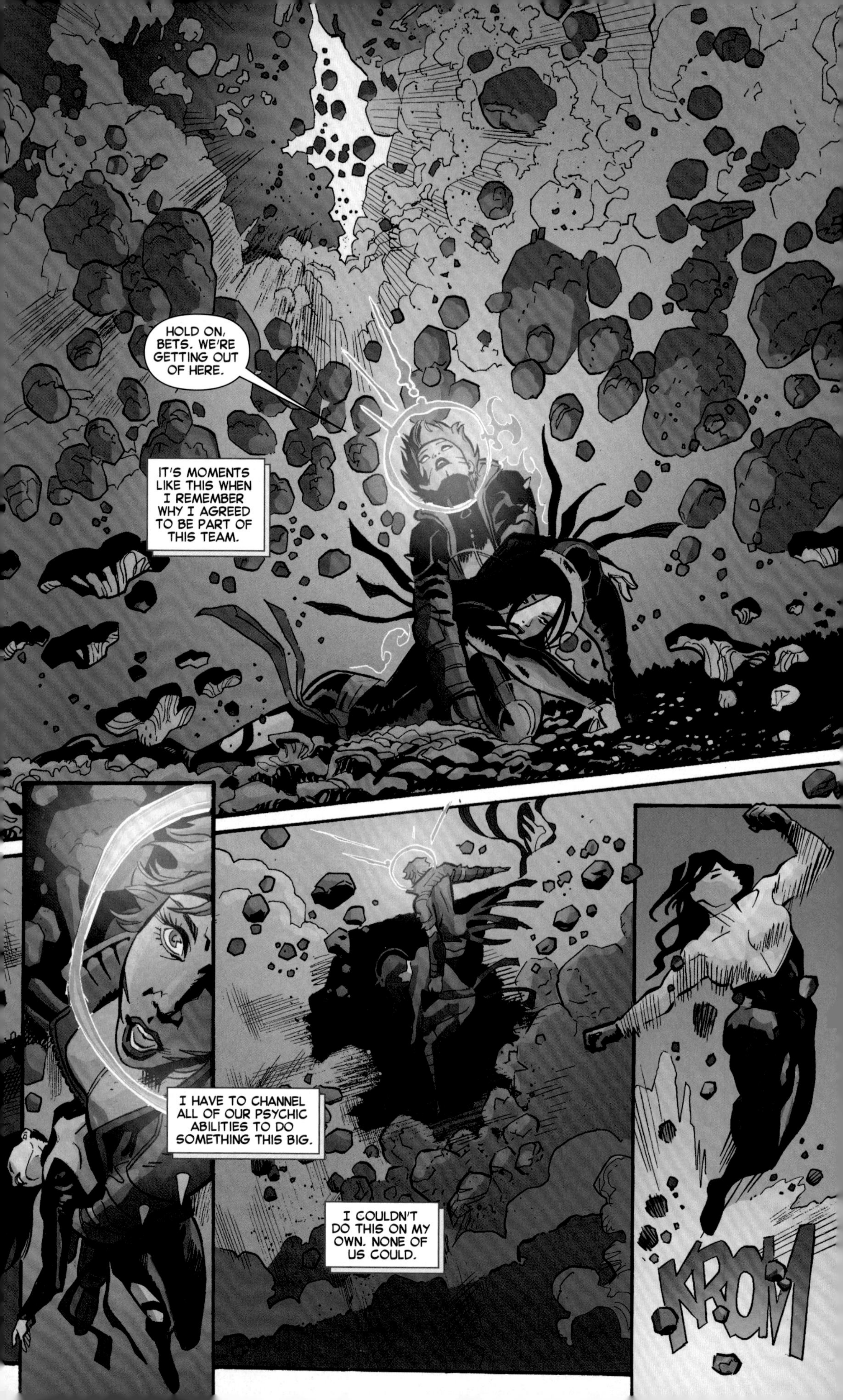
HOLD ON, BETS. WE'RE GETTING OUT OF HERE.
IT'S MOMENTS LIKE THIS WHEN I REMEMBER WHY I AGREED TO BE PART OF THIS TEAM.
I HAVE TO CHANNEL ALL OF OUR PSYCHIC ABILITIES TO DO SOMETHING THIS BIG.
I COULDN'T DO THIS ON MY OWN. NONE OF US COULD.
KRAKOOM

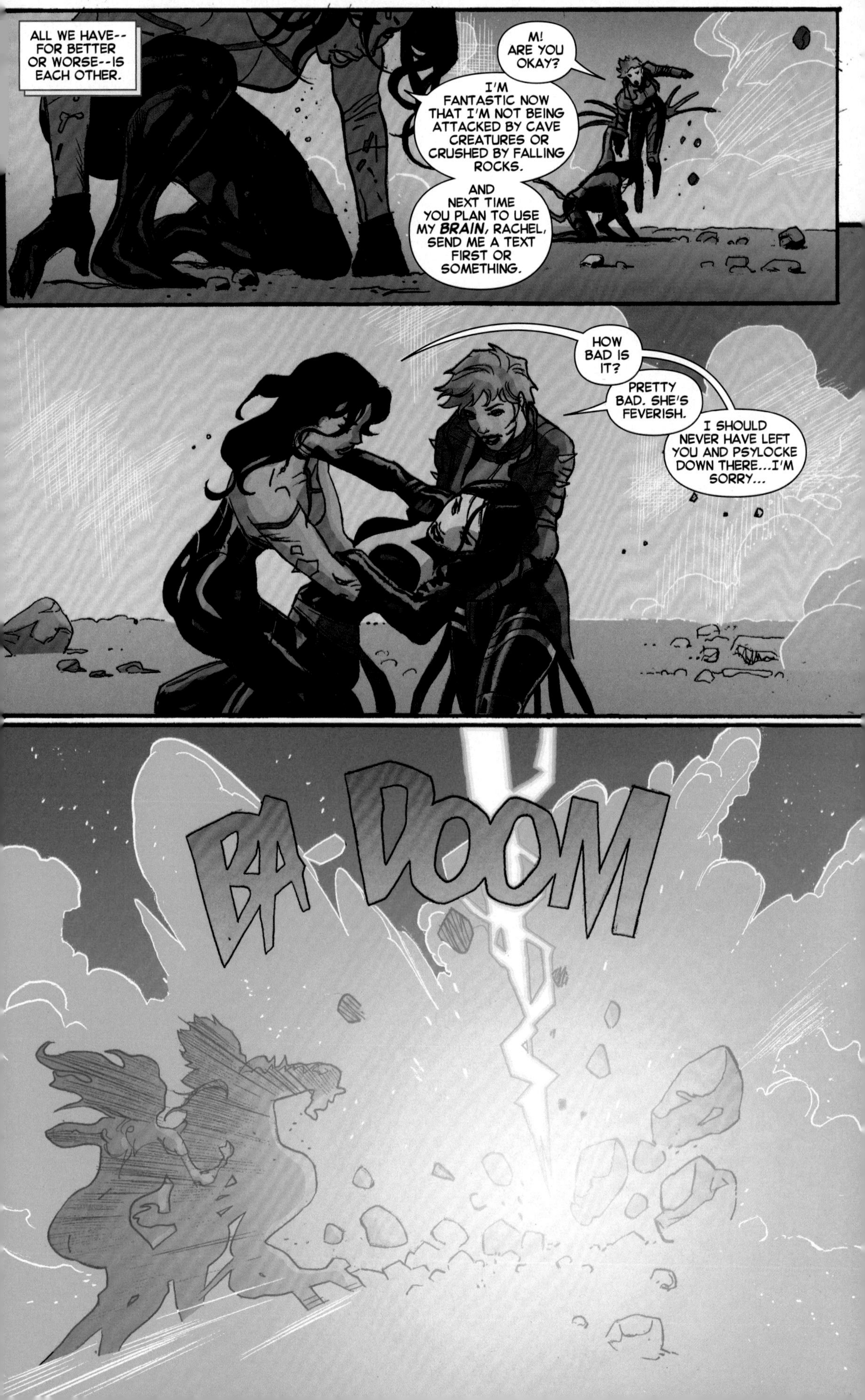
ALL WE HAVE-- FOR BETTER OR WORSE--IS EACH OTHER.
M! ARE YOU OKAY?
I'M FANTASTIC NOW THAT I'M NOT BEING ATTACKED BY CAVE CREATURES OR CRUSHED BY FALLING ROCKS.
AND NEXT TIME YOU PLAN TO USE MY **BRAIN**, RACHEL, SEND ME A TEXT FIRST OR SOMETHING.
HOW BAD IS IT?
PRETTY BAD. SHE'S FEVERISH.
I SHOULD NEVER HAVE LEFT YOU AND PSYLOCKE DOWN THERE...I'M SORRY...
BA-DOOM

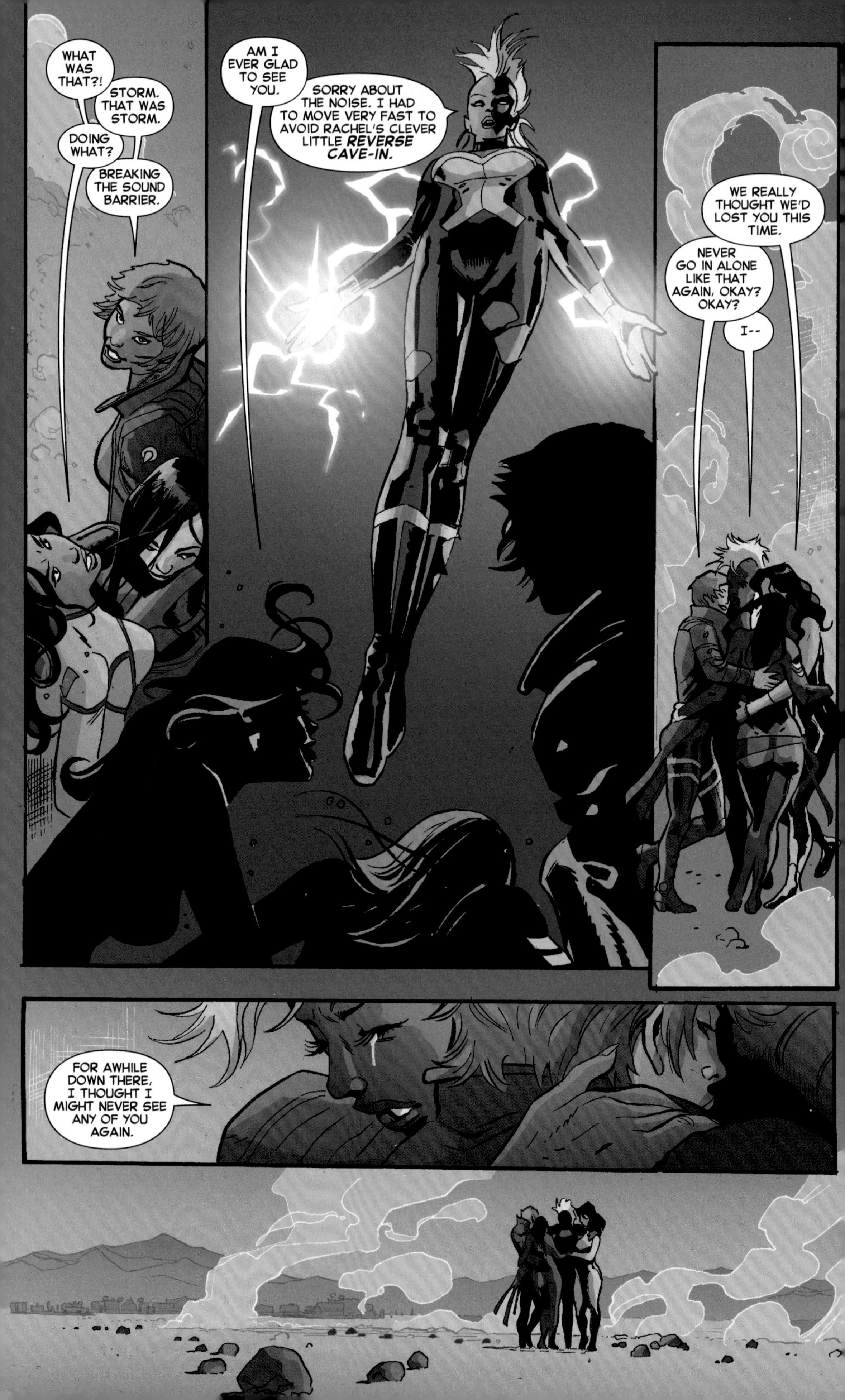
WHAT WAS THAT?!
STORM. THAT WAS STORM.
DOING WHAT?
BREAKING THE SOUND BARRIER.
AM I EVER GLAD TO SEE YOU.
SORRY ABOUT THE NOISE. I HAD TO MOVE VERY FAST TO AVOID RACHEL'S CLEVER LITTLE *REVERSE CAVE-IN.*
WE REALLY THOUGHT WE'D LOST YOU THIS TIME.
NEVER GO IN ALONE LIKE THAT AGAIN, OKAY? OKAY?
I--
FOR AWHILE DOWN THERE, I THOUGHT I MIGHT NEVER SEE ANY OF YOU AGAIN.

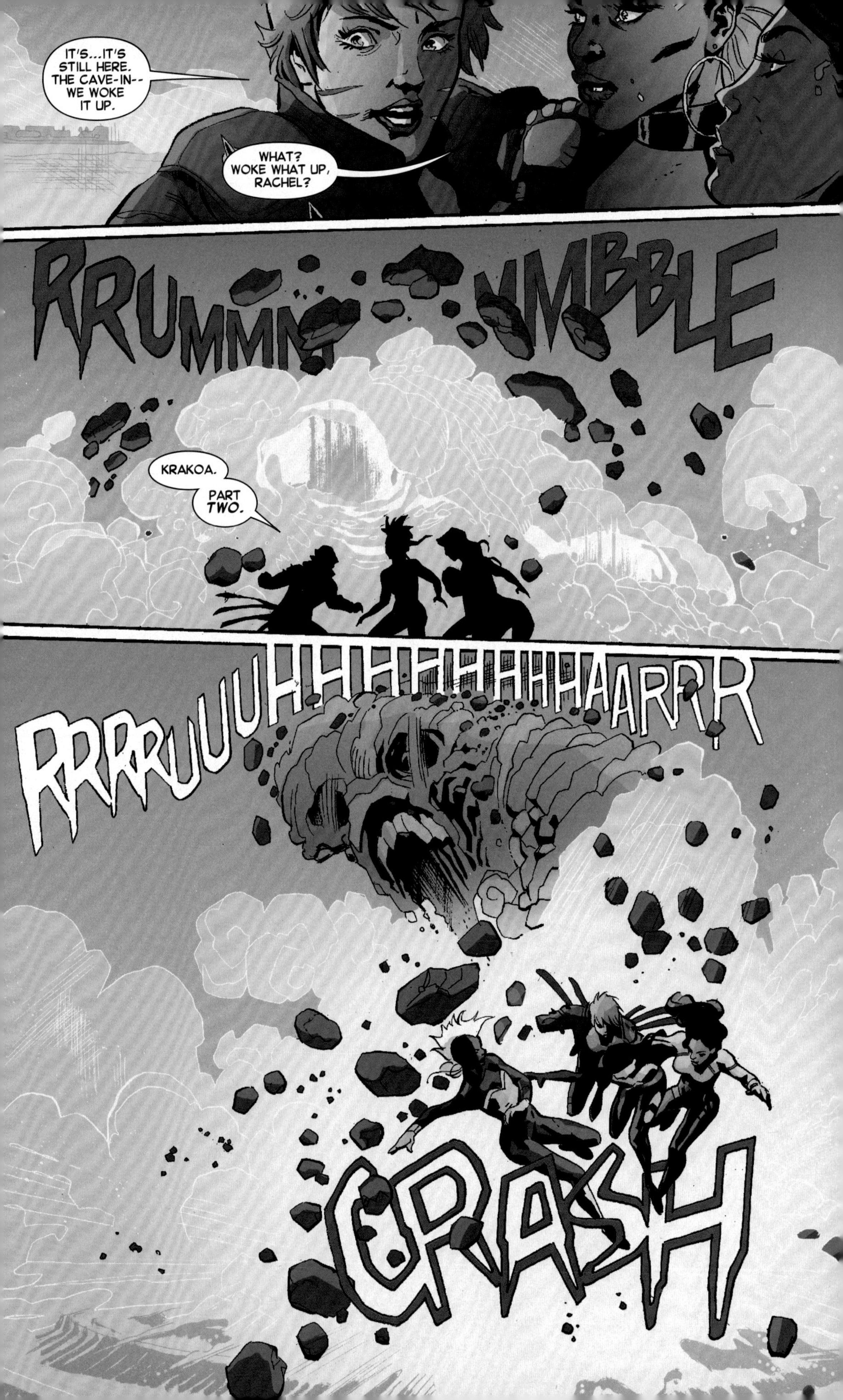
IT'S...IT'S STILL HERE. THE CAVE-IN--WE WOKE IT UP.
WHAT? WOKE WHAT UP, RACHEL?
RRUMMMMMBBLE
KRAKOA.
PART TWO.
RRRRUUUHHHHHHHHHHHAARRR
CRASH

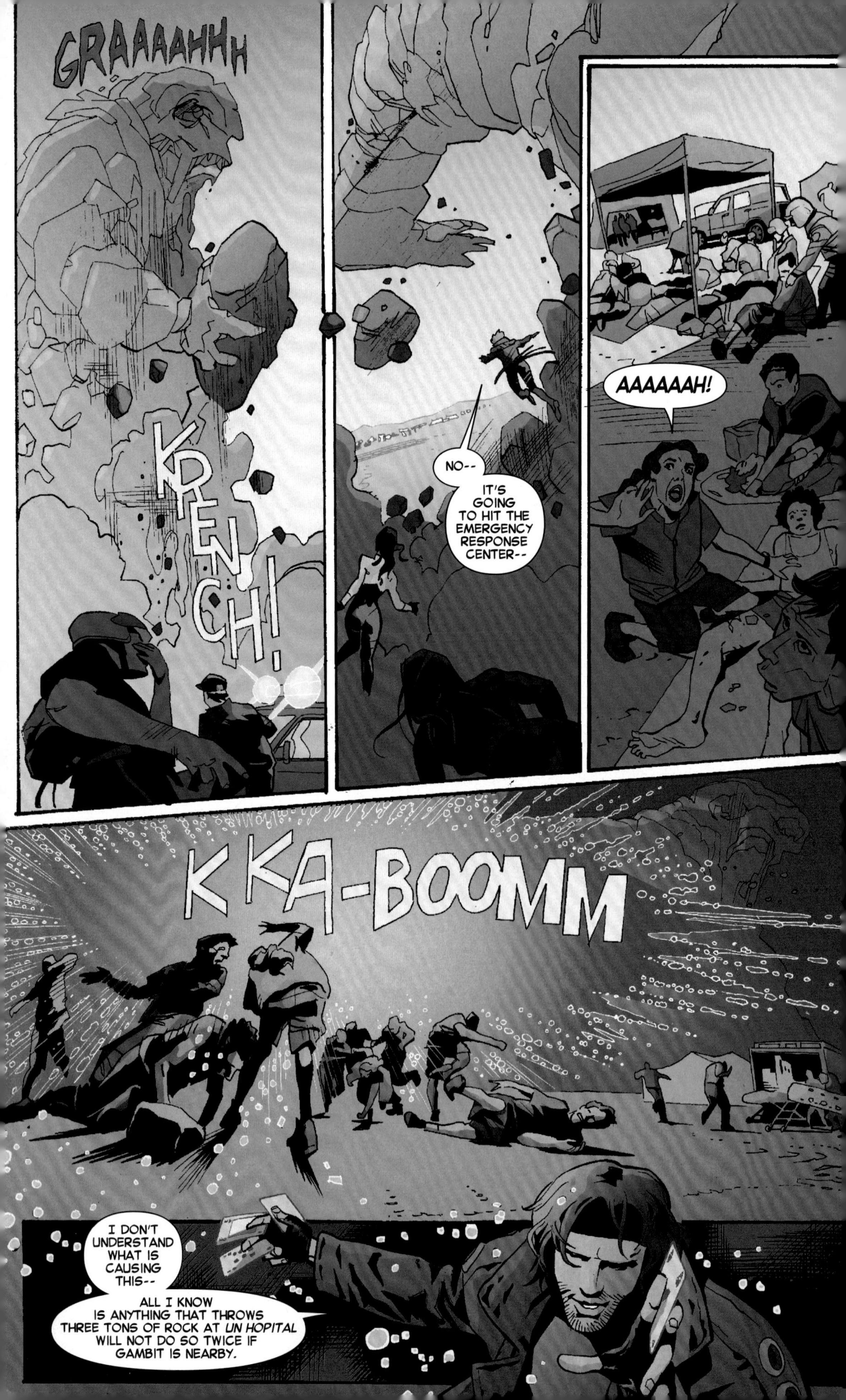
GRAAAAHHH
KRENCH!
NO--
IT'S GOING TO HIT THE EMERGENCY RESPONSE CENTER--
AAAAAAH!
KKA-BOOMM
I DON'T UNDERSTAND WHAT IS CAUSING THIS--
ALL I KNOW IS ANYTHING THAT THROWS THREE TONS OF ROCK AT *UN HOPITAL* WILL NOT DO SO TWICE IF GAMBIT IS NEARBY.

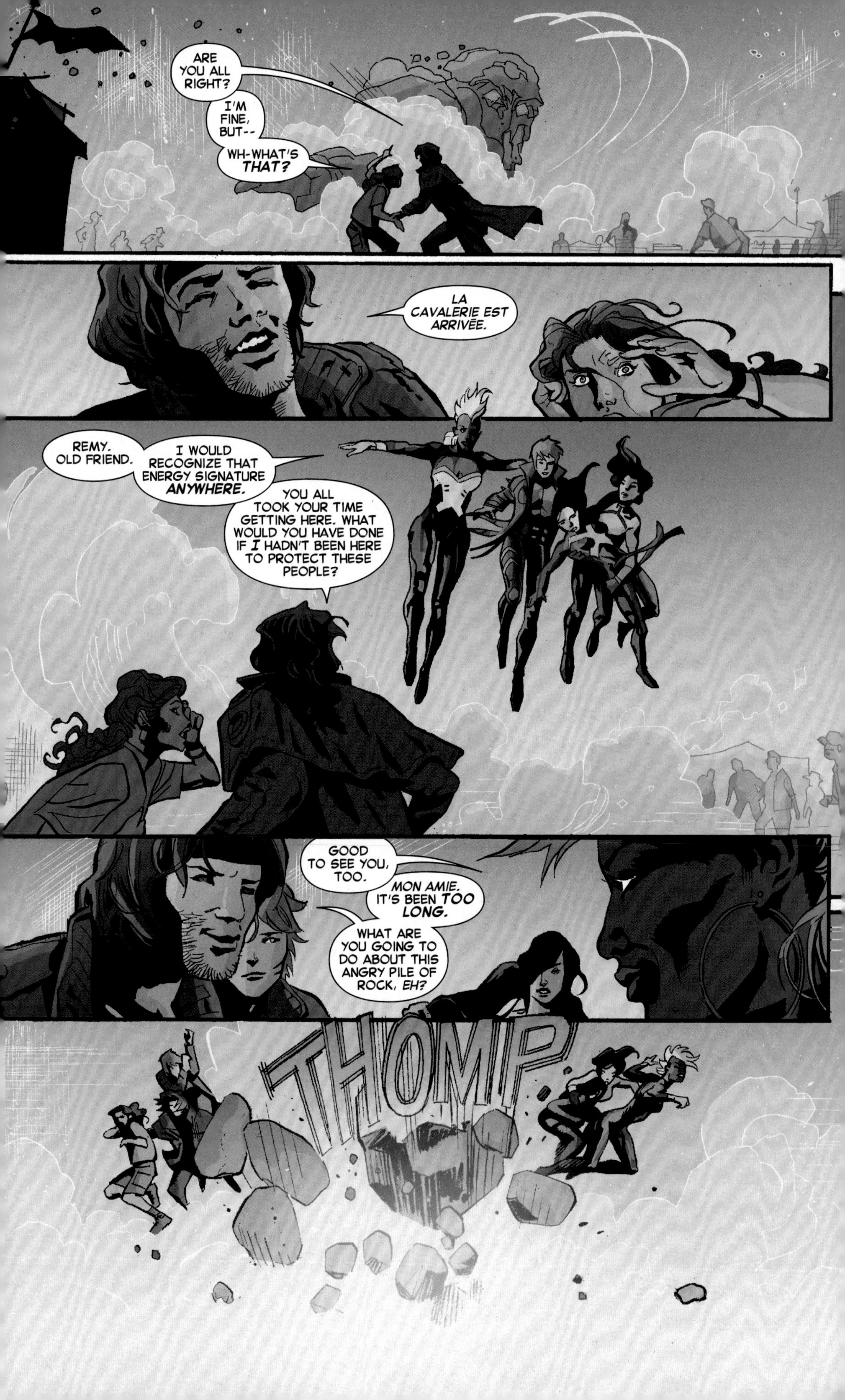
ARE YOU ALL RIGHT?
I'M FINE, BUT--
WH-WHAT'S *THAT?*
LA CAVALERIE EST ARRIVÉE.
REMY. OLD FRIEND.
I WOULD RECOGNIZE THAT ENERGY SIGNATURE *ANYWHERE.*
YOU ALL TOOK YOUR TIME GETTING HERE. WHAT WOULD YOU HAVE DONE IF *I* HADN'T BEEN HERE TO PROTECT THESE PEOPLE?
GOOD TO SEE YOU, TOO.
MON AMIE. IT'S BEEN *TOO LONG.*
WHAT ARE YOU GOING TO DO ABOUT THIS ANGRY PILE OF ROCK, *EH?*
THOMP

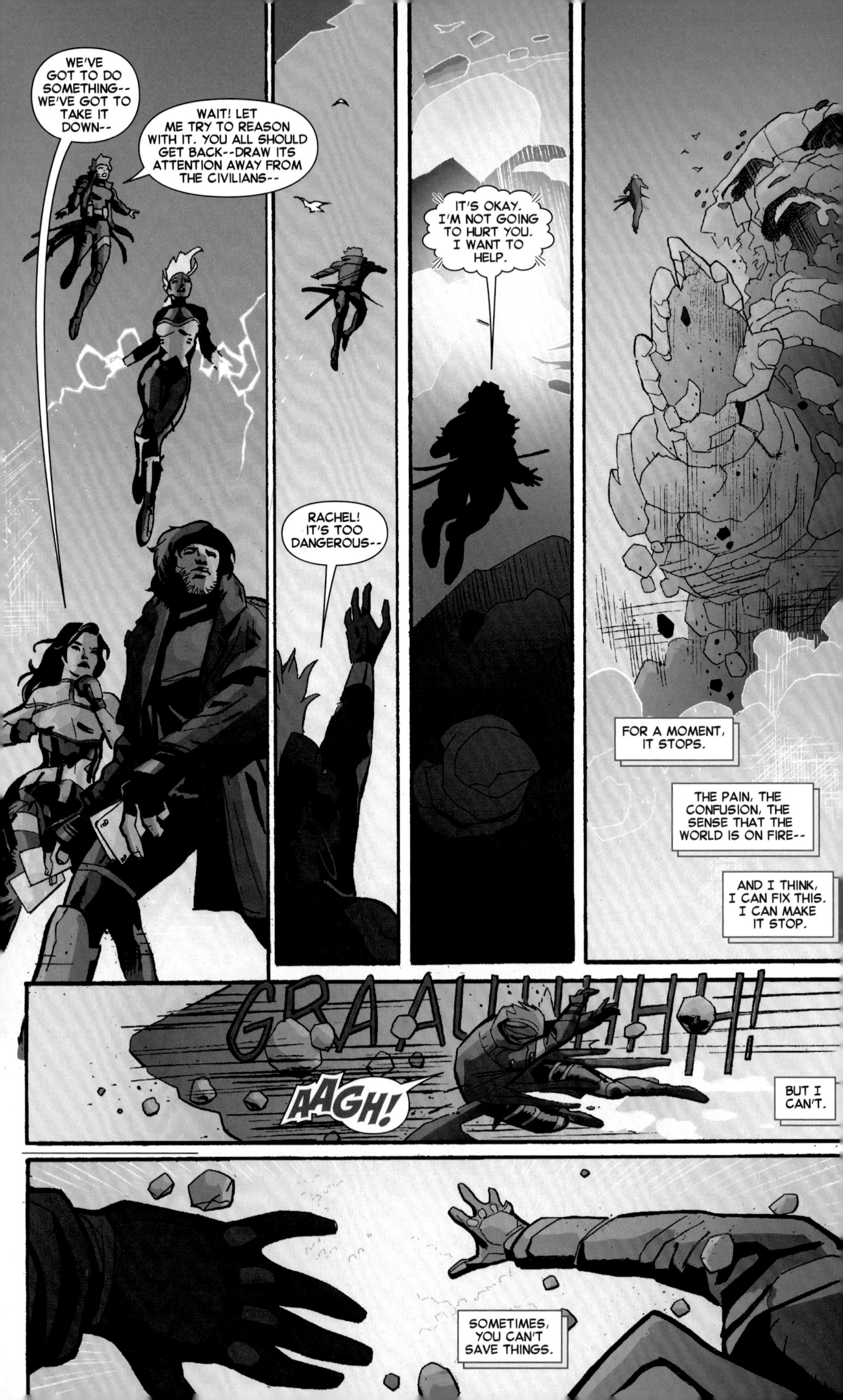
WE'VE GOT TO DO SOMETHING--WE'VE GOT TO TAKE IT DOWN--
WAIT! LET ME TRY TO REASON WITH IT. YOU ALL SHOULD GET BACK--DRAW ITS ATTENTION AWAY FROM THE CIVILIANS--
RACHEL! IT'S TOO DANGEROUS--
IT'S OKAY. I'M NOT GOING TO HURT YOU. I WANT TO HELP.
FOR A MOMENT, IT STOPS.
THE PAIN, THE CONFUSION, THE SENSE THAT THE WORLD IS ON FIRE--
AND I THINK, I CAN FIX THIS. I CAN MAKE IT STOP.
GRAAUUHHH!!
AAGH!
BUT I CAN'T.
SOMETIMES, YOU CAN'T SAVE THINGS.

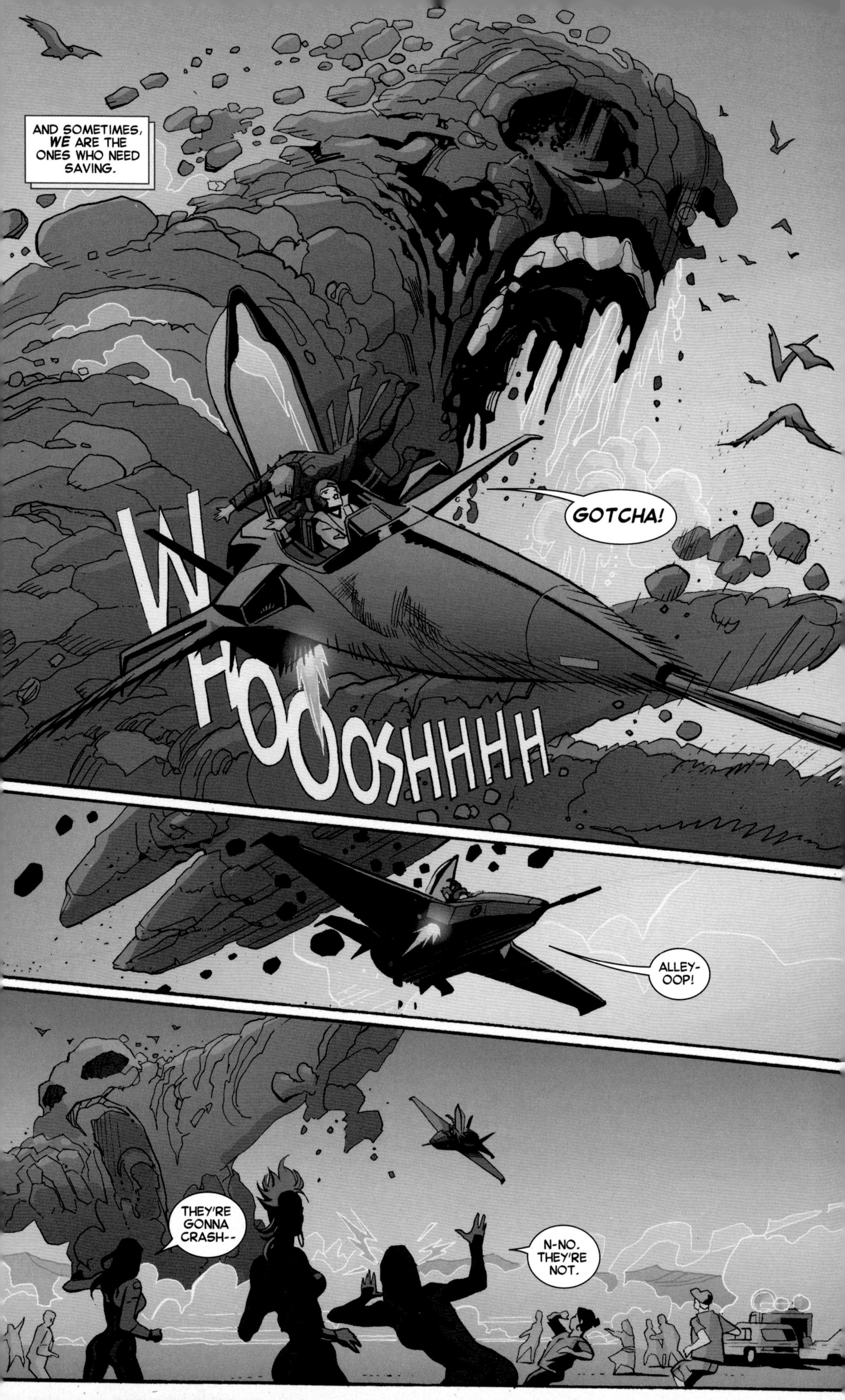
AND SOMETIMES, WE ARE THE ONES WHO NEED SAVING.
GOTCHA!
WHOOOSHHHH
ALLEY-OOP!
THEY'RE GONNA CRASH--
N-NO. THEY'RE NOT.

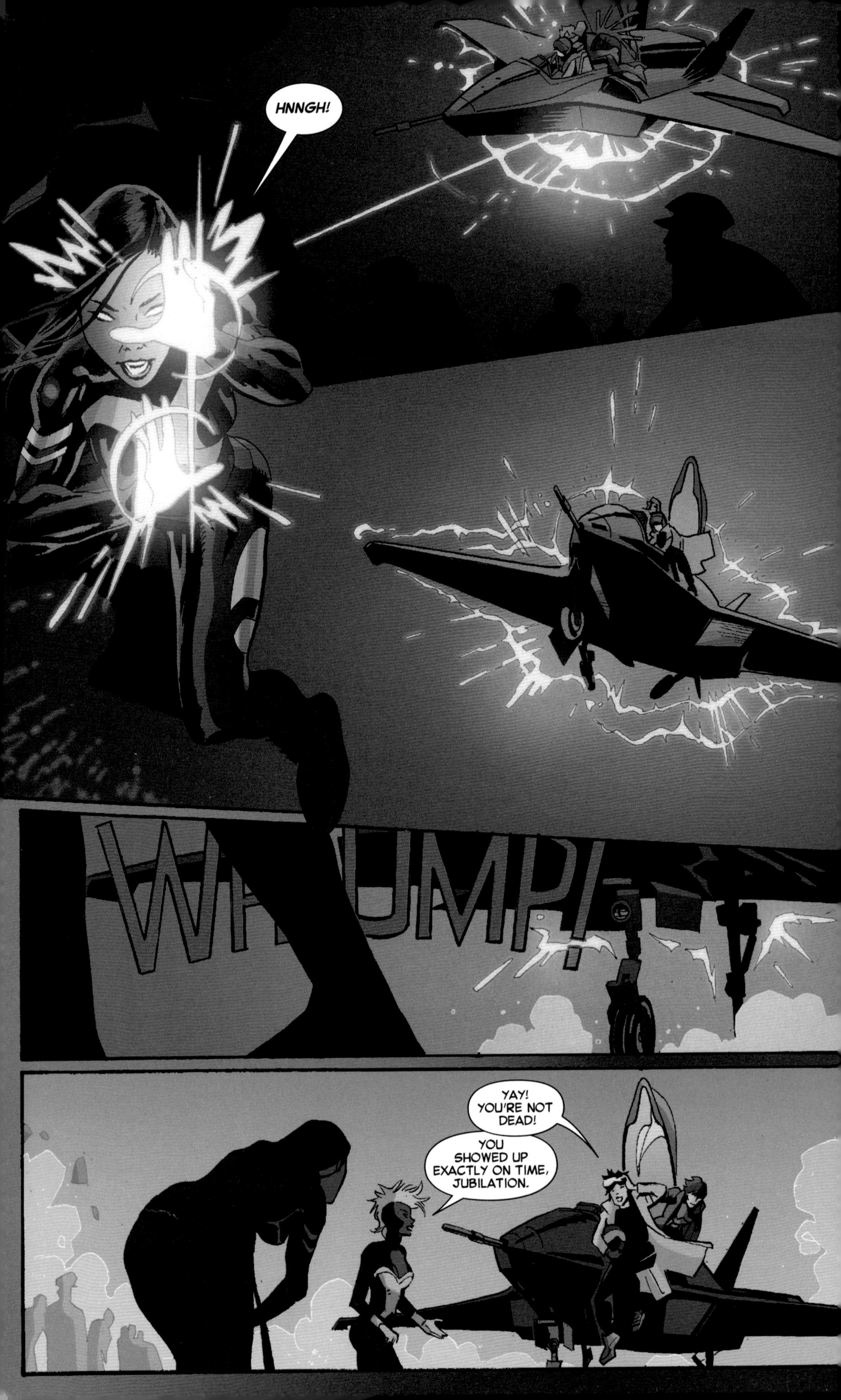
HNNGH!
WHUMP!
YAY! YOU'RE NOT DEAD!
YOU SHOWED UP EXACTLY ON TIME, JUBILATION.

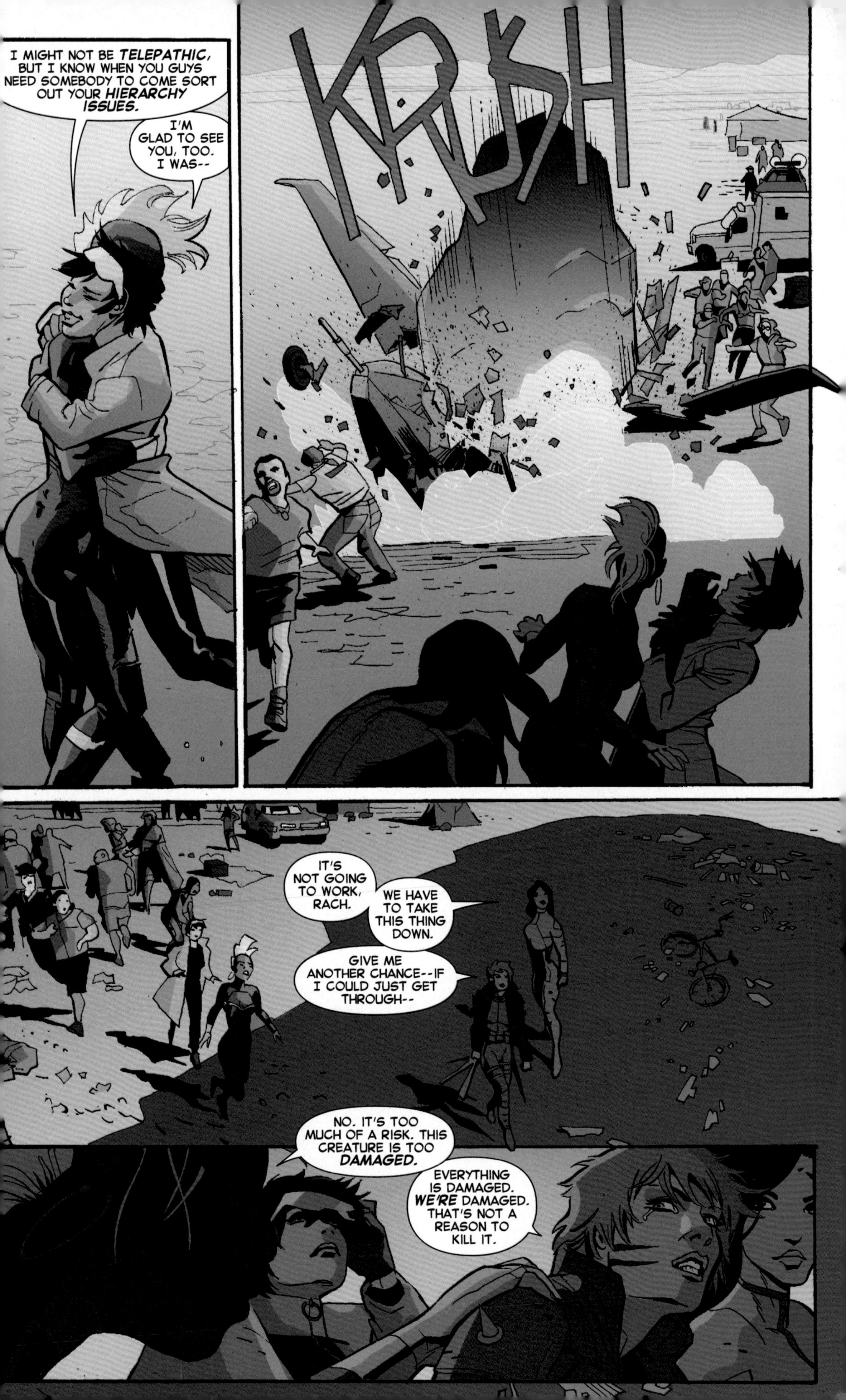
I MIGHT NOT BE TELEPATHIC, BUT I KNOW WHEN YOU GUYS NEED SOMEBODY TO COME SORT OUT YOUR HIERARCHY ISSUES.
I'M GLAD TO SEE YOU, TOO. I WAS--
KRUSH
IT'S NOT GOING TO WORK, RACH.
WE HAVE TO TAKE THIS THING DOWN.
GIVE ME ANOTHER CHANCE--IF I COULD JUST GET THROUGH--
NO. IT'S TOO MUCH OF A RISK. THIS CREATURE IS TOO DAMAGED.
EVERYTHING IS DAMAGED. WE'RE DAMAGED. THAT'S NOT A REASON TO KILL IT.

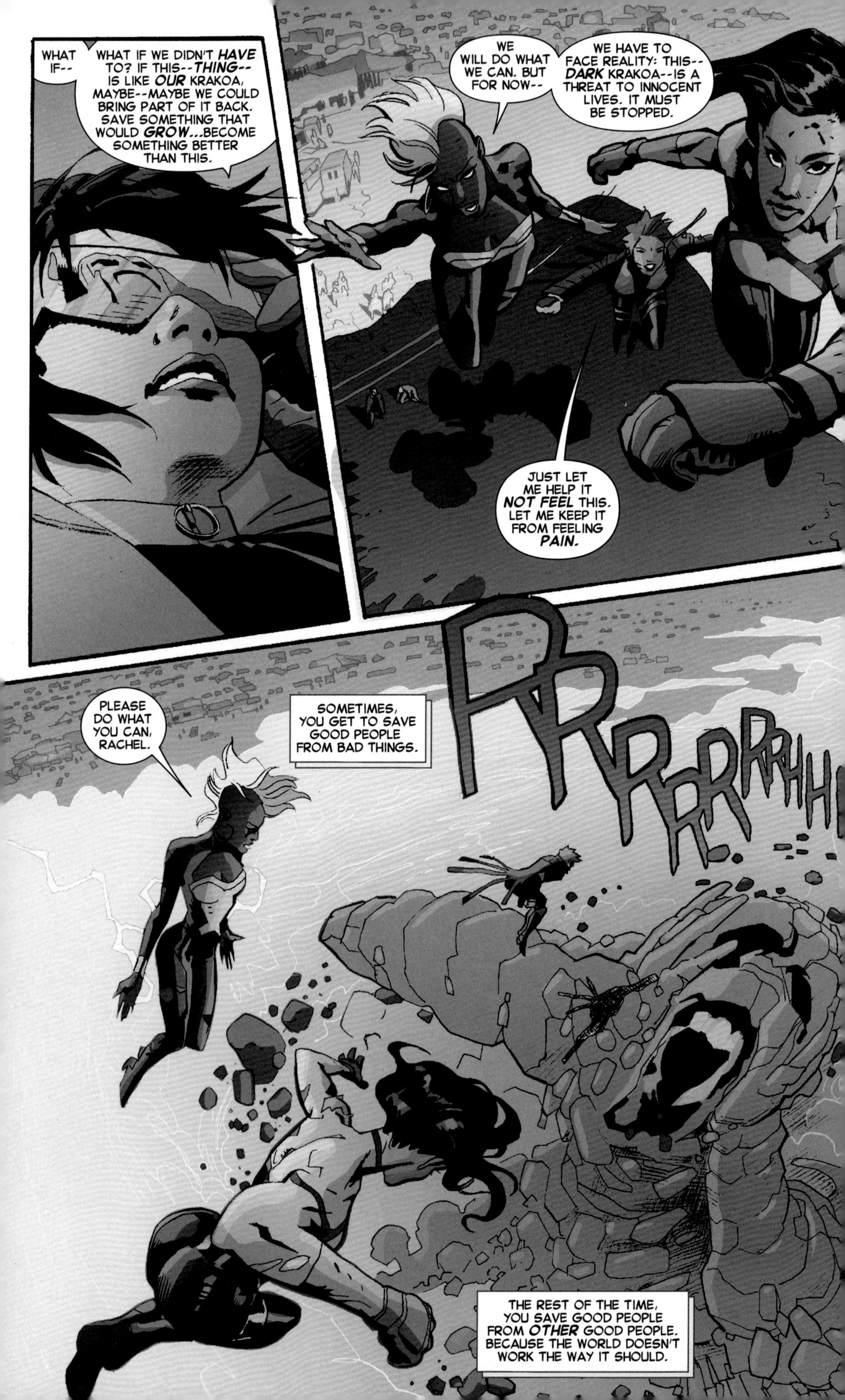
WHAT IF--
WHAT IF WE DIDN'T HAVE TO? IF THIS--THING--IS LIKE OUR KRAKOA, MAYBE--MAYBE WE COULD BRING PART OF IT BACK. SAVE SOMETHING THAT WOULD GROW...BECOME SOMETHING BETTER THAN THIS.
WE WILL DO WHAT WE CAN. BUT FOR NOW--
WE HAVE TO FACE REALITY: THIS--DARK KRAKOA--IS A THREAT TO INNOCENT LIVES. IT MUST BE STOPPED.
JUST LET ME HELP IT NOT FEEL THIS. LET ME KEEP IT FROM FEELING PAIN.
PLEASE DO WHAT YOU CAN, RACHEL.
SOMETIMES, YOU GET TO SAVE GOOD PEOPLE FROM BAD THINGS.
RRRRRRRHH
THE REST OF THE TIME, YOU SAVE GOOD PEOPLE FROM OTHER GOOD PEOPLE. BECAUSE THE WORLD DOESN'T WORK THE WAY IT SHOULD.

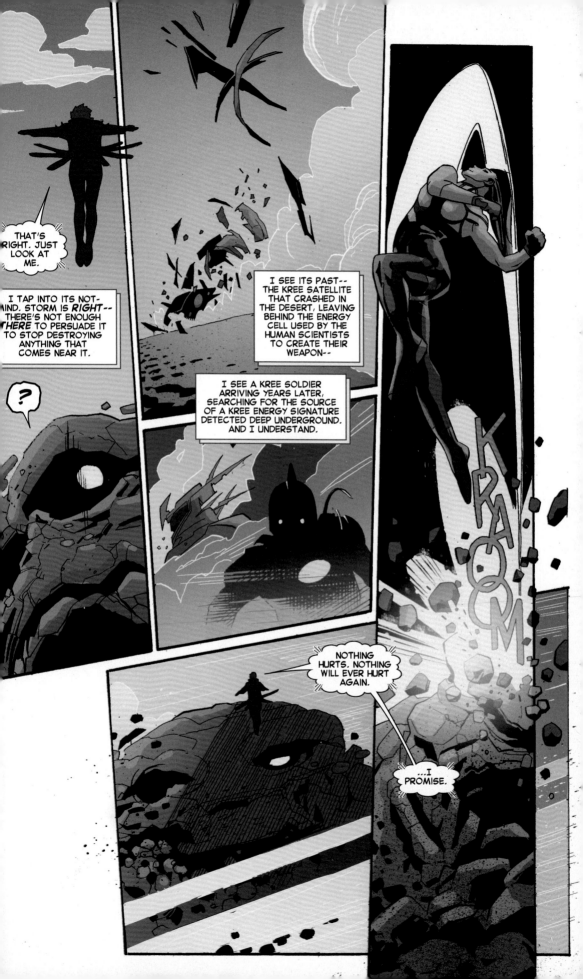

THAT'S RIGHT. JUST LOOK AT ME.

I TAP INTO ITS NOT-MIND. STORM IS *RIGHT*-- THERE'S NOT ENOUGH *THERE* TO PERSUADE IT TO STOP DESTROYING ANYTHING THAT COMES NEAR IT.

?

I SEE ITS PAST-- THE KREE SATELLITE THAT CRASHED IN THE DESERT, LEAVING BEHIND THE ENERGY CELL USED BY THE HUMAN SCIENTISTS TO CREATE THEIR WEAPON--

I SEE A KREE SOLDIER ARRIVING YEARS LATER, SEARCHING FOR THE SOURCE OF A KREE ENERGY SIGNATURE DETECTED DEEP UNDERGROUND. AND I UNDERSTAND.

KRAOOM

NOTHING HURTS. NOTHING WILL EVER HURT AGAIN.

...I PROMISE.

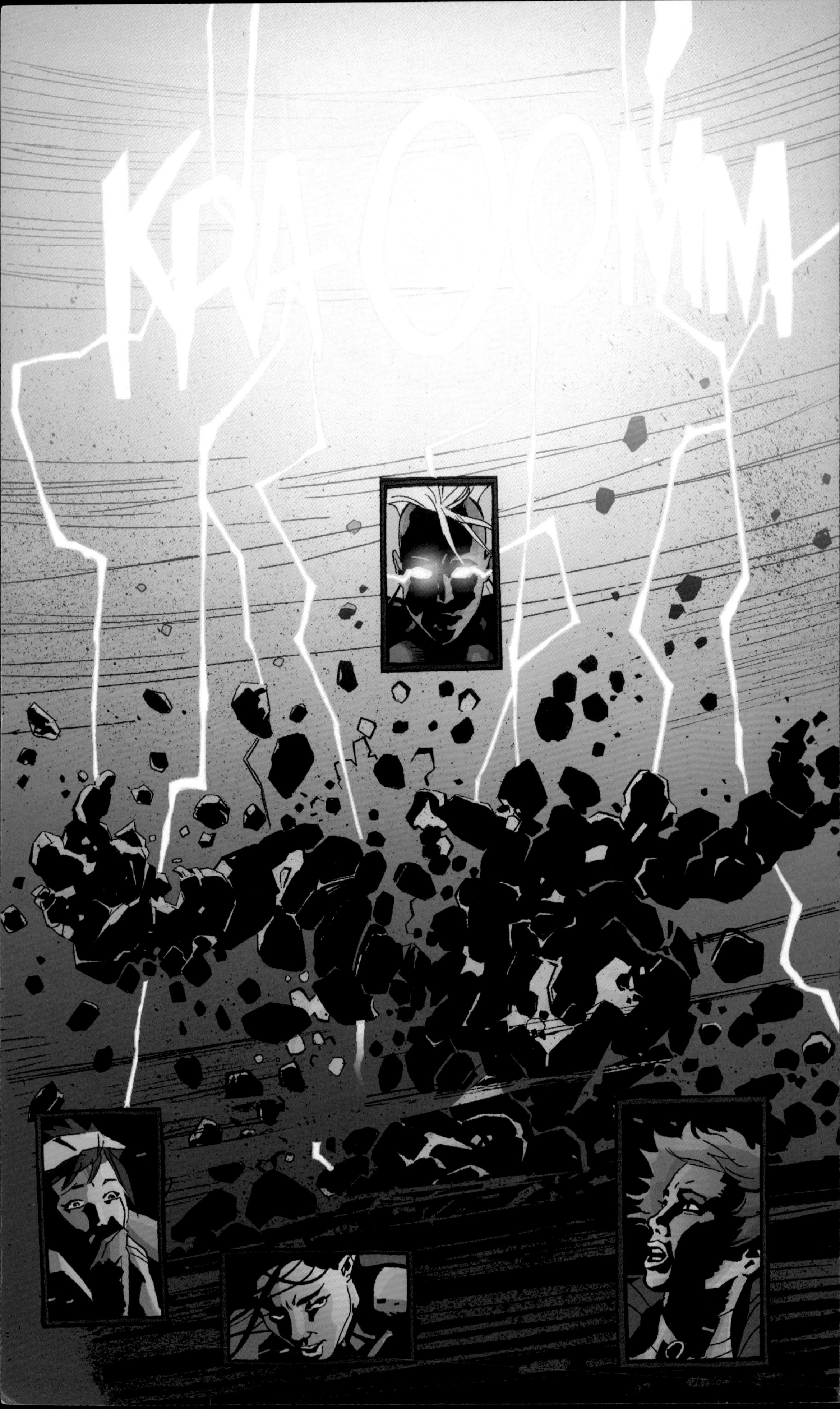
KRA-KOOMM

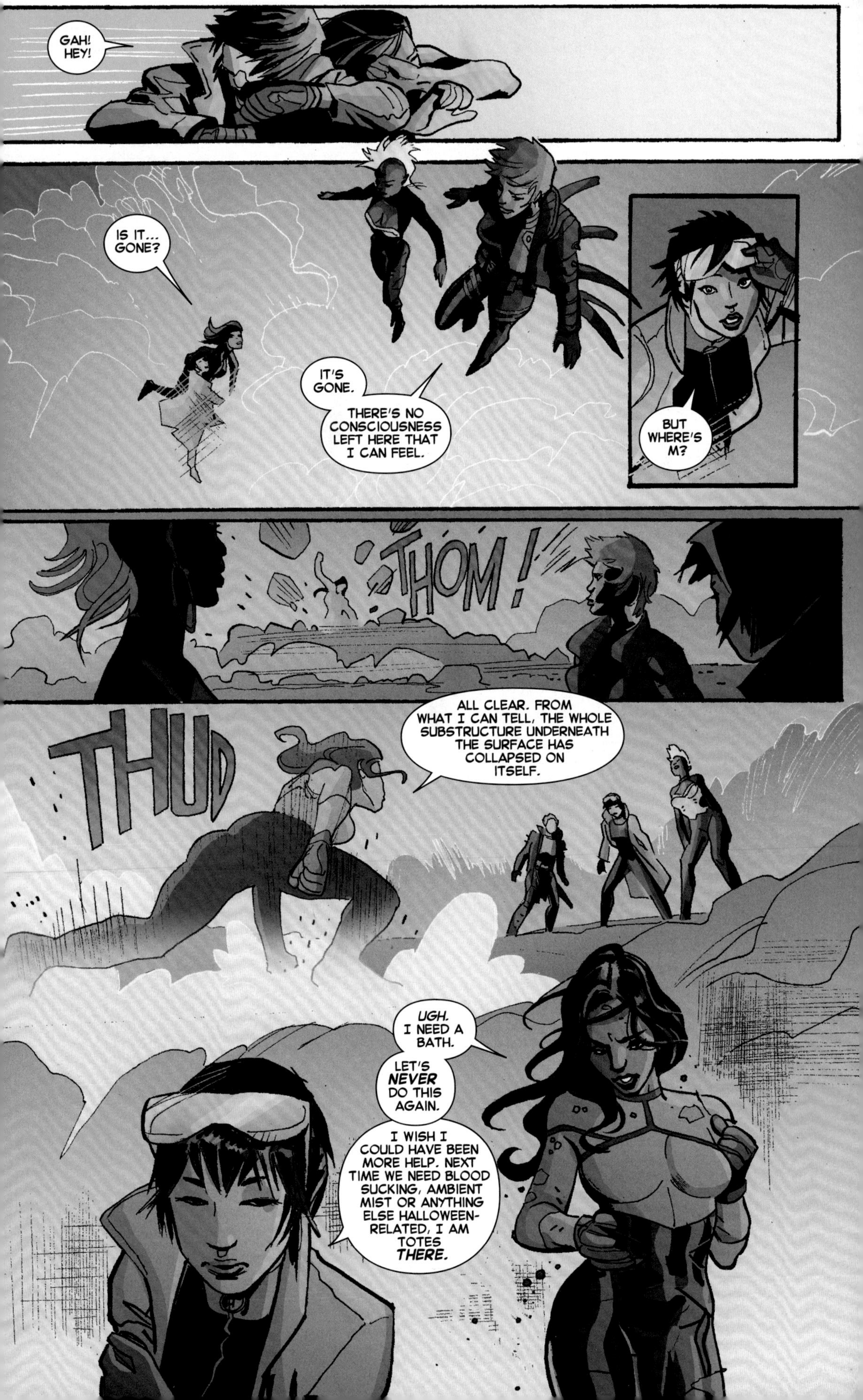
GAH! HEY!
IS IT... GONE?
IT'S GONE.
THERE'S NO CONSCIOUSNESS LEFT HERE THAT I CAN FEEL.
BUT WHERE'S M?
THOM!
THUD
ALL CLEAR. FROM WHAT I CAN TELL, THE WHOLE SUBSTRUCTURE UNDERNEATH THE SURFACE HAS COLLAPSED ON ITSELF.
UGH. I NEED A BATH.
LET'S *NEVER* DO THIS AGAIN.
I WISH I COULD HAVE BEEN MORE HELP. NEXT TIME WE NEED BLOOD SUCKING, AMBIENT MIST OR ANYTHING ELSE HALLOWEEN-RELATED, I AM TOTES *THERE.*

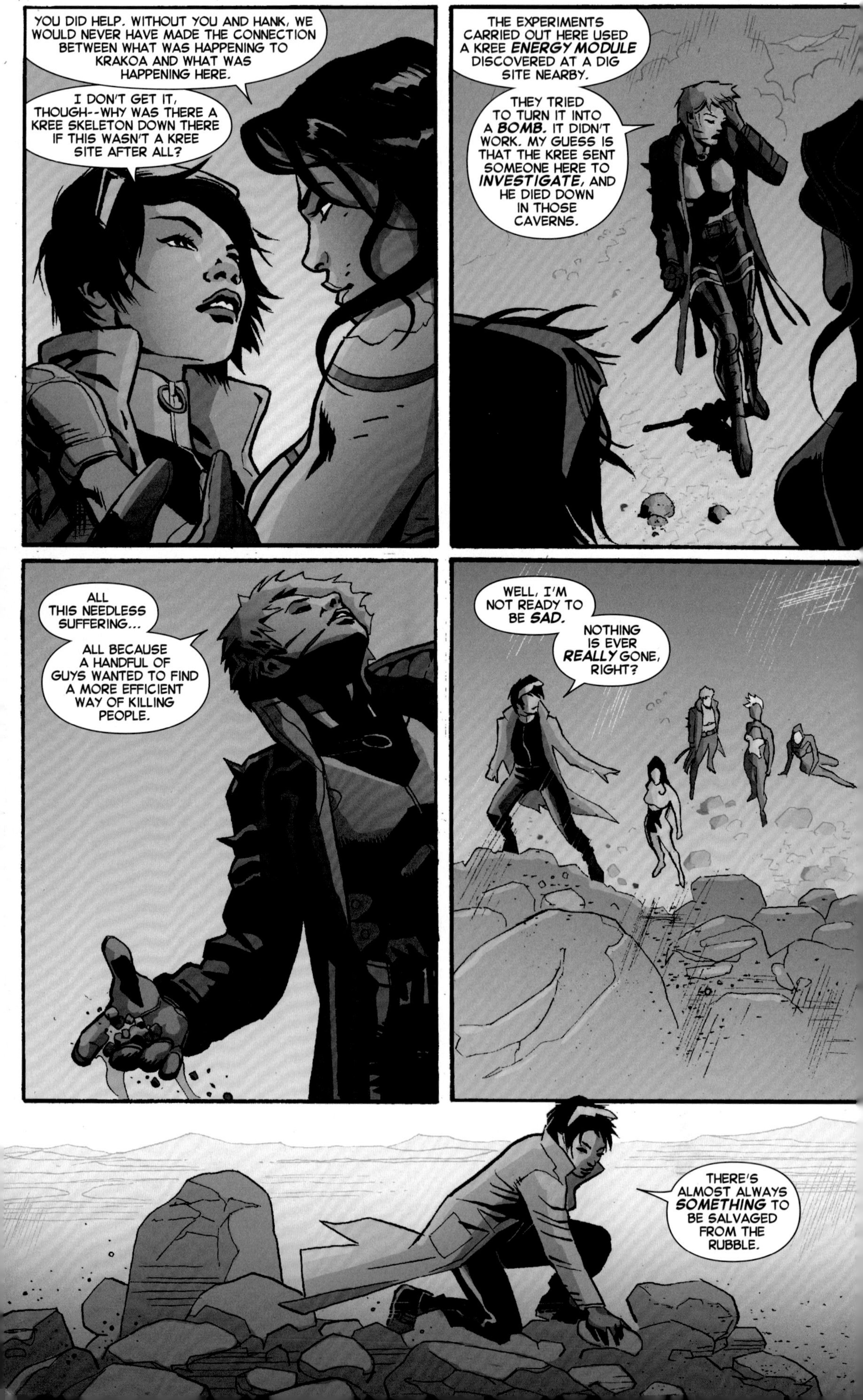
YOU DID HELP. WITHOUT YOU AND HANK, WE WOULD NEVER HAVE MADE THE CONNECTION BETWEEN WHAT WAS HAPPENING TO KRAKOA AND WHAT WAS HAPPENING HERE.
I DON'T GET IT, THOUGH--WHY WAS THERE A KREE SKELETON DOWN THERE IF THIS WASN'T A KREE SITE AFTER ALL?
THE EXPERIMENTS CARRIED OUT HERE USED A KREE ENERGY MODULE DISCOVERED AT A DIG SITE NEARBY.
THEY TRIED TO TURN IT INTO A BOMB. IT DIDN'T WORK. MY GUESS IS THAT THE KREE SENT SOMEONE HERE TO INVESTIGATE, AND HE DIED DOWN IN THOSE CAVERNS.
ALL THIS NEEDLESS SUFFERING...
ALL BECAUSE A HANDFUL OF GUYS WANTED TO FIND A MORE EFFICIENT WAY OF KILLING PEOPLE.
WELL, I'M NOT READY TO BE SAD.
NOTHING IS EVER REALLY GONE, RIGHT?
THERE'S ALMOST ALWAYS SOMETHING TO BE SALVAGED FROM THE RUBBLE.

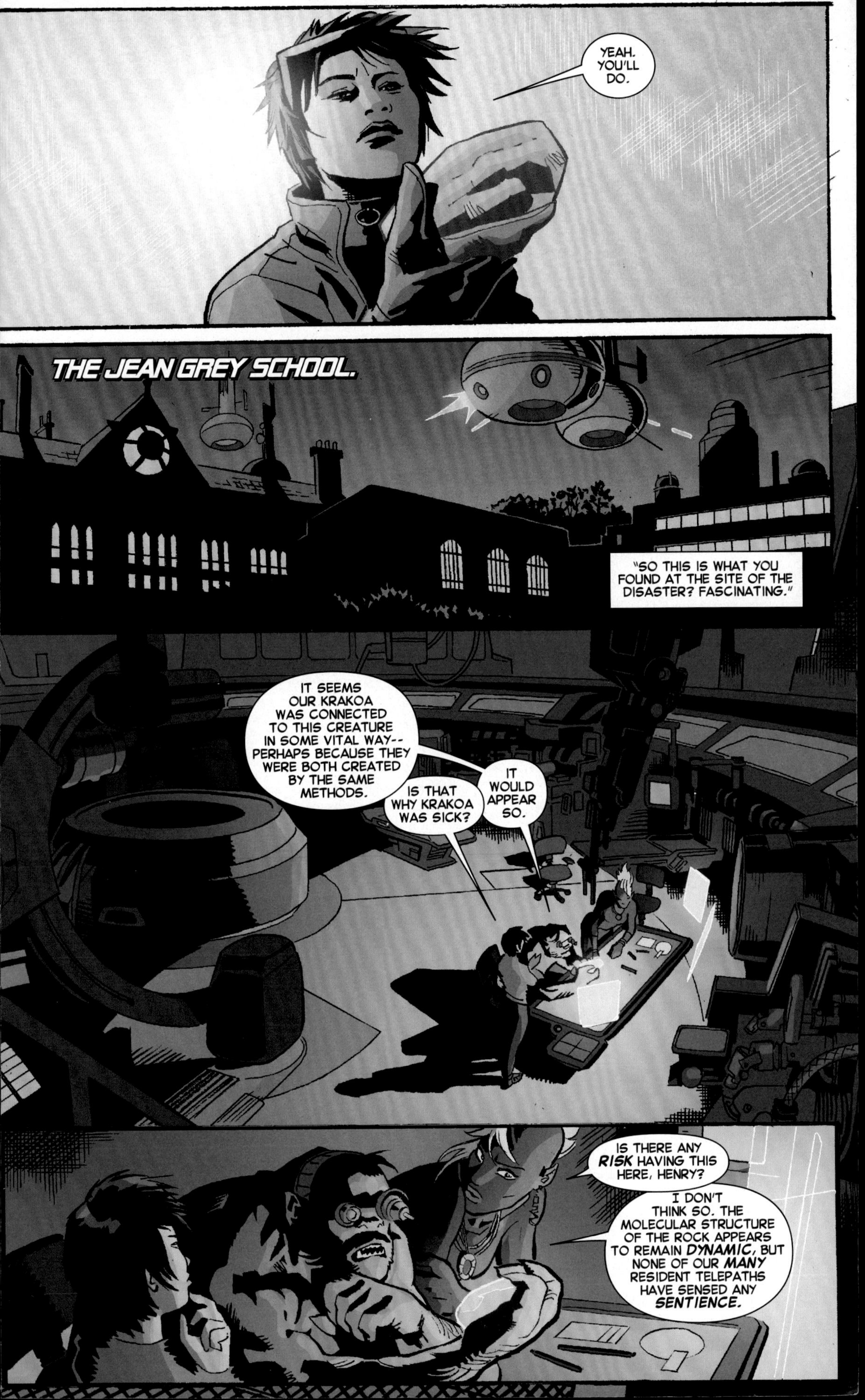
YEAH. YOU'LL DO.
THE JEAN GREY SCHOOL.
"SO THIS IS WHAT YOU FOUND AT THE SITE OF THE DISASTER? FASCINATING."
IT SEEMS OUR KRAKOA WAS CONNECTED TO THIS CREATURE IN SOME VITAL WAY-- PERHAPS BECAUSE THEY WERE BOTH CREATED BY THE SAME METHODS.
IS THAT WHY KRAKOA WAS SICK?
IT WOULD APPEAR SO.
IS THERE ANY RISK HAVING THIS HERE, HENRY?
I DON'T THINK SO. THE MOLECULAR STRUCTURE OF THE ROCK APPEARS TO REMAIN DYNAMIC, BUT NONE OF OUR MANY RESIDENT TELEPATHS HAVE SENSED ANY SENTIENCE.

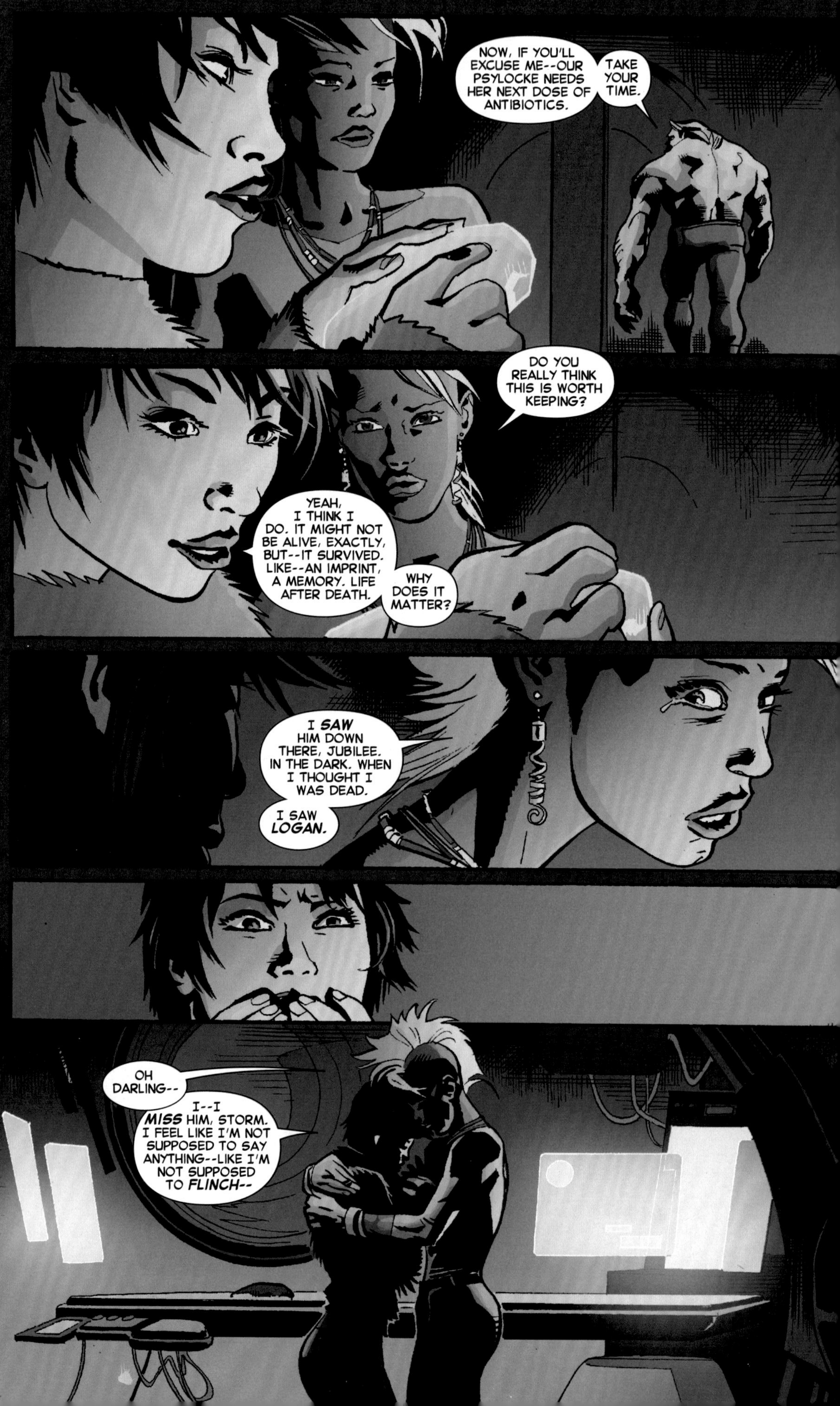

NOW, IF YOU'LL EXCUSE ME--OUR PSYLOCKE NEEDS HER NEXT DOSE OF ANTIBIOTICS.
TAKE YOUR TIME.
DO YOU REALLY THINK THIS IS WORTH KEEPING?
YEAH, I THINK I DO. IT MIGHT NOT BE ALIVE, EXACTLY, BUT--IT SURVIVED. LIKE--AN IMPRINT, A MEMORY. LIFE AFTER DEATH.
WHY DOES IT MATTER?
I SAW HIM DOWN THERE, JUBILEE. IN THE DARK. WHEN I THOUGHT I WAS DEAD.
I SAW LOGAN.
OH DARLING--
I--I MISS HIM, STORM. I FEEL LIKE I'M NOT SUPPOSED TO SAY ANYTHING--LIKE I'M NOT SUPPOSED TO FLINCH--

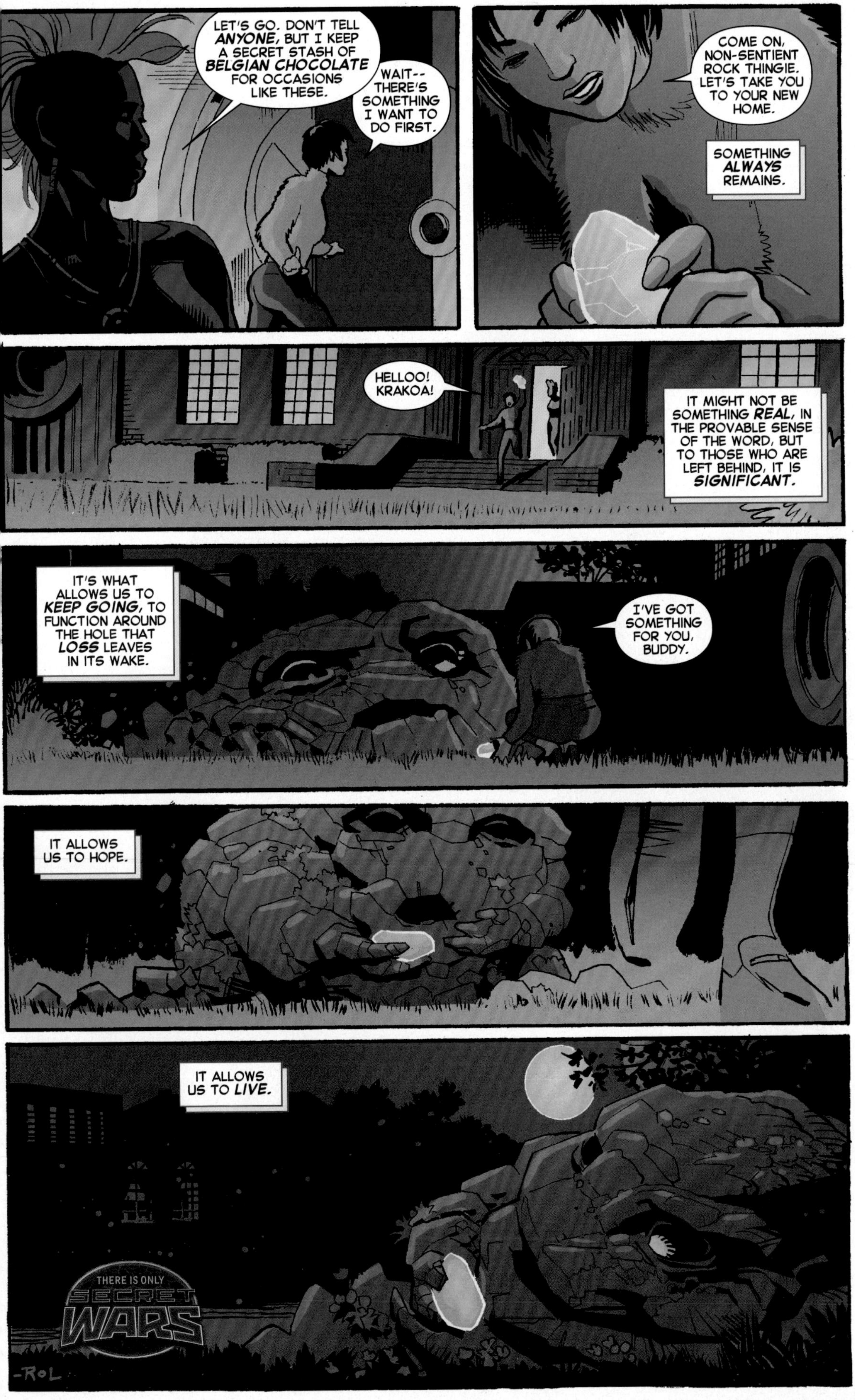
LET'S GO. DON'T TELL ANYONE, BUT I KEEP A SECRET STASH OF BELGIAN CHOCOLATE FOR OCCASIONS LIKE THESE.
WAIT-- THERE'S SOMETHING I WANT TO DO FIRST.
COME ON, NON-SENTIENT ROCK THINGIE. LET'S TAKE YOU TO YOUR NEW HOME.
SOMETHING ALWAYS REMAINS.
HELLOO! KRAKOA!
IT MIGHT NOT BE SOMETHING REAL, IN THE PROVABLE SENSE OF THE WORD, BUT TO THOSE WHO ARE LEFT BEHIND, IT IS SIGNIFICANT.
IT'S WHAT ALLOWS US TO KEEP GOING, TO FUNCTION AROUND THE HOLE THAT LOSS LEAVES IN ITS WAKE.
I'VE GOT SOMETHING FOR YOU, BUDDY.
IT ALLOWS US TO HOPE.
IT ALLOWS US TO LIVE.
THERE IS ONLY SECRET WARS
-ROL

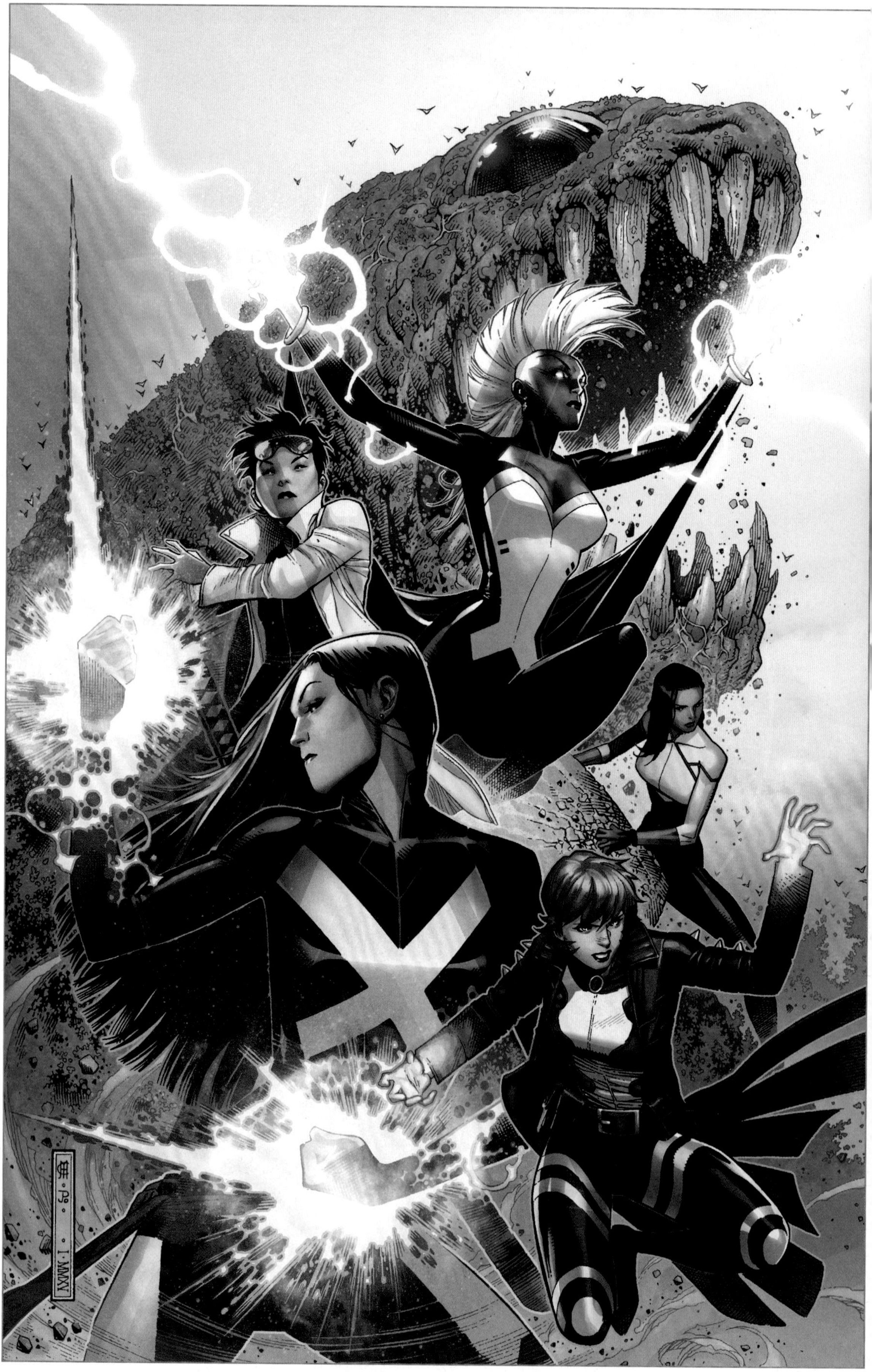

X-MEN #25 VARIANT

BY JIM CHEUNG & JUSTIN PONSOR

#25, PAGE 2 ART PROCESS

BY ROLAND BOSCHI & MARK PENNINGTON

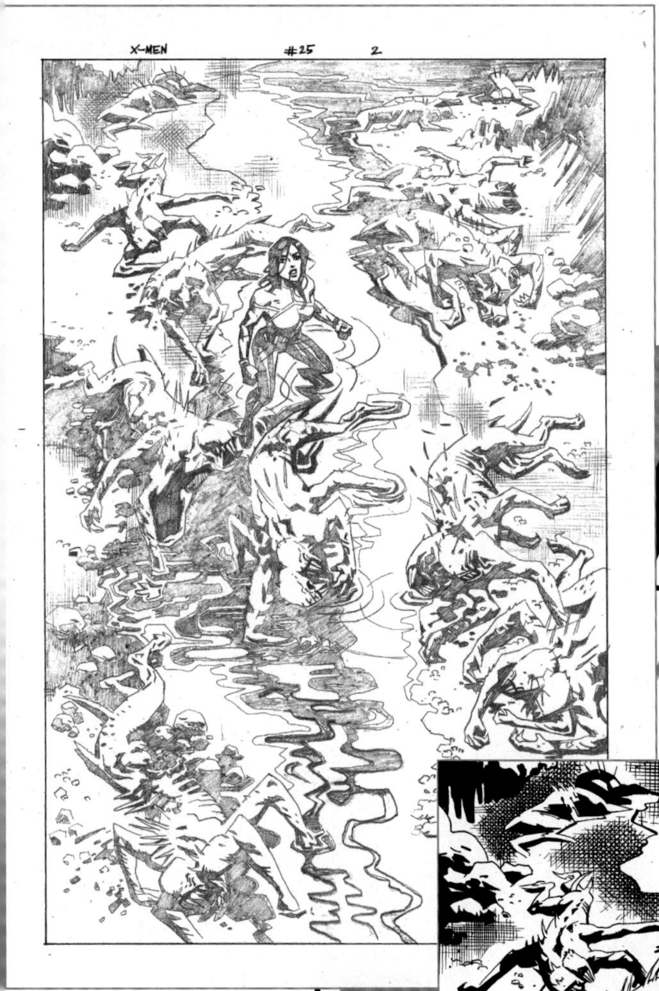
X-MEN #25 2

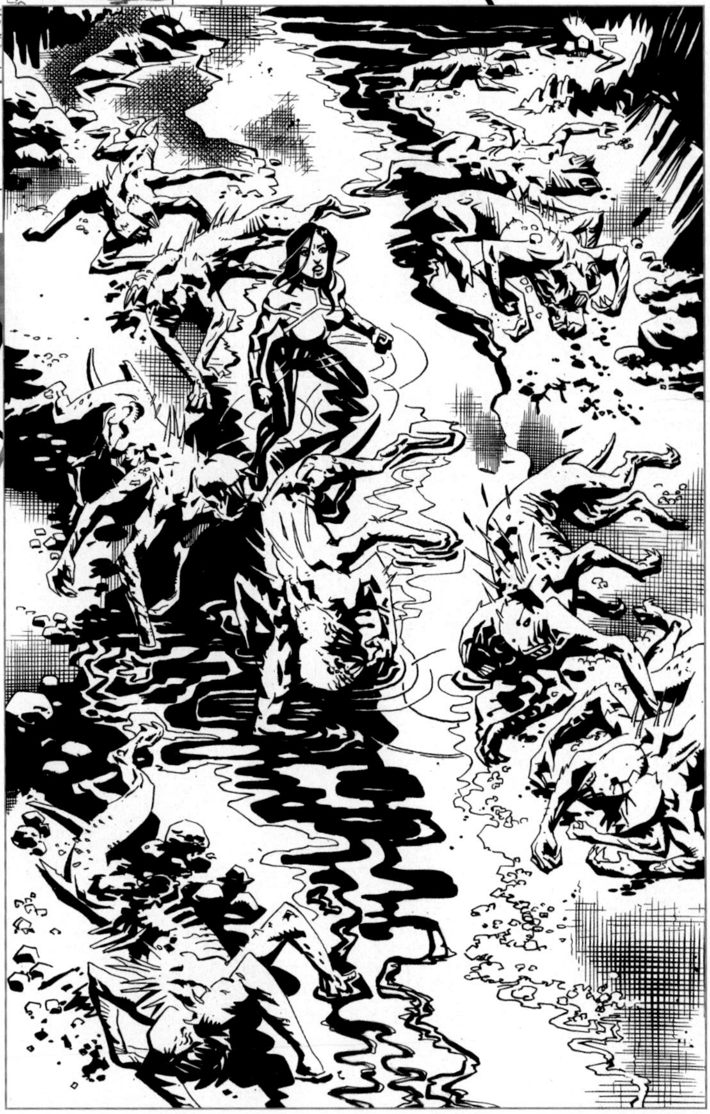

#25, PAGE 5 ART PROCESS

BY ROLAND BOSCHI & MARK PENNINGTON

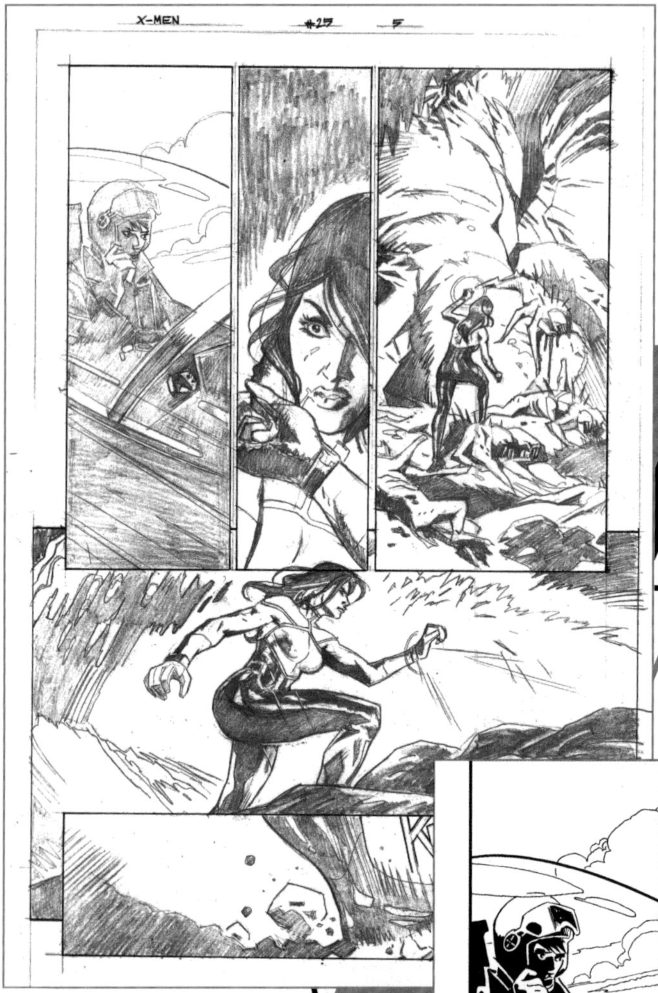
X-MEN
#25
5

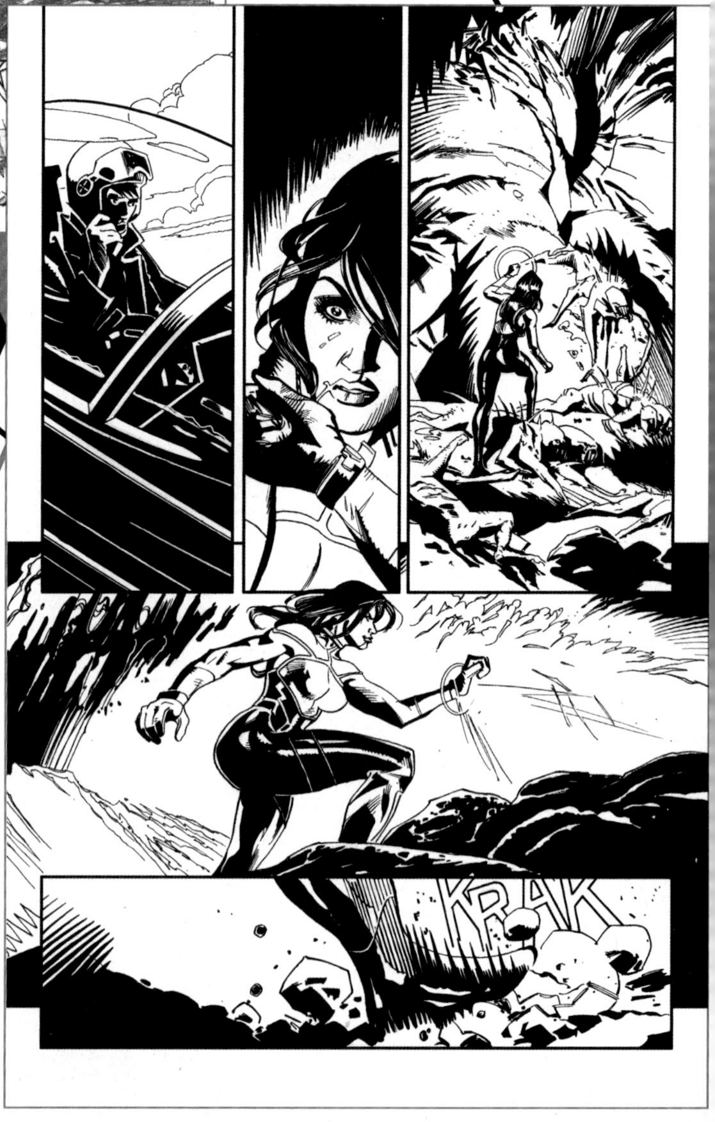
KRAK

#25, PAGE 6 ART PROCESS

BY ROLAND BOSCHI & MARK PENNINGTON

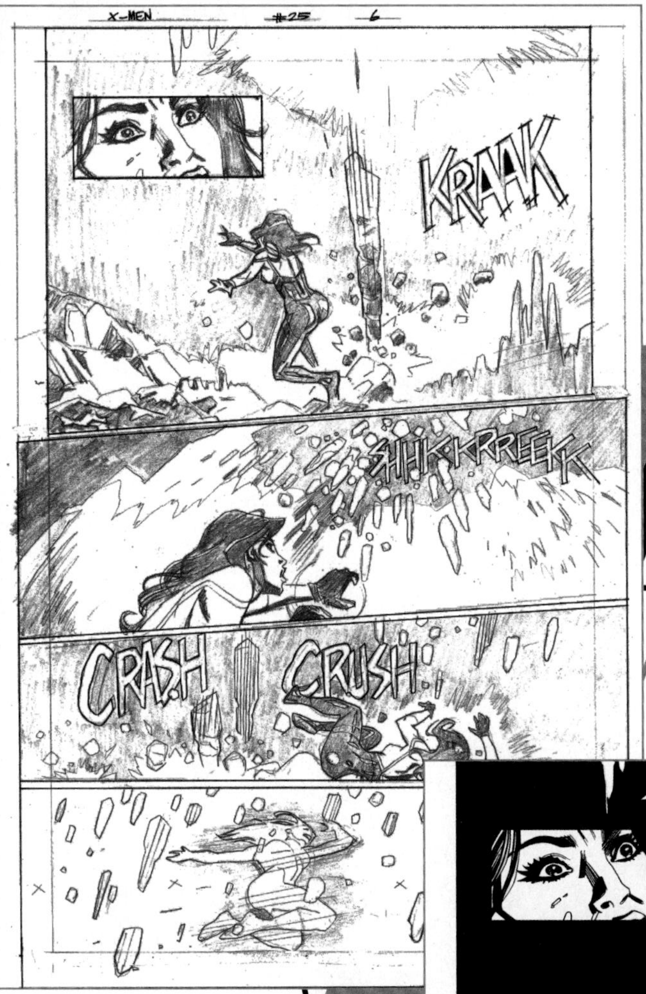

X-MEN #25 6
KRAAK
SHHK-KRREEKK
CRASH
CRUSH

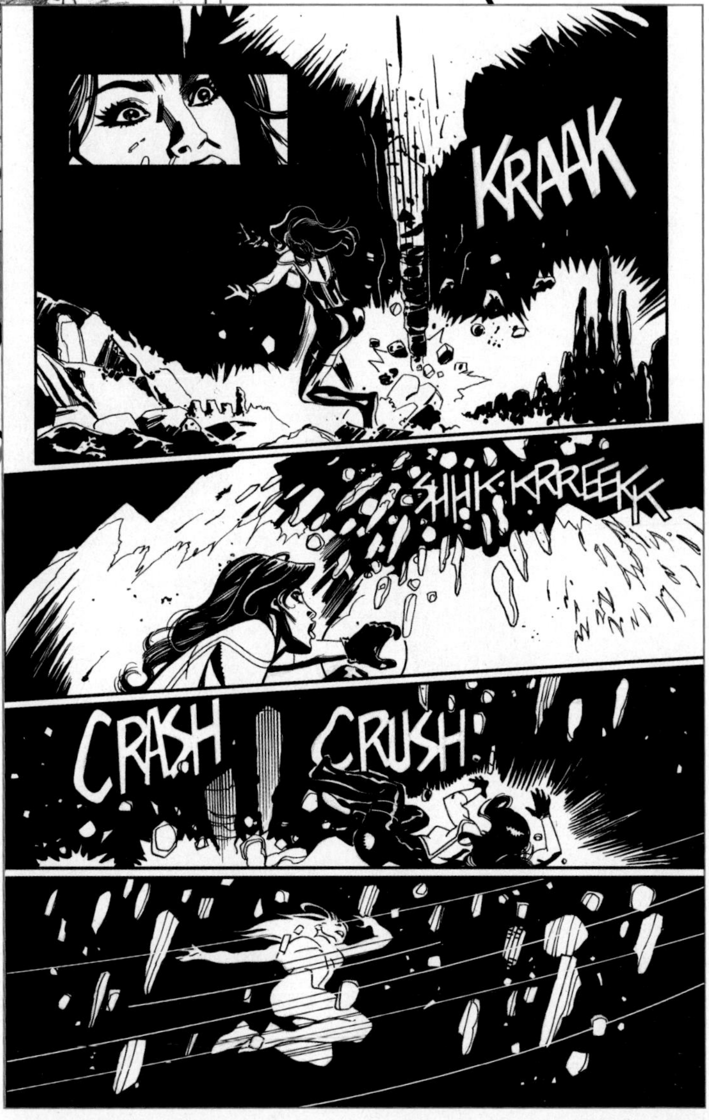

KRAAK
SHHK-KRREEKK
CRASH
CRUSH

#25, PAGE 7 ART PROCESS

BY ROLAND BOSCHI & HARVEY HUGONNARD-BERT

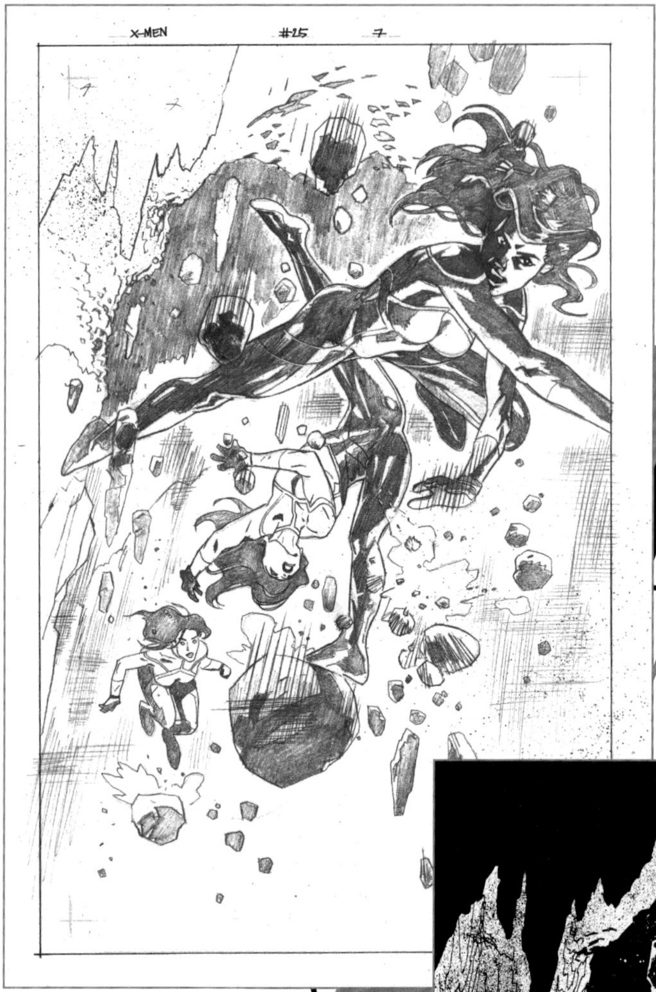
X-MEN
#25
7

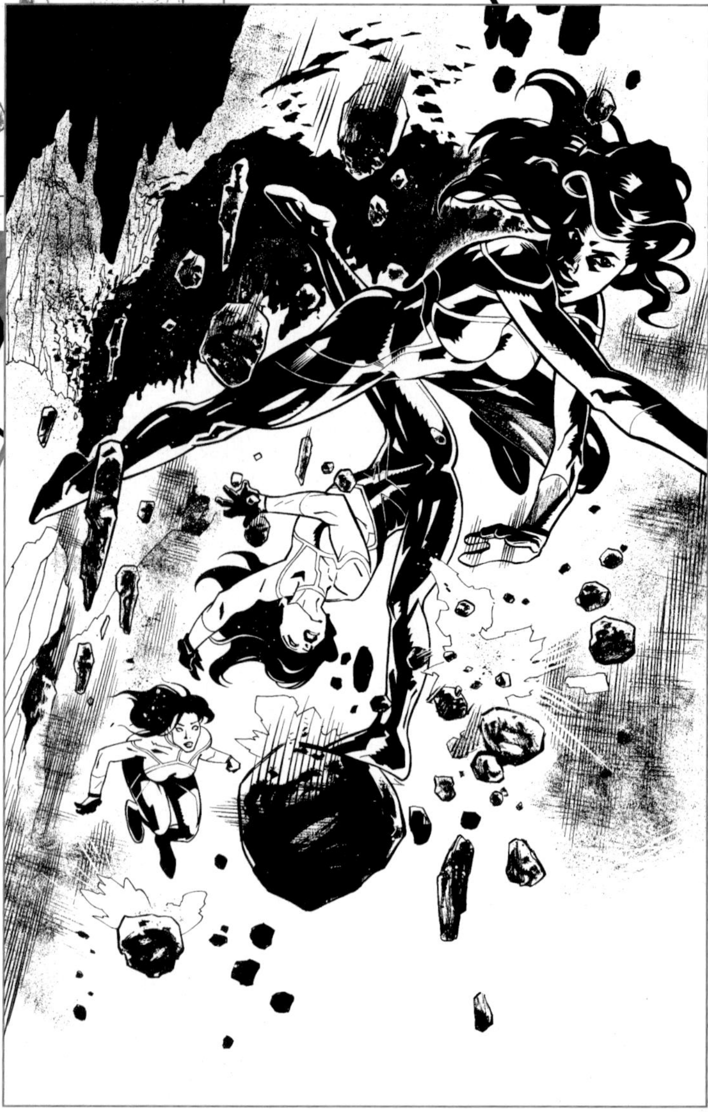

#25, PAGE 8 ART PROCESS

BY ROLAND BOSCHI & MARK PENNINGTON

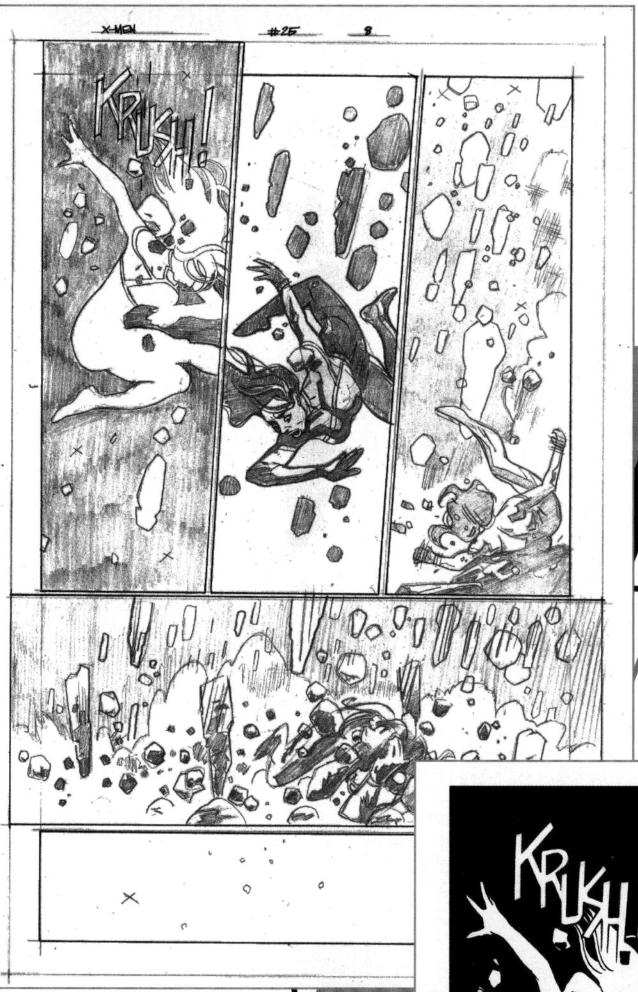

X-MEN #25 8
KRUKSH!

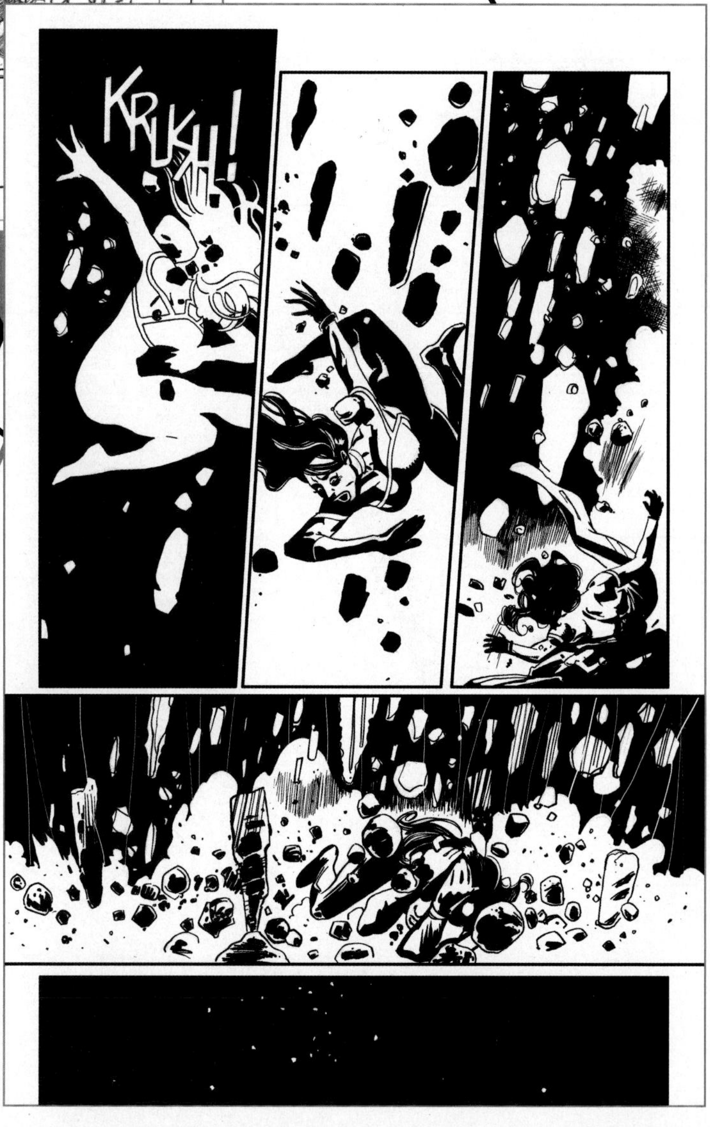

KRUKSH!

#25, PAGE 9 ART PROCESS

BY ROLAND BOSCHI & HARVEY HUGONNARD-BERT

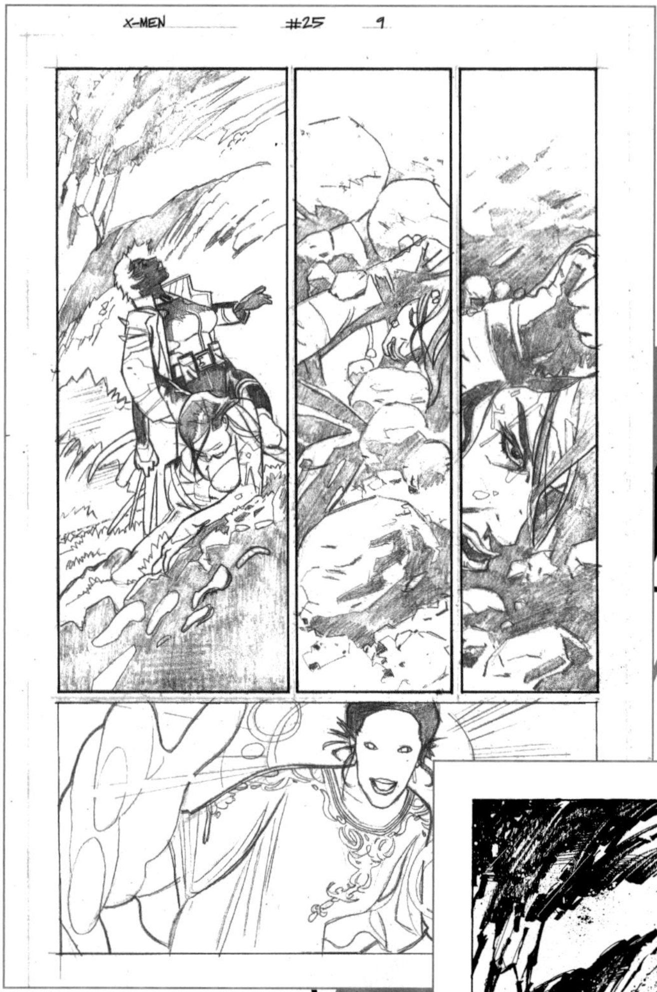
X-MEN
#25
9

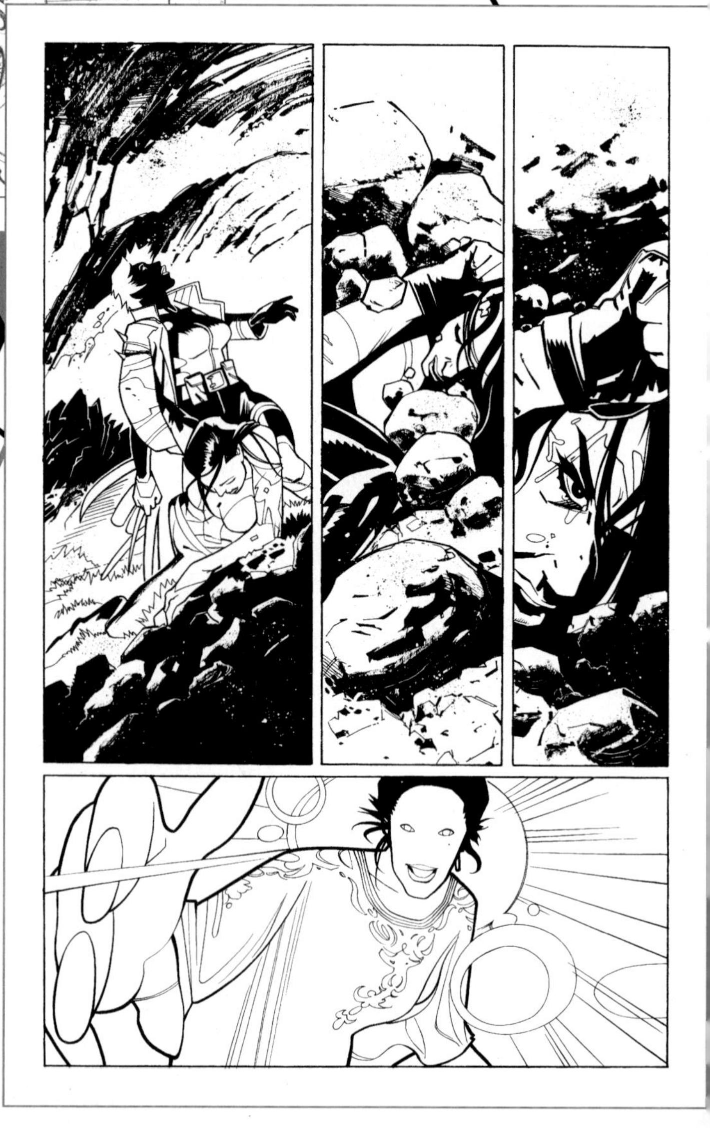

#25, PAGE 14 ART PROCESS

BY ROLAND BOSCHI & HARVEY HUGONNARD-BERT

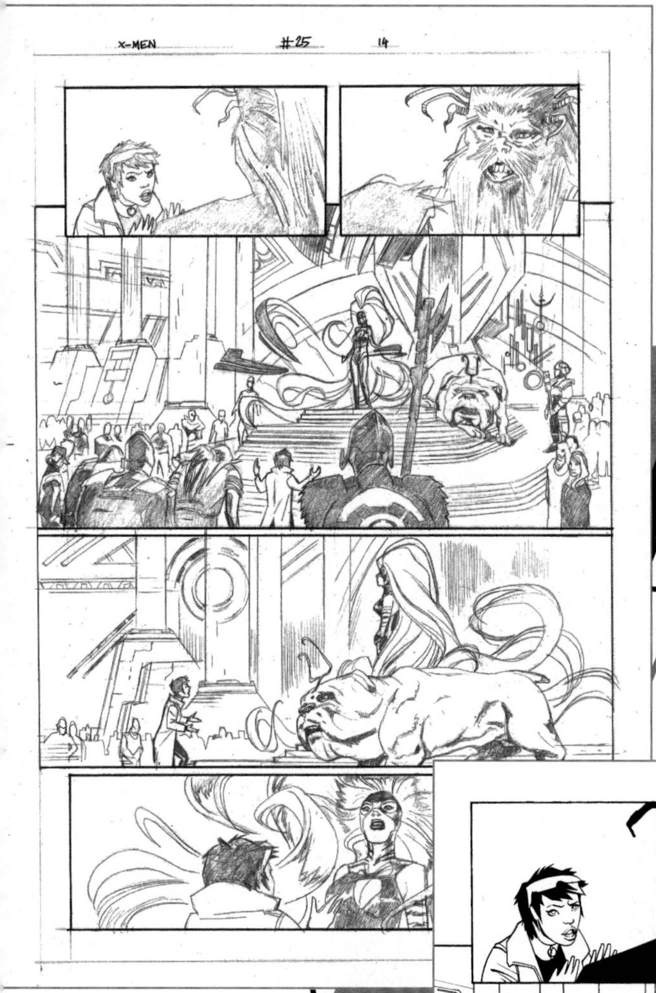
X-MEN #25 14

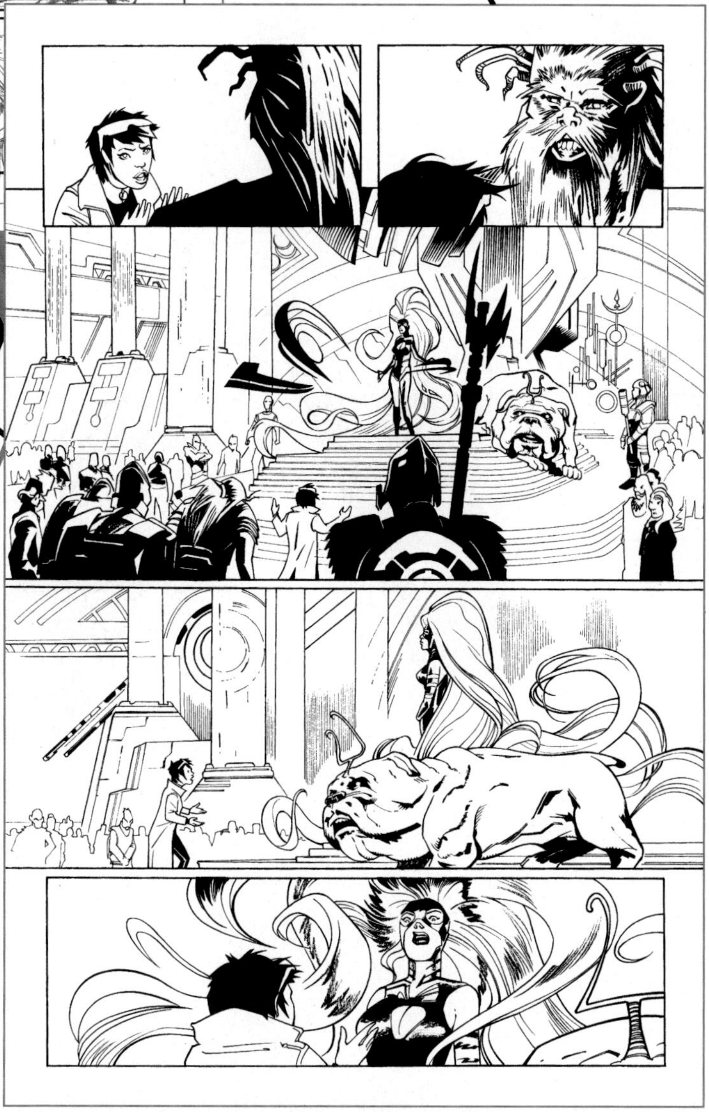

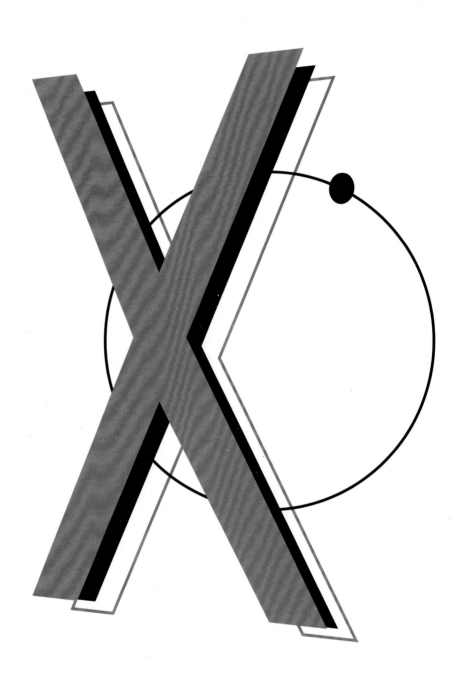